W9-CES-861

Great Americana

Across the Great Southwestern Prairies

VOLUME I

George W. Kendall

Across the Great Southwestern Prairies

VOLUME I

by George W. Kendall

READEX MICROPRINT

LIBRARY OF CONGRESS CATALOG CARD NO. 66-26348

MANUFACTURED IN THE UNITED STATES OF AMERICA

Foreword

A grim but fascinating account of one of the most extraordinary marches in the history of Anglo-Mexican relations is the *Narrative of the Texan Santa Fé Expedition* (New York, 1844) by George W. Kendall, founder of the New Orleans *Picayune* and a participant in the ill-fated expedition. Kendall's *Narrative,* first published in New York, was reprinted in London in 1845 with the title *Narrative of an Expedition across the Great Southwestern Prairies, from Texas to Santa Fé.* It is from the London edition that this reproduction is made. The *Narrative* created considerable excitement in the United States and a sixth edition was published in New York in 1850. It helped to create anti-Mexican sentiment and to prepare the American public for war with Mexico. A modern version was edited by Milo M. Quaife and published in Chicago in 1929. A facsimile reproduction was brought out in Austin, Texas, in 1935.

The author was an adventurous journalist who conceived the notion of publishing an inexpensive newspaper in New Orleans, which he called the *Picayune* because of the trifling coin that went by that name. His first issue appeared in January, 1837. As he explains in his preface to the *Narra-*

tive, he was induced to join the Santa Fe expedition by a desire for adventure and a determination to find a fresh source for "copy" for stories that he wanted to write for his newspaper. He got more than he bargained for, but the result was a book that for a time was a best seller.

The expedition, organized in 1841 to go from the new Republic of Texas to Santa Fe, New Mexico, was conceived by the republic's president, General Mirabeau B. Lamar, who believed that the people of New Mexico, oppressed by the Mexicans, would rise with enthusiasm, cast off their yoke, and unite with Texas. His calculations were mistaken. The expedition, which got under way in May, was ill-planned and ill-supplied. It made its way across the Indian country to the borders of New Mexico, where forces under Governor Manuel Armijo made prisoners of the whole lot and eventually sent them marching on foot to Mexico City.

Although Kendall protests that the group bound for Santa Fe was merely intent upon opening up a new trade route, he protests too much and admits that they carried along proclamations by President Lamar, printed in Spanish and English, promising the New Mexicans a welcome if they wanted to throw off the Mexican yoke and join Texas. Since the Mexican authorities knew about the real purposes behind the expedition before it arrived in their territory, it is small wonder that they treated the group as a hostile invading force. The cruelty of Armijo and his summary execution of some of the Texans, and the later cruelties of the sadist, Salazar, who marched the prisoners to Chihuahua, doubtless merited the bitter words that Kendall lavished upon them.

The long march from Santa Fe to Mexico City is described in graphic detail by Kendall, who proved an excellent reporter. He gives an immense amount of information about the country and the people with whom he came in contact, and his *Narrative* helps to explain the buildup of hatred of the Mexicans by the Texans and other western Americans. Kendall at last was freed and allowed to make his way to Vera Cruz, where he took a ship for New Orleans.

Kendall was the author of *The War Between the United States and Mexico. Illustrated* (New York, 1851). His articles in the New Orleans *Picayune* were designed to whip up zeal for an open break with Mexico. After the United States declared war, Kendall went to the front as a correspondent, along with a score of others, and organized a service that gave the Mexican War the best news coverage of any conflict up to that time. Information about Kendall may be found in the *Dictionary of American Biography*. See also N.W. Stephenson, *Texas and Mexican War* (New Haven, 1921).

Across the Great Southwestern Prairies

VOLUME I

SCAMPER AMONG THE BUFFALO.

NARRATIVE OF AN EXPEDITION

ACROSS THE GREAT

SOUTH-WESTERN PRAIRIES,

FROM

TEXAS TO SANTA FÉ;

WITH AN ACCOUNT OF

THE DISASTERS WHICH BEFEL THE EXPEDITION FROM WANT OF FOOD AND
THE ATTACKS OF HOSTILE INDIANS;

THE FINAL CAPTURE OF THE TEXANS AND THEIR SUFFERINGS
ON A MARCH OF TWO THOUSAND MILES
AS PRISONERS OF WAR, AND IN THE PRISONS AND LAZARETTOS OF MEXICO.

BY GEORGE W. KENDALL.

In Two Volumes.

VOL. I.

LONDON:
DAVID BOGUE, FLEET STREET.
MDCCCXLV.

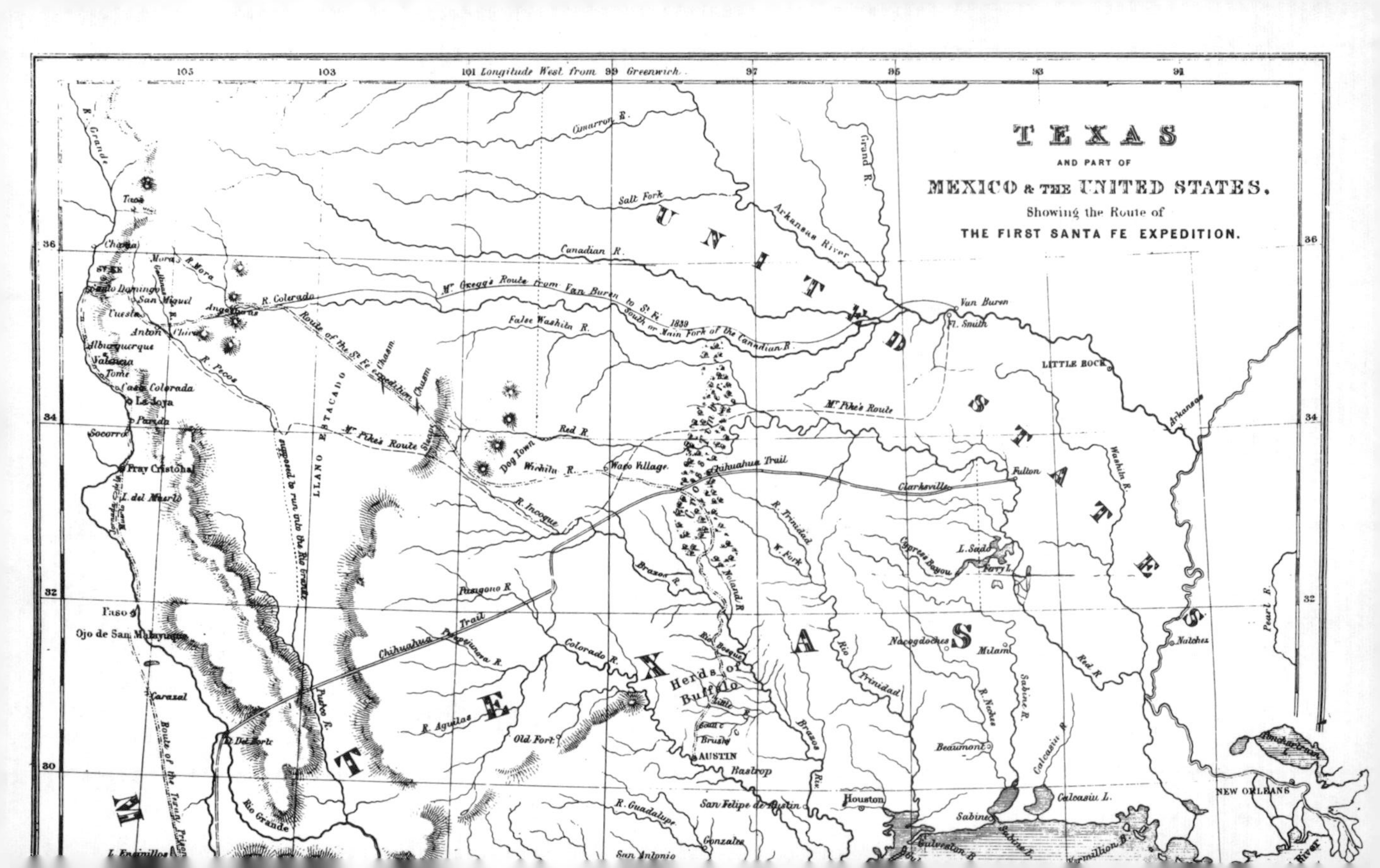

TEXAS
AND PART OF
MEXICO & THE UNITED STATES.
Showing the Route of
THE FIRST SANTA FE EXPEDITION.
101 Longitude West from 99 Greenwich
105
103
97
95
93
91
36
34
32
30
UNITED STATES
TEXAS
Cimarron R.
Salt Fork
Canadian R.
Arkansas River
Grand R.
Mr. Gregg's Route from Van Buren to St. Fe. 1839
South or Main Fork of the Canadian R.
False Washita R.
Route of the St. Fe expedition
Chasm
LLANO ESTACADO
Mr. Pike's Route
Red R.
Dog Town
Wichita R.
Waco Village
Chihuahua Trail
R. Incogue
supposed to run into the Rio Grande
R. Pecos
R. Colorado
Van Buren
Ft. Smith
LITTLE ROCK
Arkansas
Washita R.
Fulton
Clarksville
R. Trinidad
W. Fork
Noland R.
Cypress Bayou
L. Sado
Ferry L.
Brazos R.
Pasigono R.
Colorado R.
Herds of Buffalo
Chihuahua Trail
Puerco R.
R. Aguilas
Old Fort
AUSTIN
Bastrop
Brazos
Rio Trinidad
Nacogdoches
Milam
Sabine R.
R. Neches
Beaumont
Calcasiu R.
Calcasiu L.
Sabine
Sabine L.
Galveston B.
Houston
San Felipe de Austin
R. Guadalupe
Gonzales
San Antonio
Red R.
Natchez
Pearl R.
NEW ORLEANS
Pontchartrain L.
River
Vermillion B.
Rio Grande
Taos
Chama
Mora
R. Mora
San Miguel
Santo Domingo
Cuesta
Anton Chico
Angosturas
Albuquerque
Valencia
Tome
Casa Colorada
La Joya
Parida
Socorro
Fray Cristobal
L. del Muerto
Paso
Ojo de San Malayuque
Carazal
Route of the Texan Prisoners
L. Encinillos
R. Grande

GULF OF MEXICO
Loredo
Salado R.
Salt Lake
Padre I.
Rio Grande
R. San Juan
Matamoros
R. de San Fernando
L. Parras
Cerro Gordo
El Gallo
R. Nasas
Cuencame
Saltillo
Durango
Route of Col. Cooke's
Mazepilo
Lojos
Charcoal Pt.
Sombrerete
Saenea
New Santander
Santander Bar
Fresnillo
Teresa
Zacatecas
party of Texans
Escandon
Tordo Bar
S. Diego de Hussuquilla
Salina
R. Grande
R. Panuco
Tampico
Aguas Calientes
San Luis
Tepic
El Jaral
Tamiegua L.
C. Roxo
Lagos
San Felipe
Leon
Silao
Guanajuato
Guadalajara
Salamanca
Queretaro
Jalopa
L. Chapala
R. Lerma
San Juan del Rio
Zagualtipan
Tula
Villa de la Purificacion
Valladolid
Perote
Jalapa
MEXICO
Vera Cruz
Orizava
Colima
Puebla
Longitude West from Washington
28
26
24
22
20
18
16
14
D. Bogue 86, Fleet Street

LONDON:
THOMAS HARRILD, PRINTER, SILVER STREET,
FALCON SQUARE.

PREFACE.

A word with you, kind reader, before you commence the perusal of the following narrative. The object of the author has been to tell his story in a plain, unvarnished way—in the homely, every-day language which is at once understood by all. He will not, at this time, apologize for any errors of omission or any broken links in the principal chain of connexion which may be noticed; he trusts that all such faults will explain themselves in the progress of the narrative, as the difficulties he has had to encounter become apparent.

For the description of the Spanish Missions in the neighbourhood of San Antonio de Bexar, which will be found in the early part of the third chapter, the author is principally indebted to Mr. Falconer, by whom full notes were taken of these old religious establishments. The author also acknowledges his indebtedness to Mr. F. for the names of the several places through which the Santa Fé prisoners passed on their march from San Miguel to the city of Mexico, together with the dates. For dates and events previous to the capture of the expedition he has been obliged to rely upon his own memory, and upon that of such of his companions as he has been able to see and converse with since his return to the United States.

The main facts in the history of Don Manuel Armijo have been obtained from a gentleman who has known that petty tyrant and his career for nearly fifteen years. The author has only added such incidents as came under his personal observation.

In making up the map of the country between the Cross Timbers and the settlements of New Mexico, much information has been obtained from Mr. Gregg, an intelligent merchant who has been for many years engaged in the Santa Fé trade, and also from Albert Pike, Esq., of Arkansas. Both these gentlemen have travelled over the immense prairies, stretching from the western limits of Louisiana and Arkansas to the Rocky Mountains, and both agree with the author in his remarks in relation to Red River. Of course, in the construction of this map, much of what the Yankees term "guess work" has been resorted to; but it will be found, in the main, correct.

A few of the incidents in the first volume of this work, which appeared, in a series of rough sketches, in the New Orleans Picayune of 1842, have since been stolen from that journal and incorporated with the "Narrative of Monsieur Violet," written by Captain Marryat, and published in London during the fall of 1843. The author has deemed this exposition necessary, lest some of his readers, unacquainted with the circumstances, and who may peruse both books, should suspect him of having poached upon the wondrous tale of Violet. The larceny lies at the door of either the

Captain or the Monsieur—a matter they must settle between themselves.

Violet's "Narrative" also contains an attack, directly impeaching the varacity of the author in the account he has given of the murder of Golpin. It may not be deemed a work of supererogation for him simply to state, that this wanton attack is made up of deliberate falsehood. The time, place, and manner of the death of the unfortunate Texan, were precisely as the author has stated them: out of more than one hundred and eighty witnesses of the murder, many are still living to verify his account in every particular.

In speaking of the manners, customs, institutions, and character of the Mexicans, the author has simply related what came under his own observation; he has censured where he considered that reproof should fall, has praised where he deemed commendation due. Should his strictures not meet the approval of the leading men of that country, the blame cannot attach to him; for if the Mexican government, in its wisdom, saw fit to deny a friendly traveller the privilege of viewing aught save the darker shades of life while within the limits of that republic, it certainly cannot upbraid him for painting them in all their deformity. In whatever light a government or an individual may choose to "sit for a portrait," it is certainly the duty of every honest artist to give it with scrupulous fidelity.

In commenting upon the weakness and inefficiency of his own government, as regards its external or foreign policy, the author has approached the subject with much reluctance. American born and American at heart, he has always felt a just pride in the achievements of his countrymen, in their firm and untiring opposition to all usurpation and tyranny, and to every infringement upon their liberties. The people of the United States—the mass from whom all power emanates—although ever ready to sustain their rulers in the protection of the humblest of their countrymen while abroad, are too frequently kept in ignorance of the wrongs they suffer through the inattention of those who are bound to redress every encroachment upon their rights. Were it not that the exposure of errors and abuses is the only means of ensuring their correction, the author would shrink from lifting the curtain which conceals almost the only weak point in the administration of his government. For proof of the correctness of his strictures he has only to refer to every American who has visited Mexico.

Another word or two, and the author will throw himself upon the kindness of his reader. His attempt has been to interest and amuse; should it be thought that he has thrown too much levity amid scenes of suffering and of gloom, his excuse must be that he belongs rather to the school of laughing than crying philosophers — to a class who would rather see a smile upon the face of melancholy than a tear in the eye of mirth.

Contents of the First Volume.

CHAPTER. I.

Objects of the first Texan Santa Fé Expedition.—Determination to accompany it—The Western Limits of Texas.—Her claim to the Rio Grande.— —Colonel Butler's contemplated Expedition to Santa Fé.—Causes of its Failure.—Preparations for joining the Texans.—Departure from New Orleans.—Arrival at Galveston.—City of Houston.—Houston Horse Jockeys.—Leave Houston for Austin.—Race with a Thunder-shower. Arrival at Austin.—Mr. Falconer.—English Travellers.—Party to San Antonio made up.—Jim the Butcher sent to the Stable.—Mexican Mountain Pony.—His Mustaches, and Powers of Endurance - Page 13

CHAPTER. II.

Leave Austin for San Antonio.—A regular Soaking.—Crossing the Colorado.—Venison for supper.—Damp Lodgings.—Serenade of Wolves.—The Saint Mark's.—Head Springs.—Arrival of friends from Austin.—Journey towards San Antonio renewed.—Encounter with a Texan War party. Hostile Indians about.—A Texan killed.—Amusing Adventure. —The Guadalupe.—The Salado.—Night Entry into San Antonio.—A Mexican Dance.—Monte.—Comparative Merits of Floors.—Difference between Plank, Stone, and Earth.—Rough Life in Perspective - 32

CHAPTER. III.

Description of San Antonio. Climate.—The old Spanish Missions.—Objects for which they were constructed.—The Alamo.—Conception.—San Juan.—San José.—La Espada.—Bowie and Crockett.—Church of San Antonio.—Return to Austin.—Incidents upon the Road.—A Texan Leather Stocking.—An Adventure.—Out-tricking a party of Indians.—Fruitless Chase after Camanches.—Hog-wallow Prairie.—Arrival at Camp.—More of the Camanches.—Plain Supper and good Appetite.—Once more at Austin.—A Fall in the Dark.—Consolation under Misfortune - - - - - - - - - - - - - 50

CHAPTER IV.

Visit from General Lamar.—Preparations for a Start,—Bright side of the Picture.—Speculations as to the Reception of the Expedition at Santa Fé.—Senor Navarro.—A Jersey Waggon provided.—Adieu to Civilization.—A modern Athens.—Its sudden Rise, and more sudden Fall.—

President Lamar in Camp.—Arrival at the Brushy.—General Joy among the Pioneers.—Order of March.—Tricks of young Oxen.—Arrival at the San Gabriel.—Camp Stories.—Opossum Creek.—A night Storm.—Buffalo in Sight.—Petrifactions.—Methods of Hunting the Buffalo.—A regular Chase.—Falconer among the Buffalo.—Returns of Killed and Wounded. Arrival at Little River - - - - - - - - - - Page 67

CHAPTER V.

Sending back for more Cattle.—Rations of Beef for each Man.—Idle Hours in Camp.—Night Alarms.—A Dutchman shot at.—Improvident Waste of provisions.—Sickness of General M'Leod.—Once more on the Road.—Bird's Battle Ground.—A Visit from Mustangs.—The "White Steed of the Prairies."—Cow Creek.—Plenty of Buffalo.—Repairing Waggons.—Out of Water.—Fourth of July on the Prairies.—Celebration among the Clouds.—A troublesome Visiter.—Rattlesnakes and Tarantulas.—Death of Flint.—Crossing the Bosque.—The Antelope, or Mountain Goat.—Simplicity of this Animal. Another Branche of the Bosque. —Difficulty of crossing—A Stampede!—Singular Effect of Fright upon Horses and Oxen.—A Private Stampede.—Laughable Antics - - 90

CHAPTER VI.

The Valley of Cedral Creek.—Singular Natural Road.—Arrival of General M'Leod with additional Cattle.—Valley of the Brazos.—Fondness of our Animals for its Waters.—Prairie on Fire.—Out of Water again.—Sufferings of Man and Beast.—A cool Spring discovered.—Fresh Indian "Sign." —A recently-deserted Village.—The Camanche Peak.—"Seeing the Elephant."—The "Cross Timbers."—Description of this singular Forest. —Arrival at Noland's River.—Destruction of our Tents.—Deserted Indian Village.—Latitude and Longitude taken.—Our last Day in the "Cross Timbers."—A gloomy Night.—Once more upon the open Prairie.—Speculations as to the Route we had taken.—The Banks of Red River supposed to be visible - - - - - - - - - - 107

CHAPTER VII.

Trail of the Chihuahua Traders.—Causes of the Failure of that Enterprise. —A fresh Indian "Burn."—Indian Dogs.—Their forlorn Appearance.—Exciting Scene.—An Indian Buffalo Chase.—A recently-deserted Indian Camp.—A white Flag sent out.—Beautiful Camping-ground.—An Eclipse.—Once more on Horseback.—Singular Chase.—Both Parties mistaken.—A Soaking.—Carlos, a Mexican, joins the Spy Company.—Plausibility of his Stories.—The supposed Red River.—Parley with a Party of Wacoes.—Arrival at a Waco Village.—Its desertion by the Inhabitants.—Beautiful Location of the Town.—Its Houses and Corn-fields.—An Indian Musical Instrument.—High State of Civilization of the Wacoes.—Causes of the Hostility of the Wacoes to the Texans.—Fear of the Prairie Indians of Artillery.—Origin of this Fear - - 129

CHAPTER VIII.

Join the Spy Company.—Farther Speculations egards Red River.—Beautiful Streams and cool Arbours.—Visit from Mustangs.—A dashing wild Horse.—Different Modes of catching Mustangs.—Indians in Sight.—Guarding against a Night Attack.—Arrival at a Fresh-water Stream.—Carlos thinks Himself at Home.—General Joy in Camp.—Scanty Rations.—A Shower and a Stampede.—Cross the supposed Red River again.—Scarcity of "Sign,"—Mountains a-head.—A hunting Adventure. Get lost upon the Prairie.—Hopelessness of my Situation.—Ruminations upon the Horrors of being Lost.—Fortunate Escape from Difficulty.—A Ride through a Rattlesnake Region.—Once more among my Friends.—Unpleasant Dreams.—A Mesquit Prairie.—Carlos again "at Home."—Three of the Texans sent forward to the Settlements.—A Buffalo Chase.—River seen to the South.—An Adventure with Deer.—A severe Case of the "Buck Ague"—Symptoms and general Appearance of that singular Disease - - - - - - - - - - - - - Page 155

CHAPTER IX.

Brackish Water.—Los Cuervos, or The Crows.—Carlos and his Speculations.—Stream on our Left visited.—Opinion of "Old Paint."—Startling Surmises.—Endurance of the Mule.—Water seen in the Distance.—Perilous Descent of a Bluff.—Arrival at the River.—More Brackish Water.—An Alarm.—Fire in Camp.—Terrific Spread of the Flames.—Explosion of Cartridges.—Night Ascent of the Bluffs —Ravages of the Fire.—Magnificent night Scene.—Our Camp by Daylight.—Compelled to fall back upon First Principles.—Again on the March.—Intolerable Suffering from Thirst.—A Beautiful Camp.—Disappearance of Carlos and Brignoli. Horrors of our Situation.—Lost, and without a Guide upon the Prairies.—Shower on the Espy Principle.—Party sent out to Explore.—Gloomy Prospects.—Return to Camp.—Ten Miles for a Draught of Water.—"Doing" our Washing.—Company of Spies sent out.—Rations reduced.—Sufferings now commencing.—Return of one of the Spies.—Again on the March.—Visit to a Commonwealth of Prairie Dogs.—Description of these singular Animals - - - - - - - - - 185

CHAPTER X..

A Meal of Prairie Dogs.—Arrival at another brackish Water Camp.—Shower at Night, with fresh Water in the Morning.—Return of the Spy Company.—Report of the Spies.—Indians in Camp.—Horses stolen.—Daring of the Indians.—Once more on the Road.—Dog Towns.—Meeting with a Party of Indians.—Horse Meat far from being bad Eating.—Wolves about.—A dreary Desert.—Delicious fresh-water Stream.—Latitude and Longitude again taken.—Pleasant Prospects.—Again encompassed with Difficulties.—A Passage out found.— Steppes.—Mesquit Prairie and Prairie Dogs.—Mountains in the Distance.—Delusive Hopes.—More Horses stolen.—Bed of Large River crossed.—Arrival at the

Quintufue.—Large Indian Camp discovered.—Cayguas on all Sides.—Indian Provisions.—A Party sent out.—Farther Advance impossible.—A Night without Water.—Exciting News.—Firing of Guns heard.—Lieutenant Hull and four Men killed by Cayguas.—A Chase after Indians.—Return to the Quintufue.—Determination to divide the Command.—Description of the Cayguas - - - - - - - Page 208

CHAPTER XI.

Departure of the Advance in search of the Settlements.—Summit of the Steppe gained.—Level Prairie before us.—Speculations in relation to Red River.—A Bear Chase.—Sagacity of a Mule.—Arrival at a singular Chasm.—Impossibility of crossing.—A heavy Prairie Shower.—Appearance of our Men.—Description of the Chasm.—A Crossing found.—Loneliness of the Prairies.—Scarcity of Game.—Arrival at another awful Abyss.—Farther Difficulty in crossing.—Singular Birds.—Mustangs and Antelopes —Curlews.—A Buffalo descried.—Preparations for a Chase to the Death.—Tom Hancock and his Skill.—Endurance of Jim the Butcher. Description of the Chase.—Poor Prospects of a Supper - - - 230

CHAPTER XII.

A successful Search.—The Buffalo brought to Bay.—Prospects of another Shower.—Adventure with a Rattlesnake in the Dark.—Fortunate Escape. —Buffalo found in the Morning.—March resumed.—Swimming our Animals. — Singular Method of Cooking. — Encounter with a Drove of Mustangs.—Mountains discovered a-head.—Leave the grand Prairie.—Singular Hills.—Compelled to abandon our Course.—Suffering and Starvation.—Large fresh-water Stream discovered.—Speculations as to its Name. — Mexican "Sign" seen.—Plum Patches.—Carlos and Brignoli seen.—Their Sufferings.—The Texans driven to the greatest strait for Food.—Compelled to eat broken-down Horse Flesh.—Fairly among the Rocky Mountains.—A beautiful Valley.—A Feast of Catfish.—Arrival at the Angosturas. — Encounter with a Party of Mexicans. — Advance towards the Settlements.—Farther Sufferings of the Texans.—Meet with an immense Herd of Sheep.—Mexican Shepherds and their Dogs - 255

CHAPTER XIII.

Farther Feasting.—Party sent to the Settlements.—Objects of sending the Party a-head.—News respecting Howland and his Companions.—Encounter with Mexican Muleteers.—Farther Information in relation to Howland.—Manuel sent back.—Suspicious Horsemen seen.—Arrival at Anton Chico.—Consternation of the Inhabitants.—Scanty Raiment of the Women. — Confidence restored. — Description of Anton Chico.—Scantiness of the Furniture.—A Dinner under Cover.—Start for San Miguel.—Compelled to return.—A Night at Anton Chico.—A suspicious Visiter.—Report that we were to be arrested.—Start again from Anton Chico.—Valuables concealed.—Arrival at Cuesta.—Commotion in the

Village.—Our Party surrounded by Mexican Troops.—Apparent Frankness of their Leader, Dimasio Salazar.—Our Arms taken from us.—Consultation of Salazar and his Officers.—Mexican Duplicity.—Prompt Interference of Vigil in saving our Lives.—Kindness of the Women.—Don Jesus, and his Attempt to tie us.—Description of our Guard.—Puertecito.—Arrival at San Miguel.—Our first Night in Prison. Page 287

CHAPTER XIV.

Ordered to march towards Santa Fé.—Departure from San Miguel.—Gloomy Anticipations.—Our Guard increased.—Meet with a Party of Mexican Troops.—Brutality of their Leader.—Lewis, Van Ness, and Fitzgerald tied with Cords.—Our first Interview with Governor Armijo.—His Reception.—Conduct of Lewis.—Armijo's last Command.—Carlos seen.—First Appearance upon a Donkey.—A heavy night Shower.—Once more at San Miguel.—Barbarous Execution of one of our Comrades.—We are ordered before the Governor.—An exciting Trial.—Howland condemned to Die.—Cruel Mode of Execution.—Noble Conduct of Howland.—Kindness of a young Priest.—Departure of Mexican Troops for Anton Chico.—News of Colonel Cooke and his Men.—Plans of Armijo.—Particulars of the Capture of Howland.—Description of Manuel Pino.—News of the Capture of our Friends at Anton Chico.—Great Rejoicings at San Miguel - - - - - - - - - 310

CHAPTER XV.

New Quarters. Our Party taken before Armijo.—His bombastic Account of the Soldiers of New Mexico.—Appearance of Armijo.—Description of our Prison.—Overrun with Chinches.—The Family next Door.—The Zapatero's Wife.—A singular Custom.—The Senora Francisca abandons her Paint.—Dress of the Females of New Mexico.—Its Scantiness.—Freaks of Fashion.—Description of the Reboso and Mantilla.—Beauties of the Women of Mexico.—Kindness of the Girls of San Miguel.—Colonel Cooke's Men marched through San Miguel.—Lieutenant Lubbock's Account of the Surrender.—Agency of Lewis in the Affair. Prison Occupations.—Chances of an Escape canvassed.—Arrival of Caravans from the United States.—A seasonable Supply of Luxuries.—The Author assured of his personal Release.—A Mexican Loafer.—Tomas Bustamente.—Employ him as our principal Agent.—Thomas Rowland.—His Release from Arrest.—Bustamente sent on a Mission to Lewis.—Its unsuccessful Result.—Bustamente's Trickery found out - - - 334

CHAPTER XVI.

Arrival of a Party of our Companions as Prisoners.—Great Excitement in San Miguel.—Recognition of our Friends, and their Departure.—Don Antonio Bacca.—"Old Paint" Caldwell and Nine of his Men brought in Prisoners.—The Patron Saint brought from his Niche in the Church.—A Mexican Procession—Programme of the Procession.—An old Priest with queer Spectacles.—A Pair of Musicians.—More of San Miguel, the Patron Saint.—End of the Procession.—Startling Information.—Great Rejoicing in San Miguel.—General M'Leod and other Texans brought into the Plaza.—Mr. Falconer.—Arrival of all the Prisoners.—Dreadful Appearance of the Texans.—Lewis arrives.—Division of the Spoils.—Agency of Lewis in the Transaction.—A Visit from Lewis.—More of his Trachery and Rascality.—His Departure for Santa Fé.—A veritable History of Don Manuel Armijo, from his Youth upward, being a short but faithful Narrative of his thieving, gambling, assassinating, and other base Acts and Propensities - - - - - - - - Page 357

CHAPTER XVII.

Unrealized Hopes.—We are quartered with our Companions.—Arrival of "Old Paint."—Joy at seeing the Veteran.—Another Meeting with Friends.—Stories of Suffering.—Armijo and Lewis.—Departure for the City of Mexico.—A long and gloomy March before us.—The Brute Salazar in Command.—Bustamente and the Women of San Miguel.—Causes of the Failure of the Santa Fé Expedition.—Arrival at a deserted Mission.—Sufferings of the Prisoners from Cold.—More of Salazar's Brutalities.—The dreary March continued.—Arrival at Pino's Rancho.—Farther Sufferings.—Horrible Threat of Salazar.—Santo Domingo.—Kindness of the Women.—San Felipe.—First sight of the Rio Grande.—Algodones.—A Second "Black Hole of Calcutta."—Arrival at the Indian Village of Sandia.—A singular Rite.—Description of the Inhabitants.—Alameda.—Scene in an Oven.—Misery makes us acquainted with strange Bedfellows.—Sufferings on the Increase.—Bottoms of the Rio Grande; their Fertility.—Albuquerque in Sight.—Herons and Wild Geese.—A dashing Mexican Horseman.—Lieutenant Hornsby abducted.—Arrival at Albuquerque.—The Family of Armijo.—Farther Kindness of the Women.—General Pike's Journal.—The Pretty Girl of Albuquerque - - - - - - - - - - - - - - - 386

CHAPTER XVIII.

Los Placeres.—Another Dark Leaf in Salazar's Character.—Reappearance of Lieutenant Hornsby.—His singular Story of Adventure.—Arrival at Valencia.—Farther Sufferings of the Prisoners.—Death of Ernest.—An American Traveller.—Cruel Murder of M'Allister.—Its effect upon the Prisoners.—Casar Colorada.—A comfortable Camp.—Appearance of the Valley of the Rio Grande.—Uses of the Cotton-wood.—Salazar and the Alcaldes.—The Mexican Button Market.—A Story of Stump.—Magoffin's Waggons passed.—Arrival at Joya.—A Fandango, Salazar Drunk.—Conduct of the American Drivers on the Occasion.—Arrival at Socorro.—A short Rest allowed.—Character of the Inhabitants.—A party of Apaches.—Anecdote of the Priest of Socorro.—Head Chief of the Apaches.—His dignified Bearing.—Obsequiousness of Salazar.—Recrossing the Rio Grande.—The Camp of Fray Cristobal. A Snow-storm at Night.—Appearance of the Prisoners by Daylight.—Colds and Coughs - - 412

NARRATIVE

OF THE

FIRST TEXAN SANTA FÉ EXPEDITION.

CHAPTER I.

Objects of the first Texan Santa Fé Expedition.—Determination to accompany it.—The Western limits of Texas—Her claim to the Rio Grande. —Colonel Butler's contemplated Expedition to Santa Fé —Causes of its Failure.—Preparations for joining the Texans.—Departure from New Orleans.—Steam-ship New-York.—Captain Wright's Specific against Thirst.—Arrival at Galveston.—Frank Combs.—City of Houston.—Stories of old Hunters and Campaigners.—Houston Horse Jockeys.—Choice of an Animal.—Leave Houston for Austin.—Ladies on Horseback —Race with a Thunder-shower.—Incidents upon the Road.—Arrival at Austin.—Mr. Falconer.—English Travellers.—Party to San Antonio made up.—Jim the Butcher sent to the Stable.—Mexican Mountain Pony.—His Mustaches, and Powers of Endurance.

"WHAT were the objects of the Santa Fé Expedition?" and "What induced *you* to accompany it?" are questions which have been so often asked me, that I cannot carry my reader a single mile upon the long journey before us until they are answered. Without preamble or preface, then, I will to the task.

In the early part of April, 1841, I determined upon making a tour of some kind upon the great Western Prairies, induced by the hope of correcting a derangement of health, and by a strong desire to visit regions inhabited only by the roaming Indian, to find new subjects upon which to write, as well as to participate in the wild excitement of buffalo-hunting, and other sports of the border and prairie life.

The determination to take an excursion of this kind once made, my next object was to fix upon the route. The prairies west of St. Louis, the hunting-grounds of the Pawnees and other savage tribes, had been explored by Charles Augustus Murray, and described by his graphic pen; here was no new opening. Again, M. C. Field, one of my assistants in the "Picayune," had made the journey to Santa Fé by way of Independence, Missouri, and a series of articles written by him, upon the subject of his adventures, had found favour in the eyes of the public, being much copied into other journals. Here was another beaten and well-known road; yet I determined to traverse it if no other offered.

About the first of May of the same year, a number of young gentlemen of my acquaintance set on foot the project of an excursion to the prairies and buffalo-grounds, taking either Fort Towson or Fort Gibson in the route, and roaming through the Osage country and over a part of that section visited by Washington Irving in his foray upon the prairies. While canvassing the chances and merits of a trip of this kind, I met with Major George T. Howard, then in New Orleans, purchasing goods for the Texan Santa Fé Expedition.

Of the character of this enterprise I at once made inquiry. Major Howard informed me that it was commercial in its intentions, the policy of the then President of Texas, General Mirabeau B. Lamar, being to open a direct trade with Santa Fé by a route known to be much nearer than the great Missouri trail. To divert this trade was certainly the primary and ostensible object; but that General Lamar had an ulterior intention —that of bringing so much of the province of New Mexico as lies upon the eastern or Texan side of the Rio Grande under the protection of his government—I did not know until I was upon the march to Santa Fé. He was led to conceive this project by a well-founded belief that nine-tenths of the inhabitants were discontented under the Mexican yoke, and anxious to come under the protection of that flag to which they really owed fealty. I say a well-founded belief; the causes which influenced him were assurances from New Mexico—positive assurances—that the people would hail the coming of an expedition with gladness, and at once declare allegiance to the Texan government.

With the proofs General Lamar had, that such a feeling existed in New Mexico, he could not act otherwise than he did—could not do other than give the people of Eastern New Mexico an opportunity to throw off the galling yoke under which they had long groaned. Texas claimed, as her western boundary, the Rio Grande; the inhabitants within that boundary claimed protection of Texas. Was it anything but a duty, then, for the chief magistrate of the latter to afford all its citizens such assistance as was in his power?

Texas claims, as I have just stated, the Rio Grande as her western boundary; yet, so isolated were Santa Fé, and such of the settled portions of New Mexico as were situated on the eastern side of that stream, that the new Republic had never been able to exercise jurisdiction over a people really within her limits.* The time had now arrived, so thought the rulers of Texas, when rule should be exercised over the length and breadth of her domain—when the citizens of her farthest borders should be brought into the common fold—and with the full belief in their readiness and willingness for the movement, the Texan Santa Fé Expedition was originated. On its arrival at the destined point, should the inhabitants really manifest a disposition to declare their full allegiance to Texas, the flag of the single-star Republic would have been raised on the Government House at Santa Fé; but if not, the Texan commissioners were merely to make such arrangements with the authorities as would best tend to the opening of a trade, and then retire. The idea, which has obtained credence to some extent in the United States, that the first Texan Santa Fé pioneers were but a company of marauders, sent to burn, slay, and destroy in a foreign and hostile country, is so absurd as not to require contradiction; the attempt to conquer a province, numbering some one hundred and fifty thousand inhabitants within its borders, was a shade too Quixotical to find favour in the eyes of the three hundred and twenty odd pioneers who left Texas, encumbered with wagons, merchandize, and the implements of their different trades and callings. The expedition was unfortunate, and as a natural consequence, the censorious world has said that it was conceived in unwise policy. In the progress of my narrative, it will be seen that its failure arose from causes purely fortuitous; in a word, that the enterprise

* Santa Fé is situated some fourteen miles east of the Rio Grande, on a small branch of that stream.

had failed and been broken up long before those engaged in it had reached the confines of New Mexico.

The expedition was to leave Austin, the capital of Texas, about the last of May or first of June. The route to be taken had not been determined upon when Major Howard was in New Orleans, but it was thought that the pioneers would follow up the San Saba road, from San Antonio to Santa Fé; a route extending in nearly a northwest, and, as was then thought, a direct line. Fearing that there might be a scarcity of water on this trace, the direction was afterward changed.

That an enterprise, so purely commercial in its aspect, was intended for a hostile invasion of Mexico, did not, as I have already stated, enter the mind of any one at the time—at least not in Texas, where the inhabitants should be best able to judge. That a military force of some three hundred men accompanied the expedition is well known, and it is equally well known that the route across the prairies, whether by the San Saba or the Red River, would lead directly through the very heart of the Camanche and Caygüa country—inhabited by Indians who are foes alike to both Mexicans and Texicans. It cannot be considered very strange, then, that in a country so infested with hostile savages as Texas is, where a man hardly dares go out to catch his horse without a rifle and pair of pistols about him, a military force accompanied this expedition. The number of men was really not larger than that which accompanied the earlier Missouri enterprises; and large as it was, it did not prove sufficient for the purposes intended, many valuable lives being taken, and a large number of horses stolen, by the Indians we encountered on the route. These remarks I have made to counteract assertions put forth by the ignorant few, that the very fact of a military force being sent with the expedition was proof sufficient of its original hostile intentions. They would have had us, forsooth, start off with walking-sticks and umbrellas, and been scalped to a man in order to prove our object pacific. Perhaps their knowledge of the barbarians, through whose territory we were to pass, was of a piece with that of a very worthy agent sent to Texas, some years ago, by the French government. This gentleman planned an excursion after buffalo, directly into the hunting-grounds of the Camanches, to be accompanied only by two of his friends with servants. On being told of the certainty that he would be killed, he confidently remarked that he should carry the flag of France with him—*the Camanches would never dare insult that!*

It was while making inquiries, as to the nature and objects of the Texan expedition, that I first heard of an enterprise somewhat similar, then in contemplation in the United States. A company, under the command of Colonel Pierce M. Butler, formerly governor of South Carolina, and well known as an efficient and gallant officer, was to leave a point high up on Red River for Santa Fé, having for escort a body of United States dragoons. What was the object of this enterprise, whether to counteract the Texans in their attempt to divert the New Mexican trade or otherwise, I am unable to say. It was abandoned, at all events, for the reason that Colonel Butler could not make all his preparations in season to ensure a sufficiency of grass and water upon the prairies; but had it started, I should have made one of the party.

Thus foiled, I finally resolved upon accompanying the Texans. My intentions were, on joining this expedition, to leave it before it should reach Santa Fé, so as in no way to commit myself, and then to make the entire tour of Mexico—visiting the cities of Chihuahua, Durango, Zacatecas, San Luis Potosi, Guanajuato, and others on the road to the capital. These intentions I made known to all my friends in New Orleans, not one of whom thought I should in any way compromise myself as an American citizen, or forfeit my right to protection, by the route I proposed pursuing. By a law of Mexico—a law of which I must confess myself at the time ignorant—a foreigner is prohibited from entering that country through the territory of Texas; but the only punishment for this offence is being ordered out of Mexico by the nearest road, a penalty which would have been very willingly submitted to by me at any moment while I was in that country.

Having made every other preparation for my tour through Texas and Mexico, I went, on the morning of the 15th of May, 1841, in company with James H. Brewer, Esq., to the office of the then Mexican vice-consul at New Orleans, and obtained from him a passport, which gave me permission to enter, as an American citizen, any place in the so-called Republic of Mexico. Thus fortified, and with intentions the most pacific towards both the countries through which I was to pass, on the 17th of May I sailed from my native land, in the steam-ship New York, Captain Wright, for Galveston. On bidding adieu to my friends, I anticipated an exciting and interesting tour of some four months' duration, and expected to meet with the usual dangers and participate in the usual sports to be met with on the borders and prairies—nothing more.

Our voyage from New Orleans to Galveston was characterized by little worthy of remark. Some of the passengers were seasick, and all such were laughed at: some of them asserted, very positively, that if they could once set foot upon shore, they never would be seen out of sight of it, while others said they cared but little whether they ever saw land again. One circumstance I well remember: our captain told me that a piece of raw hide, placed in the mouth while suffering thirst, would impart much moisture, and consequent relief; and months afterward, when in a situation to try the experiment, I found that there was much truth in the recipe of our experienced skipper.

Early on the morning of the 19th of May we reached Galveston. This, in a commercial point of view, is the most important place in Texas; yet no vessel larger than an ordinary sloop of war can cross the bar, at the highest tide. The harbour is considered far from safe; yet it is one of the best on the entire coast, from the mouth of the Rio Grande to the Sabine, and must be the point from which a large portion of the cotton and other products of Texas will always be shipped.

At Galveston I found every one talking of the proposed Santa Fé Expedition. It was looked upon as nothing more than a pleasant hunting excursion, through a large section of country, much of which was unknown to the white man. Such portions of the route as had been previously explored were known to abound with buffalo, bear, elk, antelope, and every species of game, besides fish and wild honey. The climate was also known to be dry and salubrious; in short, until a point high up on Red River should be gained, the trip promised to be one of continued interest and pleasure. But beyond that point the country was a perfect *terra incognita,* untrodden save by wild and wandering Indians, and all were eager to partake of the excitement of being among the first to explore it.

At Galveston I became acquainted with young Frank Combs, son of General Leslie Combs, of Kentucky. He had partially made up his mind to accompany the expedition, in the hope of recovering his hearing, which had been for some time defective; on learning that I intended to start that evening for Houston, on my way to Austin, he made hurried preparations to set off in my company on board a steamer. The next morning we were landed safely at Houston.

Here all was bustle and preparation. A company of volunteers, comprising some of the most enterprising young men residing in and about Honston, had been formed, and all were busy in making arrangements for their departure for Austin, the point whence the expedition was to take the line of march for Santa Fé. Every gunsmith in the place was occupied, night and day, in repairing guns and pistols; every saddler was at work manufacturing bullet-pouches, and mending the saddles and bridles of the volunteers—all was hurry, preparation, and excitement.

To give some idea of the opinions entertained at Houston of the objects of the expedition to Santa Fé, I will here describe the general tone of conversation. Hardly a word was said of any hostile collision with the inhabitants of New Mexico; on the contrary, a chase after buffalo, or a brush with the Camanches or some of the hostile tribes known to be wandering about the immense Western prairies, was the principal topic upon every tongue. Old campaigners and hunters were among the speakers, and the wild stories they told of their forays upon the borders and beyond the borders of civilization, of their hair-breadth 'scapes and encounters with bears, rattlesnakes, Camanches, buffaloes, and other inhabitants of the boundless prairies, with the thousand and one tales of the marvellous these frontier Leather Stockings always have at their command—either ready made or easy of construction at the time of need—all served to render those who had already made up their minds to join the party more eager than ever, and induced the lukewarm to "pack up," and follow their example.

I remained at Houston, some three or four days, in which I made additional arrangements for the tour. Determined to be in no way connected with the expedition, farther than travelling with it at my own pleasure, and for such time as might suit my own interest and convenience, I had scrupulously avoided involving the Texan government in the least expense in providing the minutest article of my outfit. My rifle — short, but heavy barrelled, and throwing a ball,* with great strength and precision, a long distance — I had purchased of the well-known Dickson, of Louisville, Ky., and a most excellent rifle it was. My pistols, powder and lead, bowie and other knives, blankets, accoutrements for my horse, and other implements and articles necessary for a prairie tour, I had picked up here and

* Twenty-four to the pound.

there—some having been given me by my kind friends in New Orleans, while others I had purchased before leaving that city. My necessities now required little save a horse, and as this was one of the most important points in an efficient "fit out," I determined to take my time, and obtain a good one.

Any one who has entered the Houston horse-market with the intention of purchasing, is well aware that it is easy enough to buy a nag, but not so easy to procure one of the right sort.

When it became known that I wished to operate a little in horseflesh as a purchaser, all sorts of nags were "trotted out" by the different dealers and proprietors. There was the heavy American horse, whose owner had probably entered Texas by the inland or Red River route, and wishing to return by way of New Orleans, had no farther use for him; then there were the wiry-looking Indian pony, doubtless broken down and short-winded from hard usage; the light but game Mexican; and last, the recently caught, restless and apparently vicious *mustang,* or wild horse of the prairie: all these different samples were offered for my inspection, with the usual catalogues of their many merits, particularly their great powers of endurance. From so large an assortment I found not a little difficulty in making a selection. I looked, with an eye of fondness and craving, upon a beautiful nag, half Spanish, half wild, of fine action and most delicate points. I thought of the "show off" I could make upon a horse of this peculiar description, for he had an ambling and a proud gait, but just at this moment prudence suggested the idea of the long journey I had before me, and I purchased a heavy and powerful American horse for four times the sum with which I could have bought the spotted and sprightly Spanish pony. He was far from being "a good horse to look at," but was "an excellent one to go," and never was money better invested. Bravely, and without once flagging, did he carry me my long journey through, ever ready to start off on a buffalo or other chase, and enduring to the last. "Jim the Butcher"—not a very romantic or euphonious name, but so he was called by the man of whom I purchased him—is now in the hands of the Mexicans, and sincerely do I hope they have treated him with more kindness and consideration than they did his master. Would that I had him now. Want should never overtake him until it had first conquered me.

With the purchase of my horse ended my immediate wants. I was now fully armed, mounted, and equipped for the prosecution of my journey. I cannot take leave of Houston, however, without tendering my thanks to the many kind friends I found there. To Captain Radcliff Hudson, and Lieutenants Lubbock and Ostrander, in particular, I was under many obligations. They were the officers elect of the Houston Company of Santa Fé Pioneers, and cordially invited me to mess with them as a "guest" on the expedition. Although reluctantly compelled to decline their invitation, I could still appreciate the kind motives which induced them to proffer it.

Frank Combs and myself, with one or two others also on their way to Austin, left Houston late in the afternoon. The weather was hot and sultry, and dark clouds in the southwest gave every indication of a heavy shower before nightfall. The house that had been recommended to us to stop at over night was some twelve miles distant, inducing us to gallop rapidly along with the hope of reaching our resting-place before the coming down of the shower. As we cleared the pine woods by which Houston is environed, and struck out into the prairies, we met a party of ladies and gentlemen on horseback. They, too, were pressing their nags to the utmost, evidently to reach shelter before the heavy black clouds should commence discharging their torrents; and the loud and merry laugh of the ladies, as they gayly and swiftly passed along, showed that they were perfectly at home on horseback, and heedless of any break-neck risks they might be running.

After a closely-contested race, of an hour's duration, with the shower, during which it was almost impossible to say which would come out a-head, we finally reached our stopping-place neck-and-neck—in racing parlance, made a "dead heat" of it. No sooner had we thrown ourselves from our jaded animals and hastily stripped them of their saddles, than the large and widely scattered raindrops, which usually precede a shower, gave place to a perfect avalanche of water. Our log-house quarters, however, were closely "chinked and daubed,"* and we passed a dry and comfortable night.

The heavens were still overhung with clouds on the ensuing morning, although the rain had nearly subsided. After partaking of a warm breakfast, we resumed our journey across the gently undulating and fertile prairies to be found between all the many streams which water Texas. Although not yet June, the corn was nearly as

* The process of filling, with clay, the interstices between the logs of all houses in the new countries—for there all the houses are at first made of logs—is called "chinking and daubing."

high as a man's head, and gave goodly tokens of a most abundant harvest. The following day we crossed the Brazos at San Felipe de Austin, formerly a place of some little note, but now falling to decay. Another day, after two or three tolerably severe drenchings from the almost hourly showers that were falling, carried us through Bastrop to a noted stopping-place for travellers, within some twenty miles of Austin. The proprietor of this plantation, with his brother or son-in-law, and a few others, had settled upon it long before the revolution, and in the most troublous Indian times. Frequent and bloody were the encounters between the whites and their savage neighbours, in which the former generally came off victorious, although at times they lost some one of their number. On taking seats at the dinner-table, in the house I have just mentioned, I noticed, with some little surprise, that one of the male members of the family sat down with his hat on. I thought him guilty of great rudeness or forgetfulness; but before we left the mystery was explained. In one of the early encounters with the Indians he had been shot down, tomahawked, and scalped by his brutal enemies, and then left for dead. After remaining senseless for some time, the wounded man revived. He had bled much from several wounds, and was suffering extremely from pain; yet he had strength and resolution to crawl first to a spring of water, and then to his log-shanty, a distance of several miles. He suffers to this day from nervous headache, and, I believe, always wears his hat closely drawn down. He is the second person I have seen who has survived the barbarous process of scalping, and may be looked upon as a living witness of what the honest Hibernian *said* was a fact, namely, "that a man is not always dead when he is killed!"

On arriving at Austin, I was introduced to Colonel William G. Cooke and Doctor R. F. Brenham,* two of the commissioners appointed by General Lamar to treat with the inhabitants of New Mexico. They informed me that the expedition would not leave under a week at least—probably not under ten or twelve days. This delay I did not much regret, as it would give me an opportunity of visiting San Antonio, by far the most interesting place in Texas, not only from the beauty of its location, and the old Spanish missions in its neighbourhood, but from its being the spot where some of the fiercest battles in the early part of the Texan Revolution were fought.

At Austin I first became acquainted with Mr. Falconer, a young English gentleman of high literary and scientific attainments, mild and agreeable manners, and what is rare among his countrymen when away from home, extremely sociable and companionable qualities from the first. Your English traveller, unless he is an old stager, has seen much of the world, and has learned to take the many discomforts he is sure to encounter with

* Poor Brenham! He passed safely through all the perils, hardships, and sufferings of the Santa Fé expedition, to be again taken prisoner at the sanguinary battle of Mier, fought in the early part of the past year, 1843. While again on his march as a prisoner to the city of Mexico Brenham induced his fellow-prisoners to join him in an attempt to escape. He led the attack upon the guards, had already killed two of them, and severely wounded a third, when he stumbled, and fell directly upon the bayonet of his falling enemy. Thus died Brenham, and in him Texas lost one of her bravest and most generous spirits.

composure, is prone to grumble. Nature has made him a most excellent growler, but not a traveller; and he cannot combat against her arbitrary laws. Meet him in a stagecoach, a steamboat or a railroad car, and as far as his dress goes—for no man knows better how to dress, while travelling, than an Englishman*—all is right; but attempt to draw him into conversation, and he will wrap a *hauteur* about him more impenetrable than his rough overcoat. He will answer your question it is true, but in such a way that you think he wishes to shut the gate against your asking another. His *yes* is short and quick, like the breathing of a pipestem; his *no* comes snappingly from, like the growl of a hyena when punched through the bars of his cage with a long pole. Yankey ingenuity tries, but in vain, to find out his name, his place of residence, his business—in short, *who* or *what* he is—and all this while the close observer may detect a half smile of self-satisfaction on the round and ruddy face of John Bull, as he cruelly, yet successfully puzzles his indefatigable interlocutor.

Yet, with all his coldness and unapproachability, one cannot help admiring the English traveller. There is nothing assumed or studied in his formality—all is natural. He never asks questions—never, therefore, gives you an excuse for addressing questions to him. You think him unsocial and distant, from the coldness of his

* How different with the American traveller. He must needs, on starting on a journey, array himself in his "Sunday-go-to-meeting-dress." He makes his toilet with the greatest care, alike regardless of rain, dust, or sparks from locomotives. The Englishman laughs at him, and with good show of reason; for a more absurd custom could not well be devised. I have been pleased to observe, of late, that my countrymen are gradually dropping this foolish habit.

answers: he thinks you impertinent and forward, from the boldness of your questions. Both, to a certain degree, are right—and both are wrong. Could a medium rule of conduct be adopted, I am not certain that the ethics of those little sovereignties—the stage-coach, the car, and the steamboat—would not be greatly improved.

I have said that the Englishman is not "cut out" for a traveller; nor is he. With all the comforts of home about him, he will still find something to grumble at—but when he leaves it, everything goes wrong. The roads over which he travels are bad, the landlords of the houses where he may chance to stop are unaccommodating, the servants are inattentive, the beef is over-done, the mutton is tough and unsavoury. All this may be true, to a certain extent, for your traveller cannot find everything to his liking or taste away from his own homestead; but where your American good-humouredly cracks a hyperbolical joke at the expense of the land-lord; where your Frenchman shrugs his shoulders, and grins and bears it; where your German resorts to his pipe or cigar for consolation, your Englishman "makes a muss" about it, and growls his dissatisfaction in looks and in words. While in the stage-coach, should your only companion by chance be an Englishman, you would be led to think that a sentence to six months' imprisonment on the "silent system" would be neither punishment nor bore to him; but set him down to his dinner, at a common roadside tavern, and, like Billy Bottom in the old play, he will "roar you like any lion." But in the social circle, or in the drawing-room, where the formalities of a regular introduction have been gone through, there our friend John is a different sort of personage—there an English gentleman *is* a gentleman in every sense of the word. Having now left our Englishman in comfortable quarters, where he is enjoying himself, I will return to my friend, Mr. Falconer.

He informed me that he had some little business at San Antonio, and that he should start on the ensuing day, in company with one or two friends, for that city. Here was just the opportunity I wished for. The distance from Austin to San Antonio is some eighty miles, without a single human habitation on the route. Parties of hostile Indians are continually hovering about in the vicinity of the road, ready to attack any party they may think themselves able to overcome. The bones of many unfortunate white men are now bleaching upon the prairies, between the two cities, where the travellers were waylaid and killed. At one time the wayfarer is shot at by a party of foot Indians from some cover or ambuscade; at another, he is attacked upon the open prairies by a superior number of mounted Camanches—a tribe that appear to live, move, and have their being, or, in other words, to eat, sleep, work, and fight on horseback.

Mr. Falconer's little party consisted of himself, a Kentuckian named Mat Small, and a Canadian Frenchman named Gramont. Small had received the first rudiments of a hunter's education in Kentucky, and had finished it in Texas. An experience so extensive, and formed upon such excellent models, had rendered him somewhat noted, the country round, for his science and skill as a finished borderer. Gramont, on the contrary, had been educated at Trois Rivieres for the priesthood, but had never taken holy orders. He was now, instead of selling masses and hearing confessions at so much apiece, quietly pursuing the calling of a surveyor in the country of San Patricio, to which point he was on his way. This was Mr. Falconer's entire force, and with this he had made all his arrangements for the journey; but he was now re-enforced by myself and Frank Combs, the latter having made up his mind to join the party. We thus mustered five strong, all well armed and equipped for a trip that is set down as extra-hazardous.

Wishing to give my horse every chance to gain flesh and strength before starting for Santa Fé, I left him with a livery-stable keeper at Austin, and hired a little rough-looking Mexican mountain pony in his stead. The latter was considerably advanced in years, disposed to take every advantage, and shirk from everything in the shape of hard work. He moreover had a huge pair of *mustaches* on his upper lip, appendages which belong, I believe, almost exclusively to horses from his particular section, and of his particular species; at all events, I have never seen them worn by other nags. He was tough, however, as wrought iron, and although one hour's riding would bring on a lazy fit, ten would not tire him; a fact of which I had most abundant evidence afterward.

CHAPTER II.

Leave Austin for San Antonio.—Prospects of a Shower.—Singular Conduct of Mat Small.—A regular Soaking.—Crossing the Colorado.—No Bottom for short-legged Animals.—Venison for Supper.—More of Mat Small.—Damp Lodgings.—Serenade of Wolves.—Meeting with old Friends.—The St. Mark's.—Head Springs.—Disturbance at Night.—Arrival of Friends from Austin.—Journey towards San Antonio renewed.—Colonel Cooke in search of a Short Cut.—Encounter with a Texan War party.—Hostile Indians about.—A Texan killed.—Mr. Falconer's Portrait taken while sitting upon a Mule.—Amusing Adventure.—More scared than hurt.—The Guadalupe.—The Salado.—Night Entry into San Antonio.—Yelping Curs.—Fun at a Fandango.—A Mexican Dance.—Monté.—Getting the Hang of the Game.—Return to Lodgings.—Comparative Merits of Floors.—Difference between Plank, Stone, and Earth.—Rough Life in Perspective.—Nothing after getting used to it.

THE morning of the day on which we were to start for San Antonio was unusually hot and sultry, with hardly a breath of air stirring. We had determined upon leaving Austin late in the afternoon, riding about twelve miles, and then encamping for the night on the banks of a small creek. This plan is generally adopted by persons travelling between the two places, although they are obliged, in consequence, to "camp out" two nights instead of one; but as starting early in the morning makes two long and tiresome days' marches, the former plan is deemed the most feasible and agreeable.

After dinner, while we were saddling our horses and making preparations for departure, a black cloud about the size of a buzzard was seen in the southwest. Before we were ready to mount, this cloud had spread over the whole quarter of the sky where it made its first appearance. The distant rumbling of thunder was by this time plainly heard, and the most uninitiated in the knowledge of the "weather-wise," could easily enough see that a tremendous shower was shortly to break over us. Such prudence as I was at that time in possession of, though unenlightened by experience in what most appertains to bodily comfort in the forest and prairie, suggested that if we were to send our nags to the stable until the shower, or at least the weight of it, should be over, our evening ride would be more agreeable, and the risk of catching cold far less; but instead of pursuing this course, Mat Small seemed hurrying himself to the utmost to make a start before the rain began to fall, as if anxious to get the full benefit and luxury of the shower, if any it had. He appeared to be our leader, though self-delegated; and against his experience I deemed it prudent not to raise a murmur. Not a word did he utter—his very look was law.

To a person who, like myself, had been admonished from early infancy, both by precept and example, to keep within doors as much as possible during the heavier species of showers, the prospect now was certainly neither pleasant nor flattering. Yet there was Small, tightening his saddle-girths and arranging his wallet of stores with as much unconcern as if he did not see the threatening deluge that was hanging over us, or if he did, cared nothing for it. My companions, too, appeared to be suddenly taken with a fit of haste, and hurried through the little preliminary preparations as though life and death depended upon their "getting off" before the rain commenced falling. That some of them did it for effect I am confident.

"You'll be mighty apt to get wet," said a thorough-bred Texan who stood watching our movements in front of Bullock's Hotel.

"Wet to the skin to a certainty," I answered aloud, with the hope that I might draw Small's attention to the threatening heavens; but he never once looked at the cloud. I saw that he was determined to start; and as I should only be making a laughing-stock of myself by demurring, I assumed an indifference I was far from possessing, and *pretended* to care as little for the impending flood as any of my companions. Before my journeyings were half through I got bravely over my antipathy to thunder-showers, and took them as coolly and kindly as a young duck.

The Colorado, which we were compelled to cross immediately on leaving the city, was distant some half or three quarters of a mile. We had scarcely mounted our animals before the rain commenced falling, and ere we had gone two hundred yards from shelter the full weight of the shower was upon us. It may have rained harder before, may have rained harder since—these are questions I do not feel called upon to decide; but this much I will say, that if it ever has I did not happen to be out at the time. It rained as though every window in heaven was thrown wide open, and a perfect Niagara of water was falling upon us.

By the the time we reached the Colorado I was drenched to the skin—as wet as though I had been out in the forty day's deluge without greatcoat or umbrella.

We found the river somewhat swollen by the previous rains, and the current running unusually fast; but the man Small, who appeared to have adopted the motto of "go-a-head," without taking Crockett's precaution of first ascertaining whether he was right or wrong, spurred his animal directly into the stream. Gramont and Frank Combs, well mounted on tall and spirited horses, did the same, and made the crossing without swimming; Falconer and myself, perched upon animals of smaller size and shorter limbs, were not equally successful. We were obliged to swim them across; but finally after not a little floundering, reached the opposite bank in safety.

At a brisk pace we rode through the rich and fertile bottom of the Colorado, and soon reached the green and rolling prairies. In half an hour the rain had passed over, but the sun was still hidden by dark and heavy clouds in the west. When within two miles of the place where we were to encamp, I descried a deer some distance from our trail, quietly feeding. As there was a small clump of bushes near the animal, affording a good cover for an approach, I jumped from my horse, with the determination of having a little fresh venison for supper if possible. I was fortunate enough to reach the low bushes without being seen, and after carefully peeping through them for a few moments, discovered the deer, with head erect and nostrils distended, gazing steadily in the direction of my cover. Ever and anon he would give the well-known blow or whistle, showing plainly that he scented danger, although he could not see it. I raised my rifle suddenly and fired. The smoke hung lazily on the damp atmosphere, and several seconds elapsed before I could see whether I had made a successful shot. I had been told, by old hunters, never to stir from my tracks, after firing, until I had reloaded, and this advice I now followed. On approaching the spot where, but a few moments before, the deer had stood so full of life and activity, I found him lying stiff—the heavy ball from my rifle having passed directly through his body. Although the task was difficult, I succeeded in throwing the dead animal across my horse's back, and with this extra load rode to the camp. Small gave a species of half-smothered chuckling laugh as I threw what I deemed no inconsiderable trophy of my skill to the ground. I noticed the smile, but did not, at the time, fully understand it.

In less time than it takes me to record it, the veteran hunter had cut a shoulder and some of the more delicate and eatable portions from the deer, and then, rolling the remainder and larger portion out of the way with his foot, remarked that it was but "poor doe." I told him that it was no doe at all, but a young buck—I could not say much as to its fatness. He gave another half-laugh, accompanied by a slight shrug of the shoulders and a sarcastic leer out of the corners of his eyes, and then thrust a stick through the pieces of meat which he still held in his hand. Another minute passed, and the venison, with some clumsily-cut slices of ham which Mr. Falconer had providently brought with him, was cooking before a large fire which the latter gentleman had kindled. A goodly-sized pot of coffee was also quickly boiling upon the same fire, and what with the scent of the roasting meat, and the fragrance of the old Java, I soon was the possessor of an appetite a city *gourmand* might envy. Most ample justice did I do to it in the way of eating, after the meat was cooked; and a tin cup of coffee, sweetened, it is true, but without milk, I then thought the most delicious draught I had ever tasted. It would be folly to deny that an appetite, known only in the woods and on the prairies, lent a sauce to our plain repast which neither wine and bitters, catsup, nor any of the provocatives and seasonings usually resorted to, could have given. There was one thing, however, which was running in my mind all the while, and which I could not understand—those apparently half-contemptuous and ill-suppressed laughs of Small, and his calling young buck "poor doe!" I grew wiser before I had been a month upon the prairies, and learned the full meaning of conduct which I then thought sneering. He was laughing, in the first place, to see me pack an entire deer into camp when our utmost necessities were more than supplied by less than a quarter of the animal, and among the Texan hunters the term "poor doe" is applied, regardless of gender, to any deer that may happen to be lean. Small, no doubt, thought me lamentably ignorant of the ways of that portion of the wide world in which he moved with so much credit, as indeed I was; and what was still worse for me, I had taken his honest and well-meant smile and accompanying chuckle for tokens of derision and open effrontery.

By the time we had finished our meal it was near dark, and a dense fog was rising upon the little creek, the banks of which we had chosen for our camp. My clothes were wet, my blankets were wet, the grass was wet, and the air was damp—a prospect by no means pleasant to one who, up to that time, had always been the possessor of shelter and a bed. To complain, however, would have given

Small another opportunity to indulge in one of his quiet chuckles; so I put as good a face upon the matter as was possible, spread my wet blankets upon the still wetter grass, and after rolling myself up, resigned myself, as well as I could, to the circumstances. My friends, all of whom had some little experience in "out-door" life, were huddled around me, and made themselves exceedingly merry and facetious at my expense; but all their seeming indifference to the damp and disagreeable position we were placed in I then thought assumed, and I did not believe that one of them thought of obtaining any sleep. For myself, I would have freely staked no inconsiderable sum that not the most skilful professor of animal magnetism who has ever lived, even old Mesmer himself, could have got a single wink of sleep out of me that night; but, while reflecting upon the impossibility of the thing, I absolutely fell into a sound slumber, as refreshing as though I had been upon the best bed in the world. Once or twice in the night I was awakened by the yelping and howling of a pack of sneaking, hungry wolves, drawn close to our camp, doubtless, by the scent of the deer I had killed. Otherwise my sleep was uninterrupted.

Early the next morning, while preparing our breakfast, Major Howard and Mr. George Van Ness, who had started from San Antonio the preceding day, rode up to our camp. Van Ness I had formerly known at Vermont, but had not seen him for several years. These gentlemen were on their way to Austin, on business requiring much expedition. They proposed that we should go no farther than the St. Mark's that day, and promised that they would meet us there early the next morning, and go with us to San Antonio. Although we had intended travelling to the Guadalupe, a river some distance beyond the St. Mark's, we now altered our plan and consented to their proposal. Without stopping to partake of our meal, to which we invited them, they gave their jaded animals the spur, and were soon lost to sight beyond a roll of the prairie. After finishing our breakfast, we saddled our animals and rode slowly towards the beautiful St. Mark's. By two o'clock we reached a deserted military station, near the head springs of that stream — the rendezvous appointed by our friends in the morning—and there encamped for the night. During the day, Small pointed to several large clouds of smoke rising at some distance a-head of us, and a little to the left of our route, remarking that they proceeded from Indian fires; but at the time we thought but little of them.

Than the country in the vicinity of the St. Mark's one more lovely and fertile can hardly be found. The stream rises at the base of a low chain of mountains, a short distance from the spot on which we were encamped. The St. Mark's is not formed by a series of small branches or creeks, but takes its rise and character from its fountain head, which is a large spring of clear, cool, and most delicious water, inexhaustible in its supply. But a few hundred yards below this spring we find a deep and swift-running river, stocked with a variety of fish. The bottoms on either side are wide, well-timbered, and of the greatest fertility, admirably adapted to either cotton or corn. Once clear of the bottoms, the traveller meets with gently-undulating prairies, affording nutritious grass for pasturage, and a good depth of soil of fair quality. The climate is dry and salubrious, and the settler finds himself occupying lands equally fertile, yet exempt from the bilious fevers and debilitating agues so prevalent upon the Colorado, the Brazos, and other muddy and sluggish rivers of Eastern Texas. The vicinity of the Guadalupe, another swift and clear stream which we passed on the ensuing day, resembles that of the St. Mark's, and could emigrants but enjoy facilities for getting their produce to market, no finer or more healthy openings exist in America.

We passed the night at the St. Mark's with no incident worthy of relation, other than an alarm among our animals, which were hobbled and staked close by our camp. We started up and found our beasts gazing, with pricked ears, into a darkness which to us was impenetrable. Thinking they were probably frightened by a family of noisy screech-owls, perched in a neighbouring tree, or else by a more distant pack of howling wolves, we only examined their fastenings to see that all were secure, and retired again to our blankets. From circumstances that transpired afterward, I have little doubt that Indians were prowling about our camp, and that they were either seen or scented by our beasts. It is a well-known fact that the horses or mules of a white man are invariably terrified at the approach of Indians, can scent them at a most astonishing distance, and from the circumstance that they always give the alarm, are considered excellent sentinels.

At daybreak Howard and Van Ness, now accompanied by Colonel W. G. Cooke, made their appearance. They had started from Austin at nightfall, and as the distance to the St. Mark's was some forty miles, had had a hard night's ride. The only rest they made was while we prepared a hasty breakfast; when this was over we saddled our animals and pursued our journey. The distance to San Antonio was still forty miles—not a severe day's ride for fresh and good horses—but as some of those in our company were but indifferent nags at best, and much travel-worn, the march proved extremely slow and fatiguing.

We had proceeded but a short distance, before Colonel Cooke, thinking we had lost the shortest trail to San Antonio, separated from our party and struck off across the prairies to the left at a brisk canter. He was hardly out of sight before we saw, rapidly approaching us, at a distance of some mile or mile and a half, a body of about sixty horsemen, whose character it was impossible to distinguish. Apprehensive at first that they might be Indians, we drew up in a body, with a small *mot* * of timber close by to which we could easily retreat, and awaited their approach. It proved to be a party of Texans that had been out some four months on an expedition against the Camanches. So long had they been absent from the settlements that they really bore the strongest resemblance to Indians. Their hunting-shirts had become torn and greasy, their hair long and matted, and their faces, from long exposure to the sun and only an occasional acquaintanceship with water, imbrowned nearly to the colour of mahogany. They, too, had at first mistaken us for Indians, and under this belief had approached at no inconsiderable speed: but on hearing us they discovered their mistake, and slackened their gait to one more in consonance with the feelings of their jaded animals.

Almost the first question asked by the leader of the

* In Western Texas a small clump of timber is called a *mot*.

party was, whether we had encountered Indians. On being answered in the negative, he stated that two of his comrades had started in advance, the afternoon before, for the purpose of hunting; that one of them, a man named Moore, had been killed and scalped by Indians; that his companion, Hunter, had also been wounded by the same gang, yet was enabled to make his escape, and was then safe among his men. His arm was broken by a ball, and on his name being mentioned he rode up to the advance with his wounded limb in a sling. Hunter gave us a description of the spot where he and his companion had been waylaid, and thought it singular, as we had passed directly along the trail, that we had not discovered the mutilated body of the latter. His own horse was untouched by the volley fired by the savages, and being a strong, fleet animal, brought his master off in safety. He described the Indians as being on foot, armed principally with guns and rifles, and numbering about seventy. At the conclusion of this short interview, the Texans hurried off in the direction of the St. Mark's, to find and bury their unfortunate comrade, while we continued our journey towards San Antonio. That we had made a most fortunate escape the day before, by halting at the St. Mark's, was now evident enough. Had we kept directly on we should, in all probability, have fallen into an ambuscade and been cut to pieces. It was now also rendered evident that the alarm among our animals, the previous night, was occasioned by Indians, and Mat Small's remark, that the smoke we had seen in the afternoon arose from the signal-fires of a party of hostile savages, received direct confirmation.

But we had other matters than the past to speculate

upon. Our little party was now seven strong, all well armed if not well mounted, and we doubted not being able to give a good account of ourselves should the Indians attack us. All that was necessary was to keep a bright look-out, and not fall into an ambuscade while passing the different *mots* and ravines scattered along our trail. But where was Colonel Cooke all this while? He was a-head, perfectly unconscious of the close proximity of Indians, and might be cut off and killed without our knowledge, or without our being able to render him the least assistance. This reflection caused us great uneasiness, and induced us to push forward with the hope of overtaking him.

Up to this time I have neglected to draw my friend Falconer's picture as he sat for it that day upon his mule. Hogarth might have done it justice; I shall only pretend to give it a rough outline. Although belonging to and reared in an excellent family, and accustomed to all the comforts of the polished life he had but recently left, he easily assimilated himself to the hardships and privations incident to a wild border life. The luxuries and good things of an English fireside he appeared entirely to have forgotten—the plain and simple substantials of a prairie alone occupied his attention. While at Austin he had elected himself our commissary, steward, cook — in fact, our purveyor-general — had provided a tea-kettle and coffee-pot for the general use, besides a tin cup for each man's private accommodation. With an eye to the general welfare he had also purchased a ham of goodly dimensions, besides coffee, sugar, tea, salt, and red pepper. Mrs. Bullock, the kind and attentive landlady of the best hotel at Austin, had added something like a bushel of fresh-baked biscuit to our other stock, so that we were most amply provided for. For all these nic-nacs Mr. Falconer had kindly furnished transportation on his mule, a ricketty, lame, self-willed, long-eared brute, of stature not exceeding eleven hands. If we can judge of a mule's obstinacy by the length of its ears, the animal in question was certainly endowed with a portion far exceeding that of any others of the species it has ever been my good or bad fortune to meet. And then, as I have before stated, she was lame of one leg, and had naturally a mincing, shuffling, hobbling gait with the other three. In addition to all this, the mule had a way of stumbling and tumbling down peculiarly her own—a habit which she indulged in to an excess absolutely inconvenient, besides being at times somewhat dangerous. To offset all these rare qualities, she was as hardy as a grizzly bear, and as tough and untiring as a hound. The latter quality might not have been constitutional, but rather the result of the rigid system of economy she displayed in the disbursement of her strength and speed, regardless alike of blows, spurs, cuffs, and whacks. This is a very nice point, and one upon which I dare not hazard a decision. She is now dead, poor thing, and some two months after the events I have just recorded made a meal for many a half-starved man; but even at this time I cannot help laughing at her eccentricities.

Now, upon the back of this animal I have been describing, on the morning in question, was perched my friend Falconer. He was arrayed in a costume somewhat resembling a New England washing-day dinner, inasmuch as it was picked up here and there. I have before stated that Mr. F. had kindly offered to give transportation to our *commissariat,* and this offer he fulfilled. We now have him seated upon his mule, with a double-barrelled smooth bore upon his shoulder, while around and underneath him, tied on and hanging in festoons, was a general assortment of a little of everything. There were a ham, a tea-kettle, a wallet of biscuit, half-a-dozen tin cups, a gourd, a pair of pistols, and a coffee-pot, all occupying prominent situations immediately around him. In addition, Falconer had with him a number of books and scientific instruments, and these were arranged, here an there, among the hardware and groceries. Thus arrayed and mounted he really seemed more like a gipsy or a travelling tinker than a member of the best society in London and a distinguished barrister of that city.

We had proceeded some five miles, scattered Indian file along the trail, and were growing more and more solicitous in relation to Colonel Cooke, when the sharp report of a rifle was heard some hundred yards a-head, in a narrow skirting of timber which fringed the banks of a small stream. Van Ness, who was in advance, and had reached the edge of the timber, immediately reined up his horse, and drew a pistol from his holsters. Major Howard was jogging along next to Van Ness, but at least forty yards behind him, Falconer was close to Major Howard, while myself and companions brought up the rear. The first impression with all, on hearing the report of the rifle, was that the Indians had formed an ambuscade for the purpose of cutting us off.

"Indians!" shouted Major Howard, drawing one of Colt's revolving pistols, and then putting spurs to his steed and making for the thicket.

"Where?" said Mr. Falconer, drumming his spurless heels into his mule's sides, and evincing a zeal truly laudable to be one of the first in the brush that all felt confident was about to take place.

Frank Combs, who was well mounted, came dashing by at the top of his horse's speed. This induced Falconer to redouble his kicks and exertions to force his mule along, and he had really induced the animal to make some show towards a species of Canterbury gallop as I came up with him. Just as I had reached him, and was about to pass, down went my unfortunate friend's entire establishment, strewing the road, for some ten feet, with mule, Falconer, and sundries. Although in what a Kentuckian would call "all sorts of a hurry," I could not help stopping for a moment to survey the scene, and ascertain whether my companion had injured himself. There, side and side, reposed a volume of Lord Bacon and a Kentucky ham—there too were a thermometer and a tea-kettle—tin cups, biscuits, fishing-tackle, a barometer, wallets, pistols, knives—scattered about in enviable confusion. I can only liken the scene to the promiscuous and miscellaneous appearance of the furniture of a house saved from a fire and thrown helter-skelter in the street. At any other time, after finding that my companion had sustained but little personal injury, I should have laughed outright at the ludicrous tumble; as it was I could not restrain a smile as Falconer hurriedly scrambled upon his feet. By this time the secret of the rifle-shot was fully explained by the appearance of Colonel Cooke from the timber. It seems that he had become lost in endeavouring to find a shorter trail, and discharged his rifle as the only method of making his whereabout known.

Having assisted the fallen Falconer in repacking and remounting his mule, we renewed our ride. At noon we reached the Guadalupe, without having met with any farther incident. Here we rested an hour or two under some shade trees, while our animals were feeding and fighting prairie-flies close by. Towards sundown we arrived at the Salado, a stream which sinks in the sand and rises again some distance below the regular crossing-place between Austin and San Antonio. It was on the banks of this river that Captain Caldwell, with a small number of Texans, defeated the army of General Woll, in 1842. After allowing our animals an hour's rest, we resumed our tiresome journey, and about eleven o'clock passed the old and ruined Alamo, and entered the outskirts of San Antonio. From every house some half dozen Mexican curs would jump forth and greet us with a chorus of yelps and barks, and before we had fairly entered the town the canine hue and cry was general. Those who have for the first time entered a Mexican town or city must have been struck with the unusual number of dogs, and annoyed by their incessant barking; but the stranger soon learns that they vent all their courage in barks—they seldom bite.

It was nearly midnight before I could find a resting-place for myself and horse. Late as it was, the sound of a violin drew me across the *plaza,* or principal square, and up one of the narrow streets leading to it.

Poor Power, in one of his plays, used to say that "wherever you hear a fiddle you are pretty sure to find fun;" in the present instance I found a *fandango.* As I entered the room, which was destitute of other floor than the hard earth, and lighted by two or three coarse tallow candles, a single couple were shuffling away, face to face, and keeping time to a cracked violin. Ever and anon the woman would sing a verse in Spanish, both herself and male partner standing until its completion. Then they would shuffle away again, using a species of break-down negro step, entirely devoid of grace and ease. Another verse and then another shuffle, and the dance was over. The woman was as destitute of beauty as an Egyptian mummy — in fact, if dried, would have made a very good counterfeit of one of those curiosities; her partner was even more ugly. Some half-dozen slovenly, badly-dressed, Mexican girls were sitting upon benches at either end of the room, while an old woman in one corner was selling paper cigars and vile whiskey.* I passed through an open door, leading into a back room, where were a small party of men and women betting at *monté.* I lost a couple of dollars "just to get the hang of the game," as the facetious Sam Slick would say, and then retired to my lodgings. Here I had no other bed than my own blankets and the hard earth floor; if anything can be harder than such a couch I have yet to find it, and my experience has been rather extensive. A plank really seems to have a "soft side," and those who have tried

* This was but a fandango of the lowest order. The reader must not suppose that there is no better society among the Mexicans of San Antonio than I found at this place.

both, as I have, will say that there is a species of "give," if I may be allowed the expression, to a stone floor; but a Mexican, hard-trodden, earth floor has a dead solidity about it which fairly makes the tired bones ache again. The experience of the few past days now came like an unpleasant panorama across my mind, and I began to reflect that I had a rough life in perspective; but as every one said "it was nothing after getting used to it," I resolved to "go a-head."

CHAPTER III.

Description of San Antonio.—Fondness of the Women for Bathing.—Climate.—Irrigating Canals.—Fruits.—The old Spanish Missions.—Objects for which they were constructed.—The Alamo.—Conception.—San Juan.—San José.—La Espada.—Bowie and Crockett.—Church of San Antonio.—Anecdote of General Cos.—Mexican Merchants from the Rio Grande.—Return to Austin.—Incidents upon the Road. A Texan Leather Stocking.—An Adventure.—Out-tricking a party of Indians.—Another Night at the St. Mark's.—Fruitless Chase after Camanches.—Hog-wallow Prairie.—Arrival at Camp.—More of the Camanches.—Plain Supper and good Appetite.—Insight into Astronomy.—Once more at Austin.—A Fall in the Dark.—Speculations while falling.—Broken Bones.—Dancing Days over, or the "Jig up."—Consolation under Misfortune.

BY far the most pleasant as well as interesting town in Texas is San Antonio, or Bexar as it is frequently called by the inhabitants. The San Antonio River, which heads a short distance above the town, meanders through its streets, and its limpid waters, by the different turns it makes and the irrigating canals, are brought within a convenient distance of every door. The temperature of the water is nearly the same all the year through—neither too hot nor too cold for bathing—and it is seldom that a day passes in which all the inhabitants do not enjoy the healthy and invigorating luxury of swimming. I say *all*—for men, women, and children can be seen at any time in the river, splashing, diving, and paddling about like so many Sandwich Islanders.

The women in particular are celebrated for their fondness for bathing, and are excellent swimmers.

The climate of San Antonio is pure, dry, and healthy; so much so, that the old but rather hyperbolical saying, "If a man wants to die there he must go somewhere else," appears specially to apply to the place. During the summer months, a cool and delicious breeze is almost continually blowing, bringing health and comfort. But little rain falls; and to supply this defect the rich and fertile bottoms of the river are intersected in almost every direction by irrigating ditches, which carry the limpid waters in every direction. Whenever the ground requires a moistening, the water from the canals is let over it at once; so that even should the summer pass without a drop of rain, the crop is invariably abundant. Peaches and melons arrive at great perfection, and I have little doubt that many other species of fruit could be cultivated with success. The prairies in the vicinity afford the finest pastures for cattle and horses to be found in the wide world, and so mild is the climate that they thrive at all seasons.

By far the greatest curiosities in the neighbourhood of San Antonio are the *missions*. Before I describe these immense establishments it is necessary to observe that early after the conquest of Mexico, a main object of the Spaniards' policy was to extend the authority of the Roman Catholic Church. The conversion of the Indian and the promulgation of Christianity were as eagerly sought by them as the gold and silver which first lured them to the Western World; and this missionary zeal produced some of the most remarkable incidents in the history of the country. The new doctrines were first inculcated by force and cruelty, but subsequently in a more humane temper, by allowing the superstitions of the Indian to mingle with the rites introduced among them; and to this day, the anomalous consequences of this policy are to be seen in the Indian ceremonies, some of which I will describe when I shall hereafter speak of our journey through the Mexican country. For the purpose, however, of affording protection to the Roman Catholic missionaries, there were established, at various times, settlements which still bear the name of Missions. They are very numerous throughout California, and in Texas there are several. The Alamo, at San Antonio, was one of much importance, and there were others, hardly of less consideration, in the neighbourhood, called the Missions of Conception, of San Juan, San José, and La Espada. They were all most substantially built; the walls are of great thickness; and in their form and arrangement they were frontier fortresses. They have generally, though not always, a church at the side of a square having one entrance. Seen from without, they present the form of a blank wall surrounding a square enclosure; within is a large granary, and the wall forms the back of a series of dwellings in which the missionaries and their converts lived. There was a large appropriation of the surrounding district for the support of the mission, through which small canals were made for the purpose of irrigation. Such, at least, is the case with the missions which I have mentioned. The Alamo, is now in ruins, only two or three of the houses being inhabited. The gateway of the church was much ornamented, and still remains, though deprived of the figures which once occupied its niches. But there is enough still to interest the investigator of its former history, even if he could for a moment forget the scenes which have made it celebrated in the history of Texan independence. The exact spot where the eccentric but brave Crockett fell, surrounded by a ring of Mexicans whom he had killed, is shown, as also the quarter where the heroic Bowie breathed his last. About two miles lower down the San Antonio River is the Mission of Conception. It is a very large stone building, with a fine cupola, and, though plain, magnificent in its dimensions and the durability of its construction. It was here that Bowie fought one of the first battles with the Mexican forces, and it has not since been inhabited. Though not so well known to fame as other conflicts, this fight was that which really committed the Texans, and compelled those who thought of terms and the maintenance of a Mexican connexion to see that the time for both had passed. The Mission of San José is about a mile and a half down the river. It consists, also, of a large square, and numerous Mexican families still make it their residence. To the left of the gateway is the granary. The church stands apart from the other buildings, in the square, but not in the centre; the west door is surrounded with most elaborate stone carving of flowers, angels, and apostles. The interior is plain. To the right is a handsome belfry tower, and above the altar a large stone cupola. Behind the church, and in connexion with it, is a long range of rooms for the missionaries, opening upon a covered gallery or *portales* of nine arches. Though the Texan tooops were long quartered here, the stone carvings have not been injured. The church has been repaired, and Divine service is performed in it. About half a mile farther down is the Mission of San Juan. The church forms part of the side of a square; it is a plain, simple edifice, with little ornament. The adjacent buildings are poor and out of repair. The granary stands alone in the square, and on the northwest corner are the remains of a small stone tower. The other mission, that of La Espada, is also inhabited, as well as the last. The church, however, is in ruins. Two sides of the square consist of mere walls; the other sides are composed of dwellings as in the other instances.

The church at San Antonio was built in the year 1717; and although it has suffered much from the ravages of time and the different sieges which the city has undergone, is still used as a place of public worship. When San Antonio was attacked and taken by Colonels Cooke and Milam, in 1835, General Cos made the belfry of this church his head-quarters. A well-directed cannon-shot from the Texans struck just above his head, inducing him to evacuate the place with his staff immediately. The hole made by the ball is still visible, and, in fact, all the houses in the principal square of the town are marked more or less by shot.

San Antonio is laid out and built with some little regularity. The houses are all of one story only, with few windows and thick walls. The town probably contained, at one time, a population of some twelve or fifteen thousand; but the different revolutions, the many bloody battles which have been fought within its walls, and the unsettled state of the frontiers, have combined to lessen this number materially. It is still, however, a place of no inconsiderable trade, and should peace be concluded with Mexico, will regain its former standing. While I was there a company of Mexican merchants from the other side of the Rio Grande arrived, who were allowed to trade and depart in peace; and had the expedition to Santa Fé been given up, as was at one time anticipated, I should have joined one of these companies and entered Mexico by way of Loredo.

After spending some six or eight days very agreeably at San Antonio, I set out on my return to Austin. Two days before I left, a number of wagons, loaded with goods by the merchants of San Antonio and destined for the Santa Fé market, left the former place; these we overtook at the Guadalupe, and thence journeyed towards Austin in company.

While "nooning" on our third day's march from San Antonio, or in plain terms, while stopping a couple of hours in the heat of the day to rest, I set off, in company with an original named Tom Hancock, in the hope of being able to kill a deer. This fellow Hancock was a perfect "character," as much so as the celebrated Leather Stocking of Cooper's novels. In person he was spare and gaunt, with a loose, shambling carriage of body that ill-betokened the firm-set muscles and iron powers of endurance he really possessed. When standing erect, his height may have been five feet seven or eight inches; but he had a lazy, listless stoop, which shortened his stature two or three inches, and gave him the appearance of being mis-shapen and round-shouldered. His limbs were anything but symmetrical, and seemed to hang dangling about him—this on ordinary occasions; but when the muscles were nerved, and the body straightened in the excitement of adventure, it was then that Tom appeared in his true light, a wiry, knotty imbodiment of action, power and determination.

Decidedly the best point about him was his eye, a small twinkling orb, of no definable colour, but which never allowed any object within the farthest reach of human vision to pass unnoticed. And yet, one might journey with him for days, might be in his company even for weeks, and never suppose that he was looking at or for anything. But not a footprint, not a trail, escaped the notice of that quiet-rolling eye—Tom could tell you the animal that made it, the direction in which it was going, and the time that had elapsed since it was impressed upon the surface of the prairie.

In every species of backwoods, border, and prairie strategy Hancock had his gifts, and they were such as have been vouchsafed to but few. An Indian he could circumvent and out-manœuvre at his own games, and at killing every kind of animal known in the woods or on the prairies, at fishing, or at "lining" bees, the oldest and best hunters acknowledged Tom's supremacy. He could lie closer to the ground, creep farther, expose less of his person and get nearer a deer, bear, buffalo, or enemy's camp, than any other man, and these qualities made him invaluable not only as a mere provider of meat for a camp, but as a spy. He had been in frays innumerable with the Mexicans, as well as Indians, and invariably performed some exploit that would furnish his companions with a topic for conversation. He had been a prisoner among the Camanches, but had got away from them—in short, had made hair-breadth 'scapes innumerable. Yet he never, on any occasion, boasted of his feats—never even adverted to them. Such is a rough and imperfect picture of Tom Hancock—of one nurtured amid the solitudes of the woods and prairies—whose days had been spent in the excitements and dangers of the chase or of Indian frays, and whose nights had passed amid serenades of prairie wolves and owls. He had been hired at San Antonio by Mr. Falconer—not as his servant, for Tom would scorn being the washer of dishes or brusher of clothes for any man—but simply to accompany the Santa Fé Expedition. His obligations to Mr. F. extended this far—he was to find him if lost, and to keep him in provision should other supplies fail. Such was the singular contract.

Tom's ordinary weapon, and the one upon which he most "prided" himself, was a long, heavy, flint-lock rifle, of plain and old-fashioned workmanship, for he could not be made to believe in percussion caps and other modern improvements. In the adventure I am about to describe he was armed with one of Colt's repeating rifles, which he had borrowed, his own being out of order. The spot where we had stopped to pass the heat of the day was a little prairie on the eastern side of a small branch, the borders of which were skirted by a narrow fringe of timber, running nearly north and south, and ranging in width from one hundred yards to a quarter of a mile. Tom and myself skirted along the eastern side of the trees until we had travelled nearly a mile, without seeing a living thing save two or three large prairie rabbits, which would suddenly jump up and leap off as we approached.

Thinking we might meet with deer on the opposite

side of the timber, Tom noiselessly led the way through while I followed closely upon his heels. We put up two or three turkeys near the branch, but the underbrush was so thick it was impossible to get a shot at them. When through the timber, Tom descried a couple of deer quietly feeding in the prairie. He attempted to get a shot, and laid his plans for that purpose with great judgment and every prospect of success; but the animals appeared extremely shy, and discovered him before he was within reach of them. A little farther up the prairie another deer was discovered ; but like the others, it was timid and on the look-out for danger, and ran off before my companion was within two hundred yards. "There's been Injuns round here lately, I know by the way the critters work," said Tom in his quiet way, at the same time pointing to the last deer we had started, which was rapidly bounding away in the distance.

The hunter now hesitated a moment, took a hurried but careful survey of the surrounding scene, and then kept on his course up the prairie, in an opposite direction from that in which our party were encamped. We had not proceeded a quarter of a mile, and were within about the same distance of the wood on our left, when an abrupt roll of the prairie brought us suddenly in sight of a large, and, to all appearance, recently deserted Indian camp, for the embers of some of the fires were still smouldering. "I knew it," said Tom, and pausing a moment, and circling the prairie with his eye, finished the sentence with "and some of 'em are close by, now." I said not a word, but watched every movement of the hunter. That danger was lurking near I was well aware, and if any one could combat it successfully I felt equally confident it was my companion. Although the movement appeared singular enough to me, Tom kept directly on nearly in the same direction, only so far varying his course as to leave the Indian camp fires on the right. We had advanced but a few steps before the footprints of men were plainly visible on the prairie grass. That they were footprints, and of five men, I could see myself; but which way they had gone, and what time had elapsed since the prints were formed, were matters to me of the most profound mystery. My first impulse was to hasten immediately to our camp, keeping on the same side of the wood until opposite, or nearly so, to our party; but I said not a word. Tom hastily threw himself upon his hands and knees, bent his head close to the ground, and attentively examined one of the footprints. As he rose to his feet he quietly remarked, "The grass ain't done risin' yet," his eye in the mean time following the fresh trail until it was lost in the wood at a point directly opposite where we then stood. That the Indians had but just passed was a fact brought home to my senses by the superior craft of my companion, and eagerly did I watch his farther movements. He ran his eye along the line of timber in either direction, lifted his rifle from the ground and hastily examined the lock and caps, and then, as if his mind was fully made up for any emergency, started at a fast walk for a point of the timber still farther from our camp. I followed him in silence, and I must say in astonishment, for to my understanding there was the utmost danger in the course he took; but with all my astonishment I still felt the utmost confidence in Hancock, for there was a decision in his movements that gave assurance he fully understood the nature of the dilemma in which we were placed, and had adopted the wisest measures to extricate us from it.

At a long, steady stride, and without apparently turning his eyes either to the right or left, Tom kept a straight line for the timber. The wood was soon gained, and at a pace even increased we struck directly through. I had not noticed the circumstance before, but now that we were among the trees I saw that at this point the belt of timber was much narrower, more open, and presented fewer facilities for an ambuscade. Arrived on the eastern side, Tom did not slacken his pace until we had left the woods some three hundred yards in our rear, when placing the breach of his rifle upon the greensward, giving one long breath, and casting his eye along the thicket we had just passed, he quietly remarked, "We needn't be afraid of 'em now—five foot Injuns ain't goin' to attack us in gunshot hearin' of camp, 'specially when there ain't no place for 'em to hide." Not another word did he utter, but lifting his rifle from the ground with a slight jerk, and catching it as it fell with his right hand, he leisurely took the direction back towards our camp. This little adventure, which certainly would have been fraught with some danger had it not been for the craft of Hancock, impressed me more fully than ever with a belief in his superior skill. Another fact I ascertained from our little hunting trip: the Indian camp we had discovered was the same from which ascended the different smokes that we saw while journeying from Austin to San Antonio, and undoubtedly was the general rendezvous of the large party who had killed Moore and wounded Hunter near the St. Mark's. Where the main body was, when Hancock and myself visited their premises, it is impossible to conjecture, but it was probably engaged in some marauding expedition. We were certainly fortunate in not falling in with it, and some of the warriors who composed the party were unfortunate so far as the missing a couple of scalps may go.

We arrived in camp as our companions were saddling their animals and preparing for departure, so that we had no time for rest after the fatigue of a two hours' march in the hot sun. Our nags, however, had enjoyed a rest, if we had not, and were fresh and ready for the journey. That night we spent at the St. Mark's, and after enjoying a bath in its cool waters, I had a sound and refreshing sleep. In the early part of the ensuing afternoon, some three or four of us who were a-head descried three Camanches ascending a distant roll of the prairie on horseback. We gave chase at once; but finding, after a race of some ten minutes, that they were going at least three yards to our two over the *hog-wallow** prairies, we reined up and returned to the trail.

On arriving at the spring where we were to encamp that night, we found two of our young men, who had gone out early in the morning in quest of game, busily dressing a fat buck they had been lucky enough to kill. We told them the circumstance of our having given chase to a small party of Camanches, and after we de-

* So called from the roughness of the prairie in many parts. In some places the ground has every appearance of having been torn up by hogs—*rooted*, I believe, is the expression—and hence the name. The Indian horses are early trained to run over these rough places with freedom.

scribed to them the route the Indians were taking when we first discovered them, our hunters at once said they were following on their trail. They also stated that in their morning hunt they had noticed fresh Indian "sign"* in many places, and had little doubt the Camanches we had chased had been hanging upon their path and waiting an opportunity to cut them off. They even deemed our appearance providential in saving their lives, as they had exhausted all their ammunition, and must have been massacred if the Indians had overtaken them.†

By the time our main party reached the spring where we had come up with our hunters, it was near six o'clock in the afternoon. As I had eaten nothing since daylight, and had had no little exercise in the way of riding and walking in the interim, the reader will readily imagine that I had a tolerably sharp-set appetite. At all events, I ate venison enough to satisfy a half-famished wolf; there were no other accompaniments than red pepper and

* Any evidences seen upon the prairies of the appearance, whether recent or otherwise, of animals or men, is called "*sign*." If the marks appear recent the term is "fresh sign"—if otherwise, "old sign." The term will very likely appear often in this work, and I have therefore given this short explanation.

† It may be considered singular that both these young men, before the Santa Fé Expedition reached the settlements of New Mexico, met a violent death. One of them, a young man named Lockridge, shot himself on Little River—whether by accident or not was never ascertained. He was a native, I believe of Louisiana, a lawyer by profession, of good manners, excellent education, and modest, retiring deportment. He was much beloved by all who knew him, and was buried with military honours near the spot where he breathed his last. The other, Doctor Bell, was an assistant surgeon, and a brother of his is said to be a captain in the United States army. The doctor was killed by Indians on the Grand Prairie, and his loss was deeply regretted by those who knew him best.

salt—but at that time I thought it the most delicious meal I had ever swallowed. Since then I have made a meal of the flesh of a poor, broken-down horse with far keener relish.

The next morning, after a brisk ride of some three hours, we reached Austin again in safety, having been absent nearly a fortnight. More than half of this time I had "camped out" upon the prairies, with no other bed than the ground, no other covering than the sky—blue or black, according to the state of the weather—and a Mexican blanket. I had already made considerable advancement, practically, in the science of astronomy, being able to tell the north star with much accuracy after first occupying some ten minutes in arranging the "pointers" so as to bear upon it. A friend had also promised to hunt up and make me acquainted with the "big bear" some fair night. Farther than this, I could now easily distinguish the howling of a prairie wolf from the screeching of an owl, points upon which I was sorely puzzled the first time I heard one of their concerts. But to speak seriously, I had found no bad effects from exposure so far, and was every day growing more and more reconciled to the long tour which still lay in prospect before me.

The evening after my return to Austin, however, an accident occured which not only came near preventing me from leaving for Santa Fé, but for any other place in this lower world. The day had been hot and sultry, threatening rain, and when night came the sky was shrouded in clouds of pitchy blackness. A man's hand could have been seen as plainly had it been in Kamschatka as when held before his face at arm's-length; but notwithstanding the darkness, some four or five of us made up a little party for the purpose of bathing, and started for the Colorado with that intention. As the river is approached, the traveller meets with a fork in the road, one trail leading directly down a cut-way excavated in the high steep bank, while the other conducts to the bluff and then turns abruptly off along its edge. I happened to be a-head, and unfortunately took the wrong trail; yet so confident was I that I was right, that I walked directly up to and over what may emphatically be called the "jumping-off place" of the Rio Colorado. It was no stumble, no pitching head first over a steep precipice, but on the contrary I walked directly off the giddy height—to use a common expression, went over "all standing."

It is to be presumed that a man's feelings are by no means pleasant when he suddenly finds that his feet have no footing, and that his gravity is carrying him, with a velocity absolutely uncomfortable, to say nothing of the attendant danger, from a third or fouth story window to a sidewalk, with every brick in which he is perfectly familiar; but his feelings border upon dissatisfaction and distrust when he ascertains that he is standing upon nothing, with an unknown destination before him, and has time to reflect, while descending, upon the distance he has already come and to indulge in speculations as to the distance he has yet to go. My experience in falling from high places is limited to one or two flights of this kind, and that the world may have the benefit of it, I will return to the height from which I first started, and give a plain recital of the fall and the injuries I sustained in consequence.

The distance through which I passed I have never

been able to ascertain, but it was far from inconsiderable. I was fortunate in retaining an upright position while falling, and had presence of mind to brace myself strongly, thinking that I should be better enabled thereby to meet the shock of striking the bottom, whether of earth, or stone, or water, I was at the time ignorant. My right foot reached terra firma first, the concussion shattering the ankle badly, and, as I then thought, breaking every bone in my body. My back, in particular, was so severely injured by the shock, that I was entirely bereft of the power to move. My friends hurried back as fast as the darkness of the night would permit, groped their way until they had found the road I had unfortunately missed, and were finally successful in reaching me. I was excessively faint, and called for water. One of the party soon returned from the river with his hat full, sprinkled my face and neck, and gave me a draught. They next lifted me, with as much care as possible, to their shoulders, and carried me back to the hotel we had left but a few minutes before in high and buoyant spirits; but it seemed as though every faculty of my body was paralyzed. Doctor Brenham, who was boarding at the same hotel, immediately called upon me and did everything in the power of a physician or surgeon. The next morning I was enabled to ascertain the extent of my injuries, which, though severe, were not so bad as at first supposed. My back was still weak, and pained me so much that I was unable to move without assistance; my ankle, in the mean time, was extremely swollen and entirely useless, and in addition gave me much pain. Yet my friends, one and all, said that I should be on my feet again in three or four weeks, as well as ever, and able to run down a buffalo bull on an open prairie. I could not feel quite as sanguine, but still thought that six weeks, or two months at farthest, would restore my bruised and shattered limb to its original strength. But even my expectations were wide of the mark, for some two months elapsed before I could even bear the least weight upon my lame foot, and it was three before I could walk without much pain.

Even to this day, and some two years have slipped away since I sustained the injury, the ankle is weak and far from being cured. Time was when I was able and willing to essay a cotillon with the sprightliest—when I could cut pigeon-wings and extras, and perform the double shuffle with no inconsiderable precision and activity; but those days are over now—the "jig is up." I still have one consolation, however, and one which I freely recommend to all who may be similarly situated; when a man breaks his leg he should always be thankful it is no worse—for instance, not his neck.

CHAPTER IV.

Visit from General Lamar.—Preparations for a Start.—Pleasant Anticipations.—Northers.—Bright Side of the Picture.—Speculations as to the Reception of the Expedition at Santa Fé.—No Thoughts of Fighting the New Mexicans.—Senor Navarro.—A Jersey Waggon provided.—Departure from Austin.—Adieu to Civilization.—A modern Athens.—Its sudden rise, and its more sudden fall.—President Lamar in Camp.—Arrival at the Brushy.—General Joy among the Pioneers.—Reviewed by the President.—Order of March.—Tricks of young Oxen.—Upsets.—Arrival at the San Gabrielle.—Camp Stories.—Opossum Creek.—Scene of a Fight with the Camanches.—Anecdote of Two Brothers.—A Night Storm.—Buffalo in Sight.—Petrifactions.—Stories of Buffalo.—A Youngster caught.—Methods of Hunting the Buffalo.—A regular Chase.—Buffalo on every Side.—Fitzgerald and his zeal.—Falconer among the Buffalo.—Returns of Killed and Wounded.—Arrival at Little River.—Buffalo Calves in Camp.—Manner of taking them.

THE day succeeding my unfortunate accident, I was visited, at my room, by crowds of friends, among whom was the President, General Lamar. The only topics discussed had some relation to the expedition. Preparations were going on in every quarter. The merchants were packing their goods, and mending and strengthening the heavy waggons upon which they were to be transported. Volunteers were cleaning and preparing their arms, as we were to enter an Indian and buffalo range almost immediately—in a word, all was hurry, bustle, and excitement. Every one was anticipating an exciting, a glorious frolic, the wild gossiping tales of old hunters and campaigners tending, not a little, to increase the fever of impatience to be upon the road. Not a word was said of the hardships, the dangers, the difficulties we were to encounter—the biting "northers,"* the damp and dreary bivouac, the intolerable thirst, the gnawing hunger—these were the dark sides of the picture, and were never exhibited.

As to our reception on reaching Santa Fé but little was said. Texas claims, as I have before stated, to the Rio Grande; and as Santa Fé is situated some fourteen miles from that stream, on the eastern or Texan side, no invasion of the territory of Mexico was thought of. It is true Texas had never been able to exercise jurisdiction over that section, because of its isolated position and the immense wilderness that separates it from the other portions of the Republic; but this was no reason why she should not, at some time, assert her claims. The universal impression in Texas was, that the inhabitants of Santa Fé were anxious to throw off a yoke, which was not only galling, but did not of right belong to them, and rally under the "lone star" banner; and events which have since transpired, and which I shall refer to hereafter, have convinced me that such was the feeling with the larger part of the population. Should any opposition be made to the peaceable entry of the Texan pioneers, it was thought it would come from the few regular troops always stationed at Santa Fé by the government of Mexico; and this force would easily have been put down if a large majority of the residents

* The prairies of Texas are visited, every season, by cold rains and winds from the north, called "*northers*." The winds have full sweep directly from the mountains, and not only animals, but men have frequently perished during their continuance.

were in favour of such a course. As for having anything like a regular battle, or forcibly subduing the country should the inhabitants be found hostile, such events were neither intended nor talked of. Invading armies, when hard fighting is anticipated, seldom take merchandise with them to sell to their enemies. The merchant, who sends a "venture" to some distant and barbarous shore, anticipates, on reaching his destination, either losing all or reaping a rich harvest of profit. The Texans looked for danger on the road across the prairies—nothing more. Safely arrived in New Mexico, their perils were all passed—they had, with the hopes and expectations offered them, no farther risks to incur. But adverse circumstances stepped in to thwart their bright dreams of commercial success—they were robbed of all, property and liberty—and after drinking thus deeply of the bitter cup of misfortune, have been held up, by those who knew neither the men nor their intentions, as a "gang of marauders," a "horde of land pirates."

But what, the reader will ask, induced so large a body of young men to start upon an expedition of this kind? What objects could they have in view? The answer is easy enough. They were actuated by that love of adventure, which is inherent in thousands of our race; they were anxious to participate in the excitements ever incidental to a prairie tour. What induced Washington Irving and his companions to make a trip to the prairies west of the Osage hunting grounds? Why did the Honourable Charles A. Murray spend a summer with the buffaloes and the Pawnees? And why does Sir William Drummond Stewart, year after year, leave wealth and title, to say nothing of the comforts and honours in their train, and pass his summers among the Indians high up on the waters of the Missouri and its tributaries? To our party, the incentives were unusually strong and exciting. We were to pass over a portion of country entirely unknown to the white man, and might reasonably expect to meet with a larger share of adventure than usually falls to the lot of the Western travellers. We felt confident that we should meet with large bands of Indians, known to live directly on our path, who were hostile alike to Texas and Mexico, and with whom we should have an occasional "skrimmage." We should see the American Indian, too, in his primitive and unhunted retreat. Thus fraught with adventure, the tour promised to be one of unusual interest.

While lying confined to my bed at Austin, I received, from Mr. Roberts, then acting Secretary of State, a letter written at the request of General Lamar, inviting me to join the expedition as a "guest." I was to be subject to no control, civil or military; I was free to remain with the expedition so long as it suited my convenience, and to leave it when I pleased—in short, I had no connexion, other than that of a stranger who happened to be travelling the same road, with the men whom I accompanied, or with the objects in which they were engaged. In the same letter I was kindly invited to mess with the commissioners, or civil branch of the expedition, an invitation I gladly accepted. This letter, with my passport, and other papers of importance as defining the relation in which I stood to the expedition, I placed in a secure parcel, and always kept about my person. I was determined, by no act of mine, to forfeit my claim to American protection any farther than by accompanying the expedition across wild and unknown prairies; and considering these papers the best proofs I could have to sustain me, should difficulties, which I certainly did not anticipate, arise on my reaching New Mexico, I was careful in preserving them. The obligations I considered myself under to the officers of the expedition were these: to obey all general orders for the well-being and safety of the men, and if we were attacked by Indians on the march, or met with any opposition from them to take an active part with my friends. Here my obligations ceased. I had started with the intention of making the entire tour of Mexico, and could not compromise myself so far as to take any part in the events which might occur on reaching the settlements of New Mexico, whether these events should be pacific or hostile. But to continue my narrative of the movements of the expedition.

The 18th of June arrived, and with it the time for the departure of the pioneers. It was now three days since I had met with my unfortunate accident, and I was still unable to move without assistance. A few of my friends endeavoured to dissuade me from going; but I was blessed, or cursed, as the case may be, with strongly-developed organs of self-will, obstinacy, and "go-a-headity," and made up my mind to go even if I had to be carried. "I will go it if I lose a leg," is a common yet not very classical remark among a certain class of Western men, when they have fully made up their minds to do a thing. I determined upon starting for New Mexico, although I had already as good as lost a leg, at least for all present purposes, and it is now too late to regret that I did so.

Among the Texan Commissioners was Jose Antonio Navarro, Esq.,* who, like myself, was unable to walk. For our accommodation, General Lamar provided a neat Jersey waggon, drawn by two mules, and covered so as to protect us from the sun and rain during the long marches.

As I have stated above, it was on the 18th of June that the last detachment of the expedition left Austin. This was at least one month later than it should have been, on account of both water and grass; but unavoidable delays had arisen in getting everything in readiness, and even as it was General M'Leod, the commander of the military portion, was obliged to march unprovided with many necessaries. The main body of the expedition had been lying encamped for some time on the Brushy, a small stream about twenty miles from Austin. As far as this point General Lamar accompanied the last party. I was assisted into the waggon on leaving, but still bade adieu to civilization, its comforts and enjoyments, in good spirits.

At Austin we left the last tokens of a settlement—beyond, all was in a state of wild, uncultivated nature. Singular as it may appear, the then capital of Texas was the extreme frontier town, and what may appear

* Mr. Navarro is the only member of the Santa Fé pioneers still retained a prisoner. He is a Mexican by birth, was once a senator in the Congress of that Republic, is a man of no inconsiderable abilities and influence, and has been punished with unusual severity. I found him a kind-hearted, gentlemanly man, and regret that he was not liberated with the rest of the prisoners.

still more strange, daring bands of hostile Indians have frequently been known to enter the principal streets, run off with horses tied to the very door-posts of their owners, and in some instances have even murdered the inhabitants within a few hundred yards of the government-house.

From Austin to the Brushy, the road—for here there is an old military road—runs over rolling and beautiful prairies, occasionally relieved by the slight skirting of timber which fringes the margins of the small streams, or by a small grove of timber so regularly planted by nature that it would almost seem the hand of man had assisted in its production.

To the left of the road, at the distance of some mile and a half, or two miles, is a high and delightful situation, which some visionary speculator, years since, endeavoured to convert into a stirring town.

In the first place, he purchased a beautiful site for a city—lacking only all the essentials to support a large population. Highly-coloured plans were got out, and on paper, at least, a more flourishing place never existed. There were colleges and squares, city halls and penitentiaries, public walks and public houses—and looking at the engravings, so well were they executed, a man could almost imagine he heard the carriages rattling over the pavements, and the busy hum which denotes the large and thriving city.

The name by which it was known on the plans—it cannot be found on the map of Texas—was *Athens ;* and so firmly did the visionary, who planned it, believe in his speculation, that he built a house and made some other and expensive improvements on the premises. While engaged in digging a well, assisted by some two or three negroes, he was attacked by a roaming party of Camanches and driven off, narrowly escaping with his life. The person who gave me this information said that the man never returned, and that everything remained just as he had left it. Thus fell a modern Athens.

We made a short stop, during the heat of the day, at a cool grove. Near it was a fine spring of water, and under the shade of the over-arching boughs a plain dinner was prepared. Every man appeared to be his own cook, President Lamar as well as the rest. I also observed that his excellency unsaddled and staked his own horse on a small plot of grass near by. There was a specimen of Republican simplicity—the chief magistrate of a nation cooking his own dinner and grooming his own horse! In all my intercourse with General Lamar I ever found him a courteous and honourable gentleman, possessing a brilliant intellect, which has been highly cultivated; and if Texas ever had a warm and untiring friend, it was and is Mirabeau B. Lamar.

It was late in the afternoon when we reached camp, a beautiful and romantic situation on the Brushy, near several large springs of cool and most delicious water. The camp was all animation on our arrival, as it was a token that the expedition was soon to be on the march. Many of the volunteers had been stationed at this place three or four weeks, and had become impatient of the delay; now that it was rendered certain that they were soon to be on the move to Santa Fé, all was joy, activity, and life.

General Lamar was accompanied by the Honourable Mr. Chalmers, Secretary of the Treasury, and several other gentlemen, who all "roughed it" upon the ground at night with the volunteers—a single blanket forming each man's bed. The next morning the different companies were reviewed, a neat and appropriate address was delivered by the President, after which himself and party returned to Austin.

Two days were now passed on the Brushy in reloading the waggons, and making the necessary arrangements for the long journey we had before us. Here I would state, that never since the discovery of America had such a journey been undertaken. Years before the first waggon started from St. Louis for Santa Fé every inch of the country was well known and the route that was to be taken clearly defined; all that was known in our case was, that Austin was in such a latitude and longitude and Santa Fé in another—of the principal part of the country between the two points not a man among us knew anything. That deep rivers were to be crossed, that ravines were to be encountered, that salt and dry prairies were to be met—in short, that innumerable obstacles would be found in our path, were things that every one expected: of the nature and extent of these obstacles all were alike ignorant. Yet in the face of difficulties which seemed almost insurmountable the expedition started, and after toil almost incredible they were overcome—twenty-four waggons were taken in safety over nearly a thousand miles that never had been trodden before except by the savage. At starting it was known that the direct course was almost northwest; but as it was feared there might be a scarcity of water by taking a straight line, it was deemed prudent to follow the course of the Brazos, cut through the celebrated

Cross Timbers before reaching Red River, and then follow up that stream, the course of which was supposed to be nearly east and west. By this route we made nearly a right angle, and the journey was much longer, and probably more difficult.

On the morning of June 21st, the expedition finally took up the line of march from the fertile valley and cool springs of the Brushy. Two companies, numbering some eighty men, were detailed to go forward as an advanced guard; then came the waggons, in single file, and the beef cattle that were to furnish us with meat. One company was also detailed for fatigue duty—driving the cattle and cutting away the banks of creeks, or removing any obstacles that might obstruct the passage of the waggons. This was the most irksome and laborious duty of all, and was performed by the companies in turn. The rear-guard brought up the long procession, and consisted of three companies, there being six in all. These companies were commanded by Captains Caldwell, Sutton, Houghton, Hudson, Strain, and Lewis, the latter commanding the artillery company, which had one brass six-pounder. The number of volunteers doing duty was two hundred and seventy. In addition, there were about fifty persons attached to the expedition in some way, being General M'Leod and his staff, the commissioners, merchants, tourists, and servants. None of these, except the first named, did military or guard duty.

The long train of waggons moving heavily forward, with the different companies of volunteers, all well mounted and well armed and riding in double file, presented an imposing as well as an animating spectacle, causing every heart to beat high with the anticipation of exciting incidents on the boundless prairies. On the first day many of the young oxen, "critters" that had never been yoked before, performed divers unseemly antics, diverting enough to themselves in all probability, but by no means pleasing to the drivers. The consequence was that a number of the waggons were upset, occasioning delays which made it near night before we reached our camping ground on the Sand Gabriel. The road this day was over beautiful rolling prairies, the land rich, and susceptible of cultivation.

The San Gabriel is a picturesque stream running into the Brazos. A few miles above our camp, on its banks, a settlement had formerly been made by one or two families; but they had been attacked by Indians, and those who were not killed driven off. The stream abounds with trout, perch, and catfish, as do nearly all the watercourses in this section of Texas. Some of our party, who were first in, amused themselves by fishing, and shooting alligators, the latter being too plentiful for any useful purposes.

On the arrival of the beef cattle, one of them was selected, shot, and dressed with the greatest expedition, and then followed the cooking and eating of both dinner and supper. We had made no stop during the day, which necessarily brought both meals together and good appetites to do them justice.

Our fare was simple enough—roasted or broiled beef, cooked on sticks or ramrods before the fire, with salt, coffee, and sugar. No breadstuffs were provided, unless a small quantity of rice can be dignified with that title; but the appetites we contracted during our long ride across the high, dry, and bracing prairies served us instead of bread and dessert, and a more hearty meal it has seldom been my lot to partake of.

Our meal over, knots of the volunteers would congregate, here and there, around the camp fires, telling stories of the marvellous and spinning long yarns about border forays, buffalo hunts, and brushes with the Indians of the prairies. The stories of buffalo hunting, in particular, were eagerly listened to, as it was known that in ten days we should be in the best range for these animals in Texas.

An hour or two would be whiled away in this manner, and then preparations would be made for *retiring* to sleep—a very simple process upon a campaign. A person has only to pick out a soft place upon the ground, roll himself up in his blanket, and take immediate possession of his bedroom ; and though people who have never lived " out of doors" may picture anything but comfort with such lodgings, sounder, sweeter, and more refreshing sleep never visited the downiest couch than can be found upon the earth on one of our western prairies. Should any of my readers ever undertake a tour of the kind, and find any difficulty in getting to sleep, I can recommend a plan to bring about that desirable object which has never been known to fail in a single instance : *just count the stars.*

As the days were now extremely warm, early morning starts were recommended and adopted. Accordingly, at daybreak on the 22nd of June, we were awakened by the cheering notes of the *reveille.* We had a small but tolerably well-organized band with us, including some two or three clarionets, a horn and bugle, besides fifes and drums. To the latter instruments were assigned the task of waking us in the morning; and at first there was something so inspiriting in the lively notes of the *reveille* breaking the deep stillness of the early dawn, that with me farther sleep was uncared for. I was heartily tired of it before the campaign was half over.

Notwithstanding our early start, we made but twelve miles this day, encamping on Opossum Creek, as there was no water beyond within several miles. During this day we passed the scene of an Indian fight which took place a year or two previous, and in which Major Howard, having drawn a party of Camanches into an ambuscade, gave them a severe drubbing. His men were fortunate enough to discover the Indians before these had seen their white enemies, giving the latter every advantage. Knowing, full well, that he never could come up with the Camanches in a chase, or provoke them into an open fight on the prairies, for in numbers the two parties were nearly equal,* Major H. resorted to a stratagem. Secreting his men in a thick grove of timber, he started off alone, well mounted, in the direction of the enemy. The moment the Indians saw him they considered his scalp as certain as though it was already hanging at their saddle-skirts, and with frightful yells gave chase. The gallant officer trusted to his steed, at a time when a stumble would have been inevitable destruction to both. The Texans, in their covert, could plainly hear the distant whoops of the savages, and hugged still closer the trees behind which they were sheltered. With almost lightning speed the pursued and pursuers scoured across the prairie, the former leading the savages directly

* The Camanches, even on the prairies, never attack the white unless they greatly outnumber them.

within range of his own men. When at a point opposite the Texans, and within a few yards' distance, a well-directed volley tumbled seven of the Camanches dead from their horses. So sudden and unexpected was this reception, that the Indians turned their horses and made a precipitate retreat. One only remained behind, whose heroic conduct deserves a passing remark. Among the dead was his brother, and in endeavouring to save the body from the hands of the Texans the savage lost his own life. He dismounted, and absolutely succeeded in packing his lifeless brother upon his horse amid a shower of bullets; but while mounting, a well-directed rifle-ball pierced him to the heart, and the brothers came together to the ground. Not one of Major Howard's men was injured.

In the night we passed at Opossum Creek we were visited by a tremendous storm of thunder, lightning, and wind, although but little rain fell; our tent had been pitched, and, as we thought, securely; but the first heavy gust of wind carried it completely from its fastenings, and the rest of the night, to quote the expression of one of our men, we "took plain without kiver."

Our next day's travel carried us across rolling prairies, not a tree being in sight in any direction. Here and there, in the distance, small gangs of buffaloes could be seen scampering off, the scouting parties, it would seem, of the immense herds we were soon to encounter. Several of the huge animals were run down and killed during the day by some of our hunters, and that night, for the first time, I made a meal of buffalo meat—one of those killed being a fat cow, and her flesh of fine texture and delicious sweetness. Two buffaloes had also been killed on the previous day; but they were old and poor, and nothing but their tongues was brought in.

Large numbers of petrifactions, some of them uncommonly perfect, were found in the vicinity of our camp on Deer Creek. Although the distance must be some three hundred miles from the seacoast, we still found fossil specimens of oysters and other shell-fish in abundance, and in good preservation. I remember one oyster, in particular, the shell of which, on being forced open, displayed the edible part of that delicate luxury in form and colour so natural, that I could not help thinking of pepper, salt, vinegar and a fork, at once.

The stories this night in camp were all in relation to buffalo, the abundance of "sign" in the shape of tracks, and places where the grass had been eaten close, plainly denoting that we were in the vicinity of a large herd. The old campaigners, and there were many among us, told stories of the immense number they had seen at a time, while the harum-scarum youngsters of the camp would listen eagerly to their tales, manifesting, at the same time, a restless impatience to be among the huge monarchs of the prairies.

"How many buffalo did you ever see at one time?" asked a young man, whose greatest achievement had been the bringing down a fat buck, addressing one of the oldest backwoodsmen in camp.

"Can't say, exactly—probably between two and three million!" replied the old one, with a cool, matter-of-fact indifference, as much as to say that he was keeping as near the truth as possible.

I was an attentive listener to this conversation, and could not but remark the singular expression on the countenance of the young man. At first, he partially closed his left eye, and opening his right to its utmost width, gazed intently in the face of the old hunter with a look half comic, half incredulous. Then, as if thinking he might not have fully understood the answer to his question, he turned his head to one side, somewhat after the manner of a hog in an oak grove listening for the fall of an acorn, and curving his left hand into the form of a half-moon and placing it behind his ear, so as to be certain of hearing every word, he again addressed his older and more experienced friend with "Perhaps I mistook your answer—*what* number of buffalo did you say you had seen at one time?"

"Between two and three million!" repeated the old one, with a countenance as immovable as though it had been made of cast iron.

"Y-e-s," drawled the youngster, with that peculiar tone and expression which signify that one neither believes nor disbelieves a story, or in other words, intimating that while he did not wish the old campaigner to think he altogether discredited the number, he was at the same time anxious to avoid being considered over credulous by entirely swallowing a story which might possibly be intended as a quiz. As for myself, I did not believe a word the old hunter said, but rather thought he was indulging an appetite for which all of his class are notorious, that of "stretching" their stories far beyond the line between the probable and incredible. Since then, however—in fact the very next day—I "saw sights" which induced me to alter my mind, and to give the aged borderer more credit for keeping within the bounds of probability than I was at first willing to accord him.

I do not say that I have seen "between two and three million" at the same time; but I have stood upon a high roll of the prairie, with neither tree nor bush to obstruct the vision in any direction, and seen these animals grazing upon the plain and darkening it at every point. There are perhaps larger herds of buffalo at present in northern Texas than anywhere else on the western prairies their most formidable enemies, the Indians, not ranging so low down in large parties, on account of the whites; but I was told that every year their numbers were gradually decreasing, and their range, owing to the approach of white settlers from the east and south, becoming more and more circumscribed. It would seem almost impossible, especially to one who has seen them, numerous as the sands of the seashore, on their immense natural pastures, that the race can ever become extinct; but when he reflects upon the rapid strides civilization is making westward upon the domain of the buffalo, he is brought to feel that the noble race will soon be known only as a thing of the past.

The whites have two ways of hunting these animals. One is to creep up within a short distance, and shoot them with a rifle carrying a heavy ball, or with a musket —a mode of hunting seldom resorted to except by those who are in want of meat. The other way is to sally out after them on horseback, armed with heavy holster-pistols, run alongside, while under full speed, and shoot from the saddle. Of all hunting in the world this is probably the most exciting, at the same time involving the sportsman in no little danger. The horse that has been trained to it soon gets as fond of the sport as his master, will run directly up within three or four yards of the immense animal, and is always ready to sheer off and get out of the way in case the buffalo shows a disposition to fight. When the hunter wants meat he rides in among the animals, and singles out a fat cow or young bull, which he marks for his own—if he is merely hunting for the sport, or for "grandeur" as it is called in the West, he attacks the oldest and largest bull he can find, and continues to blaze away at him with his pistols until he brings him down. He may possibly secure the tongue of the animal—the carcass is soon sought and preyed upon by the legion of buzzards which are ever on the scent.

Early on the morning of June 24th we left our encampment on Deer Creek, intending to reach Little River before night. We had travelled but a few miles before the cheering cry of "Buffalo! buffalo!" was heard along the line. Directly a-head, on the right and left of our road, innumerable small black objects could be seen more resembling stumps than aught else. As we slowly approached them, the objects became more distinct, gave signs of life, and appeared to be slowly moving about on the interminable prairie. When within half-a-mile it was evident, even to those who had only seen badly-executed woodcuts of the animal in "picture books," that they were buffalo, spread out over the immense space, and in countless numbers.

Notwithstanding orders had been given the volunteers not to break their double-file ranks, nothing could restrain the youngsters from leaving the command and sharing in the exciting chase. The merchants, and others not attached to the military, were at perfect liberty to go when and where it might please them, as a matter of course. We were soon surrounded by buffalo, and every two minutes a Texan malecontent would leave the ranks at full gallop, and dash off after some huge animal, which chance, or a more clumsy gait, had left behind his fellows. Never have I beheld a scene so full of excitement. Such of the command as did not join in the hunt continued steadily along, myself and Mr. Navarro, in our Jersey carry-all, keeping in line with them, while all around us was hurry-scurry and confusion. We had not advanced a mile, after reaching the outposts of the immense herd, before we were in their midst, seeing nothing in any direction save the immense animals speeding along at a heavy, lumbering gallop, the larger ones more resembling loads of hay in motion than anything else I can liken them to. In the distance, far as the eye could reach, they were seen quietly feeding upon the short prairie grass, and apparently unconscious of the wild riot and danger so near at hand.

Unable to mount a horse, I could not join the exciting chase; yet I could plainly see and enjoy the animated scene. At times, I could discern one of our men, apparently hemmed in on all sides by the frightened and infuriated animals, and running the greatest risk of being run over and trampled to the earth. Anon, the smoke of a pistol would rise, followed quickly by the report, and then succeeded a general and confused scattering. Perchance a bull—for the "green-horns" generally select the largest of the herd as affording a better mark—would be seen to totter, his tail lashing the air in furious circles, and then to tumble headlong to the earth; at another time, one of the animals, wounded and rendered furious by pain, would rush blindly and madly at his pursuer. The largest number of horses were entirely unused to the sport, and "fought shy" of the unsightly animals; others, again, had been regularly trained, and would eagerly carry their riders up to the buffalo, and allow them to "bang and blaze" away, pistol after pistol, without starting, or even moving a muscle. Such is a faint description of the stirring scenes I saw around me on that day's travel.

Among the merchants was a wild, frolicking Irishman, named Fitzgerald, one of the best fellows that ever the sun shone upon. Fitz, as he was universally called, was descended from one of the best families in Ireland, nearly every member of which has been distinguished as an officer in the British service. His mother was a daughter of the celebrated Archibald Hamilton Rowan, who acted so conspicuous a part in the Irish rebellion of '98, and one of his uncles, a major-general in the English army, has recently returned to England from Bombay, where he was governor. As several of Fitzgerald's brothers held commissions in the British service, his family thought it expedient to make a clergyman of him, although nature had intended him for anything but that. To carry out their plans successfully they sent him, when only some eight years of age, to a school near Boulogne, in France. There he learned the usual amount of Greek, Latin, and Hebrew, and according to his own statements, an extra amount of mischievous practices generally. At the age of eighteen he returned to Ireland, and on his peremptorily refusing to take holy orders his father ordered him to Jamaica, to fill a lucrative station he had procured for him in the customs. He set off for that island, but on getting as far as London, he saw the walls covered with handbills calling upon volunteers for General Evans's Legion, then about to embark for Spain to the assistance of Isabella. Here was just the thing that suited Fitzgerald's wild temperament and ardent impulses, and to enlist, leaving the customs at Jamaica to regulate themselves, was his first movement. Arrived in Spain, he was promoted, step by step, for his gallant conduct and finally, for skilfully and successfully leading a forlorn hope, received a captain's commission, and was also created a knight of the Order of St. Ferdinand. The return of the Legion to England left Fitz without employment; but hearing that he could obtain a commission in the Persian army, he pushed for that country to join the service. Finding, on reaching his new and singular destination, that there was little fighting and less pay, he returned to England. He next visited the Cape of Good Hope, either with or in search of his father, and from that point went to Van Diemen's Land and the parts adjacent. Thence he returned to England, taking Brazil in his route. A life of inactivity he could not endure; so hearing that there was not only fun but fighting in Texas, he embarked for that Republic by way of New Orleans. We next hear of him selling dry goods at San Antonio de Bexar. This business, however, did not prevent him from joining the different expeditions against Mexicans and Indians that were continually fitted out at that place, and in this way he became enamoured of a prairie life—a feeling which induced him to join the Santa Fé Expedition. Educated in France, he spoke the French languange, and his three years' sojourn in Spain had given him a smattering of Spanish—enough, at all events, to carry on an ordinary conversation.

Always willing, ready, and among the first to enter into any madcap, daring or break-neck scrape, as a matter of course Fitz led off the chase after the buffalo. He was mounted on a game and untiring Mexican pony, loaded down with saddlebags, water-gourd, blankets, and the miscellaneous equipage which constitues the fit-out of a campaigner; but all this did not deter him from starting off at once. Away he went in neck-or-nothing style, riding up to the first buffalo he met, and banging away with his pistols as fast as he could load and fire. In all his wanderings he had never met with buffalo before, and so exciting was the dangerous sport of riding among them that he could not command himself. In the mad chase he lost first his hat, then his blanket, and finally his saddlebags and water-gourd; but these were mere trifles when such game was in sight, and as Fitz never stopped to pick them up, they are probably now lying on the prairie in the exact places where he dropped them.

My friend Falconer, too, was seized with a fit of excitement. His horse, however, unlike that of Fitzgerald, was a sedate, quiet, slow-and-easy kind of animal, holding a gallop or canter in such special abhorrence that neither whip nor spur could induce him to indulge in either. Still Falconer must needs have a trot after the buffalo, as he could not chase them in a gallop; and it was droll enough to see a gentleman, who had started upon the expedition in search of strange weeds, stones, and the picturesque, now jogging along after buffalo, with a glass raised to his right eye. As he was armed only with a doubled-barrelled gun, loaded, probably, with bird shot, he did not essay the killing of any of the huge monsters by which he was at times surrounded.

The number of buffalo killed during the day, in our immediate vicinity, was twenty-eight; the number of prisoners taken in the shape of young calves, some ten or twelve. As to getting the number of wounded, that would have been impossible.

In the afternoon we reached Little River, where we encamped for the night, and where we had a feast of choice buffalo meat, tongue, and also the marrow bones of that animal; some of the calves also were killed, and furnished us with delicious veal. The simple things followed our men into camp without the least trouble. It was only necessary to blind their eyes with the hands for a moment, push their noses to the ground, and hold them in that position until their dams were out of sight. On raising their heads they would stare about, and the first object that caught their gaze, whether man or horse, they would follow like dogs. Thus ended our first day among the immense buffalo herds of the Western Prairies.

CHAPTER V.

Sending back for more Cattle.—Rations of Beef for each Man.—Idle Hours in Camp.—Annoying Insects.—Night Alarms.—Death of Lockridge.—A Dutchman shot at.—Improvident Waste of Provisions.—Game in our Vicinity.—Sickness of General M'Leod.—Once more on the Road.—Bird's Battle Ground.—A Visit from Mustangs.—The "White Steed of the Prairies."—Stories in relation to this Horse.—Cow Creek.—Plenty of Buffalo.—Repairing Waggons.—Profanity of the Teamsters.—Out of Water.—Fourth of July on the Prairies.—Celebration among the Clouds.—A troublesome Visitor.—Rattlesnakes and Tarantulas.—Death of Flint.—Crossing the Bosque.—The Antelope, or Mountain Goat.—Simplicity of this Animal.—Another Branch of the Bosque.—Difficulty of crossing.—More Swearing.—A Stampede!—Singular effect of Fright upon Horses and Oxen.—Falconer's Horse at his Eccentricities.—A Private Stampede.—Laughable Antics.—Falconer's Philosophy.

Before the main body of the expedition left Austin, in May, it was thought by those most familiar with the subject that the journey to Santa Fé would not occupy more than six weeks, or two months at the very farthest, and a supply of beef on the hoof was purchased, amply sufficient for that length of time. On arriving at Little River, our commissary stated that it would be imprudent to go farther without sending back for more beeves, as in the long delay on the Brushy the volunteers had consumed a large portion of those originally furnished. Had the expedition started at the time originally proposed, there would have been no necessity for a fresh supply; but inasmuch as it had been delayed three weeks, the wants of the men, admitting that the journey would occupy two months, would require some thirty head of cattle more. The regular ration to each person was three pounds of beef a day, a quantity amply sufficient for an ordinary man even when he has no breadstuffs or vegetables, as was our case. In addition to the beef, coffee enough to give each man two pints a day, with the needful sugar, was served out. Instead of breadstuffs, for which transportation could not be provided, a quantity of tobacco was served to each man.

The sending back to the settlements for an additional number of beeves occasioned a delay of five days, the time being passed in fishing and hunting by some, lounging and sleeping by others, and heavily enough by all; for the desire to be on the move was a serious drawback upon the enjoyments even of those most fond of buffalo hunting. The place where we encamped abounded with a small insect called, I believe, the seed tick, which penetrates under the skin in great numbers, raises small sores or pimples, and causes a burning and continual itching. I was completely covered, or rather filled with these annoying visitors, and lost many an hour's sleep in consequence.

We had two alarms the second night we passed on Little River. The first was about ten o'clock, and was caused by the sharp report of a rifle directly in the centre of the camp. A circumstance so unusual started every man to his feet, and the alarm was far from inconsiderable until it was ascertained that the young man Lockridge, of whom I have spoken elsewhere, had shot himself. Some two hours after, the camp was a second time thrown into excitement by the startling "Who goes there?" of one of the guard, followed by the heavy report of a musket. The hands of every man were instantly upon his gun, and every preparation was made to resist an attack from Indians, for in the hurry and alarm we could think of nothing else; but on inquiring into the affair it was ascertained that an honest Dutchman, a servant of Colonel Cooke, was returning late into camp, with a horse he had found after a long search, and that not answering the sentinel promptly, he had been fired upon. Fortunately he was untouched, although badly frightened. This second alarm satisfactorily explained, we again returned to our blankets, and the rest of the night was passed in quiet and sleep.

While encamped upon Little River, and I may say during the whole of the time we were in the buffalo and game country, there was a most improvident waste of beef, the regular rations being served out to each man. Those who could obtain choice portions of the buffalo and deer, which were now killed in immense numbers, of course threw away the coarse and tougher parts of the beef given them. These, however, soon found customers; for clouds of buzzards were immediately hovering over and lighting within the lines, playing the part of most excellent scavengers. Could we but have anticipated the horrible sufferings we were then bringing upon our heads, or rather stomachs, by this prodigality; had we thought the time was near at hand when the poorest morsels we were throwing away so lavishly would be absolutely necessary to sustain life, a more provident course would have been adopted. Some of the old campaigners spoke of this waste at the time, remarking that the buzzards were fattening upon meat of which we should all feel the want before we got to our journey's end; but by far the greater portion of us were inexperienced, and went on the principle of taking special good care of ourselves to-day, and letting to-morrow look out for itself. We gained experience and wisdom afterward, but we bought it at an enormous price.

The place where we encamped on Little River was the site of an old picket fort, garrisoned, some years previous, by a detachment of Texan soldiers, who were stationed there to keep a look-out for Indians. The location is one of exceeding loveliness, healthy, and combining every advantage for a flourishing settlement. A growth of heavy timber, some two miles in width, covers the fertile bottom, while the rich prairies afford the best of grazing for the immense herds of buffalo and deer always to be found in the vicinity. Bears and Mexican hogs, the latter a ferocious animal, are found in great numbers in the bottoms, fish of different varieties are caught in the stream, and many of the trees are filled with delicious wild honey.

While encamped at this place, General M'Leod was attacked with fever, and was carried in a waggon to Bryant's Station, some twenty miles to our right, near the Brazos. Major Howard took the command of the expedition during his illness. On the evening of the 29th of June the order was given for an early march next morning—an order received with joy by all. The next morning, therefore, saw us again on our road, crossing prairies on which buffalo could be seen in almost every direction. In the afternoon we passed the scene of Bird's celebrated battle with the Indians. With thirty-three Texans only he fought some two hundred and fifty Indians several hours, killing large numbers of them. Bird himself was killed, towards the close of the battle, which was a drawn one, both parties retiring after sustaining great loss.

At sundown a drove of *mustangs,* or wild horses of the prairie, paid us a flying visit. They were first seen ascending a hill at the distance of half a mile, and as they were coming towards us were taken for Indians. When seen on a distant hill, standing with their raised heads towards a person, and forming a line as is their custom, it is almost impossible to take them for any thing but mounted men. Having satisfied their curiosity, they wheeled with almost the regularity of a cavalry company and galloped off, their long thick manes waving in the air, and their tails nearly sweeping the ground. They are beautiful animals, always in excellent condition, and although smaller than our American horses, are still very compact, and will bear much fatigue.

Many were the stories told that night in camp, by some of the older hunters, of a large white horse that had often been seen in the vicinity of the Cross Timbers and near Red River. That many of these stories, like a majority of those told by gossipping campaigners, were either apocryphal or marvellously garnished, I have little doubt; but that such a horse has been seen, and that he possesses wonderful speed and great powers of endurance, there is no reason to disbelieve. As the camp stories ran, he has never been known to gallop or trot, but paces faster than any horse that has been sent out after him can run; and so game and untiring is the

"*White Steed of the Prairies,*" for he is well known to trappers and hunters by that name, that he has tired down no less than three race-nags, sent expressly to catch him, with a Mexican Rider well trained to the business of taking wild horses. The latter had nothing but a *lasso* or *lariat* with him — a long rope made either of hemp or horse hair, but generally the latter. One end of this rope is made fast to the pommel of the saddle, while the other is formed into a noose: the Mexican carries it coiled up in the right hand, and throws it with astonishing dexterity and precision, casting it directly over the head, feet, or even tail of the animal he may be pursuing.

The Mexican who was sent out to take the wild steed, although he mounted a fresh horse as the one he was riding became tired, was never near enough the noble animal to throw a slip-noose over his head, or even to drive him into a regular gallop. Some of the hunters go so far as to say that the white steed has been known to pace his mile in less than two minutes, and that he could keep up this rate of speed until he had tired down everything in pursuit. Large sums had been offered for his capture, and the attempt had been frequently made; but he still roamed his native prairies in freedom, solitary, and alone.* The fact of his being always found with no other horse in company was accounted for, by an old hunter, on the ground that he was too proud to be seen with those of his class, being

* Since my return I have been informed, by a Texan Gentleman, that a horse in many respects answering the description of the "White Steed of the Prairies" has been caught, after a hard chase, between the head waters of the Trinity and Brazos. He lived but a short time, however, the excessive fatigue of the race causing his death.

an animal far superior in form and action to any of his brothers. This I put down as a rank embellishment, although it is a fact that the more beautiful and highly-formed mustangs are frequently seen alone.

On the 1st of July we reached Cow Creek, killing large numbers of buffalo during the day. The 2nd we halted to repair some of the waggons which had been upset and injured. The gullies and creeks we were compelled to cross were many of them impassable until much time had been spent in cutting and digging away the steep and lofty banks. With all the cutting and digging, however, hardly a day passed in which we escaped an upset; and then the expressions made use of by the drivers and fatigue-men sounded so much like swearing of the most forcible kind, that there was no mistaking it. It appeared to be the only study of some of our teamsters to invent the most blasphemous oaths; and the cool, slow, and decided manner in which these imprecations were uttered, showed that they wished all within hearing to have the full benefit of their studies. I asked one of them, just as he had finished a long and most horrid oath which I would not dare to put on paper, why he uttered such profanities. His answer was, they saved much whipping, and that his oxen drew much better than with the common kind of swearing. Be this as it may, I believe that if the unfortunate animals had possessed the powers of understanding, they would have run away in the midst of one of the long list of blasphemies. I have heard swearing in many quarters, but for originality, deliberate utterance, and deep wickedness, I have never heard that of some of the drivers on the Santa Fé Expedition equalled.

Our route from Cow Creek led us over high and dry prairies, and after travelling some twenty miles—a long distance for waggons—we were finally obliged to encamp without water. The day had been insupportably hot, without a cloud, or hardly a breath of air stirring, and all the water in our canteens was consumed before noon. As a consequence, we suffered extremely that night; and had there been a glass of water up at auction, I should certainly have bid high for it. Visions of sherry cobblers, soda, and other cooling drinks haunted me the whole night, and when I awoke, it was to the painful reality that there was no reality in my dreams. Since that time I have gone ten miles for a cup of water.

An early start the next morning, which was the 4th of July, enabled us to reach a cool and delicious spring early in the afternoon, and here we slaked our intolerable thirst. A few seconds after we had forgotten our sufferings. A man may endure the most torturing thirst for thirty-six or forty-eight hours—thinking of water, and nothing but water the while—but the moment he has reached it, and swallowed a sufficiency, all thoughts of past suffering are at once banished.

We had no opportunity of keeping the birthday of American Independence as many of us could have wished; but the heavens got up a private celebration in the shape of a thunder-storm, and seldom have I heard such continued, heavy, and rattling peals. It always seemed to me that in the early part of summer the thunder was louder, the lightning more vivid, and the storms generally were more severe on the prairies than anywhere else. They are not, perhaps, attended with as much rain, but the accompaniments are altogether on a grander and more magnificent scale.

We had a troublesome and unwelcome visitor in camp on the night of the 4th of July. The storm had induced the mess to which I was attached to pitch a tent. The wet grass without probably drove a prairie rattlesnake to more comfortable quarters within our canvass, the first intimation we had of the vicinity of his snakeship being his crawling over one of us in an attempt to effect a lodgment under some of the blankets. A more disagreeable companionship cannot well be imagined, even if one has his choice from among all living, moving, creeping, flying, running, swimming, and crawling things ; and to assert that any of us felt perfectly easy and at home with such a neighbour among us would be saying what is not true. For myself, fearing to move lest I should molest the reptile, I rolled myself, head and all, under my blanket, and lay perfectly quiet until daylight. Where the intruder went no one could tell, and we had the very great satisfaction of seeing no more of him.

Very frequently, on the great prairies, a man wakes up in the morning and finds that he has had a rattlesnake for a sleeping partner but there is one excellent trait in the character of these reptiles—they never bite unless disturbed, and will get out of the way as soon as possible, except in the month of August, when they are said to be blind, and will snap at any and everything they may hear about them. The ordinary prairie rattlesnake is of small size, seldom being seen over three feet in length; but those living in the holes of the prairie dogs, mention of which I shall make hereafter, grow to an immense magnitude. The former, I believe, are considered not only the most vicious, but the most poisonous.

In addition to the rattlesnake, the *tarantula* is frequently met with on the Texan prairies, is also often found under the blanket of the campaigner, and is said to be as poisonous as the former. They are large, black, venomous-looking insects, with bodies about the size of a dove's egg, although their long and strong legs made them appear much larger. When attacked with a stick, they will rear up on their hind legs and attempt to bite, and are extremely ferocious in every respect. The least scratch from their long fangs throws a person into convulsions, and will produce death unless immediate remedies can be procured. The ballet of *Le Tarentule,* in which Elssler gained so much applause, is a beautiful creation, although founded upon an idle superstition of the Italians. The bite of the real tarantula drives a person to anything but dancing, subjecting him rather to fits and strong nervous excitement. The opinion prevails, among the ignorant and superstitious of many countries, that music will cure the individual who has been bitten by one of these venomous insects. What effect it might have in soothing the nervous system I am unable to say ; but were I bitten by a tarantula I should certainly prefer hartshorn, taken inwardly and outwardly, for the purpose of procuring a safe and speedy cure.

It is deemed an easy matter to keep the rattlesnake from sharing your bed while sleeping upon the prairies. It is said that they will never cross a hair *lariat,* so that by circumscribing the ground you occupy with one of these instruments, you enjoy an exemption from their more sociable visits; but this is no guard against the poisonous tarantula. Few persons, however, are bitten by either, not an instance occurring on the route, although we saw great numbers of each.

On awaking the next morning, after the adventure with the rattlesnake, we found that there had been another visiter in camp, and one from whose insatiate fangs there is no escape. Death had carried off a poor fellow named Flint. He had eaten freely of unripe grapes or berries during the previous day, which brought on a colic that no medicine could reach. He was buried at an early hour, and a volley was fired over his grave, after which the march was resumed.

We had already, and with no inconsiderable difficulty, crossed one branch of the Bosque, and on the evening of the 5th arrived at another fork of the same stream, where we encamped for the night. It abounds with excellent trout and soft-shell turtle. This day, for the first time, we saw the antelope, or mountain goat, an animal somewhat resembling both the deer and the goat, but with flesh preferable to that of either. It runs with great speed, and has a stride like a horse. How fast the animal can run when in possession of four legs is a question I am at a loss to answer, but one with a fore leg broken by a rifle ball made out to escape from one of our best horses after a long chase. On the Table-lands at the foot of the Rocky Mountains they are met with in great numbers, and many are seen on the Upper Brazos and Colorado. Although a shy, they are still a very inquisitive animal, and are frequently lured within gunshot by simply hanging a red handkerchief upon a ramrod or stick, and moving it aloft. The hunter keeps his body out of sight as much as possible, when the antelope, seeing nothing but the handkerchief, approaches, with head erect and by slow degrees, until within rifle-shot, and then pays the penalty of its curiosity with its life.

The early part of the 6th of July was spent in cutting a road through the thick belt of wood which skirts either side of the main branch of the Bosque, and in partially digging away the high, steep bank of the stream. The labour of crossing the river was incredible. In descending the abrupt banks which led to the channel, it was necessary, not only to lock the wheels, but to hold back the waggons with ropes to prevent them from pitching down, "head first" as it were; the greatest difficulty, however, was in ascending on the other side. The ascent was nearly perpendicular and some forty feet high, with no better footing than a deep sand. Some twenty yoke of oxen would in the first place be hitched to a waggon; then ropes would be attached wherever there was a place to make them fast, manned by about fifty or sixty of the fatigue party; finally, all the drivers would be called into requisition, and when all was ready for a start such a jumping, whipping, cracking, yelling, pulling, cursing, and swearing would arise, as to set all description at defiance. Bedlam itself, with five hundred Indians as an accompaniment, seemed let loose in a body. I will not pretend to say that had Bonaparte met with the Bosque while crossing the Alps he would have been compelled to return; but he would have found a serious detention at all events. Yet difficult as was the crossing, everything was safely over before the middle of the afternoon, and we still made a march of a few miles to a spring a short distance from the River Brazos. At this camp we were favoured for the first time with the magnificent but much-dreaded sight of a *stampede* among our horses.

As there was no wood near our camping-ground, some half-a-dozen men pushed on to a small piece of timber in search of it. One of them had a wild, half-broken, Mexican horse, naturally vicious, and with difficulty mastered. His rider found a small dry tree, cut it down with a hatchet, and very imprudently made it fast to his horse's tail by means of a rope. The animal took it unkindly from the first, and dragged his strange load with evident symptoms of fright; but when within a few hundred yards of camp he commenced pitching, and finally set off at a gallop with the cause of all his uneasiness and fear still fast to his tail. His course was directly for the camp, and as he sped along the prairie it was soon evident that several of our horses were stricken with a panic at his approach. At first they would prick up their ears, snort, and trot majestically about in circles; then they would dash off at the top of their speed, and no human power could arrest their mad career.

"A *stampede!*" shouted some of the old campaigners, jumping from the ground and running towards their frightened animals; "a *stampede!* look out for your horses, or you'll never see them again!" was heard on every side. Fortunately for us, the more intractable horses had been not only staked, but hobbled before the panic became general, and were secured with little difficulty, else we might have lost half of them irretrievably.

It is singular the effect that sudden fright has, not only upon horses, but oxen, on the prairies. The latter will, perhaps, run longer and farther than the former, and although not as difficult to "head," because they cannot run so fast, their onward course it is impossible to stay. Oxen, so I was informed, have been known to run forty miles without once stopping to look back ; and when they did finally hold up, it was simply because exhausted nature would allow them to go no farther. Not one in fifty of them had seen the least cause for fear, but each ran simply because his neighbour did. Frequent instances have occurred where some worthless but skittish horse has caused the loss of hundreds of valuable animals. In the instance I have above alluded to, we did not lose one, but on a subsequent occasion, no less than eighty-seven were irrecoverably lost by one *stampede*.

Nothing can exceed the grandeur of the scene when a large *cavallada,* or drove of horses, takes a "scare." Old, weather-beaten, time-worn, and broken-down steeds —horses that have nearly given out from hard work and old age—will at once be transformed into wild and prancing colts. When first seized with that indescribable terror which induces them to fly, they seem to have been suddenly endowed with all the attributes of their original wild nature. With heads erect, tails and manes streaming in air, eyes lit up and darting beams of fright, old and jaded hacks will be seen prancing and careering about with all the buoyancy of action which characterises the antics of young colts; then some one of the drove, more frightened than the rest, will dash off in a straight line, the rest scampering after him, and apparently gaining fresh fears at every jump. The throng will then sweep along the plain with a noise which may be likened to something between a tornado and an earthquake, and as well might feeble man attempt to arrest either of the latter.

Were the earth rending and cleaving beneath their feet, horses, when under the terrifying influence of a *stampede,* could not bound away with greater velocity or more majestic beauty of movement. I have seen many an interesting race, but never anything half so exciting as the flight of a drove of frightened horses. The spectator, who may possibly have a nag among them which he has been unable to get into a canter by dint of spur and whip, sees his property fairly flying away at a pace that a thorough-bred racer might envy. Better "time," to all appearance, he has never seen made, and were it not that he himself is as much astounded as the horses, there might be very pretty betting upon the race.

On one occasion, when a closely-hobbled horse was rushing madly along the prairie under the influence of fright, his owner coolly remarked, "I wish I could make that critter go as fast on my own account without hobbles, as he can on his own with them—I'd gamble on him *sure.*" And so it is. No simile can give the reader a fair conception of the grandeur of the spectacle, and the most graphic arrangement of words must fall far short in describing the startling and imposing effect of a regular *stampede!*

While upon this subject, I should not, perhaps, neglect to notice one of the little private *stampedes* my friend Falconer's horse was in the habit of occasionally getting up, principally on his own individual account and to gratify his own peculiar tastes and desires, entirely regardless, all the while, of his master's convenience as well as of the public safety.

He was a short, thick-set, scrubby, wiry nag, tough as a pine knot, and self-willed as a pig. He was moreover exceedingly lazy, as well as prone to have his own way, and take his own jog—preferring a walk or gentle trot to a canter; and so deep-rooted were his prejudices in favour of the former methods of getting over the ground, that neither whip nor spur could drive him from them. He possessed a commendable faculty of taking most especial good care of himself, which he manifested by being always found where water was nearest and the grass best, and on the whole might be termed, in the language of those who consider themselves judges of horse-flesh, a "tolerable chunk of a pony" for a long journey.

He had one bad quality, however, which was continually putting his master to serious inconvenience, and on more than one occasion came near resulting seriously to all. One day we stopped to "noon" close by a spring of water, and had simply taken the bridles from our horses to give them a chance to graze, when he improved the occasion to show off one of his eccentricities. Falconer had a way, as I have before stated, of packing all his scientific, cooking, and other instruments upon his horse, and on the occasion to which I have alluded, some one of them chanced to chafe or gall the pony, inducing him to give a kick up with his hinder limbs. The rattling of the pots and pans started him off immediately, and the faster he ran the more they rattled. We immediately secured our horses by catching up the *lariats*, and then watched the fanciful antics of the animal that had raised all the commotion.

He would run about ten jumps and then stop and kick up about as many times; then he would shake himself violently, and then start off again on a gallop. Every now and then a culinary or scientific instrument would be detached from its fastenings, when the infuriated pony would manage to give it a kick before it struck the ground and send it aloft again. The quadrant took the direction towards the sun without taking it; the saucepan was kicked into a stew; the thermometer was up to 100—inches above the ground, and fell to, worth nothing. To sum it all up, what with rearing, pitching, kicking, and galloping about, the pony was soon rid of saddle and all other encumbrances, and then went quietly to feeding, apparently well satisfied with all the trouble he had given his owner.

The whole affair was ludicrous in the extreme, defying description. The rattling of the tin, earthen, and other ware, as the pony snorted, kicked, and pranced about, made a noise resembling that produced at a *charivari*. His antics were of the most unseemly nature, too—and the cool philosophy of Mr. Falconer, as he quietly followed in the wake of the vicious animal, picking up the fragments scattered along, completed a picture which would have made the fortune of Cruickshank had he been on the spot to take it down. Some time after this adventure the Indians stole the horse, but they made a bad bargain of it.

CHAPTER VI.

The Valley of Cedral Creek.—Singular Natural Road.—Another Delay.—Arrival of General M'Leod with additional Cattle.—The March resumed.—Bad Travelling.—Delicious Spring of Water.—Valley of the Brazos. Fondness of our Animals for its Waters.—Crossing the Brazos.—Prairie on Fire.—Out of Water again.—Sufferings of a Man and Beast.—A cool Spring discovered.—Natural Bathing-tub.—Fresh Indian "Sign."—A recently-deserted Village.—Trick of a Wag.—The Camanche Peak.—"Seeing the Elephant."—The "Cross Timbers."—Description of this singular Forest.—Arrival at Noland's River.—Destruction of our Tents.—The Crossing of Noland's River.—Deserted Indian Village.—Latitude and Longitude taken.—In the Midst of our Troubles.—Our last Day in the "Cross Timbers."—A gloomy Night.—Once more upon the open Prairie.—A hearty Meal.—Speculations as to the route we had taken.—The Banks of Red River supposed to be visible.

On the evening of the 6th of July, the day after the *stampede* mentioned in the preceding chapter, we encamped in a rich and beautiful valley through which Cedral Creek meandered. Our descent into this valley was down the sides of a steep hill, and by a road so perfect that it seems almost impossible nature had any hand in making it. From the top we had a fine view of the romantic valley far below us, which was studded here and there with clumps of trees, while in the distance a dim outline of mountains and the wooded bottoms of the Brazos relieved the eye.

At first it was thought impossible to get the waggons down the steep declivity, but the spies soon found that there was a regular road winding down the sides, and by means of this we descended with ease and safety. For some two miles there was every appearance of a regular excavation on the upper, and of an embankment thrown up on the lower side of the hill; and if this road, upon which there was little vegetation, is really the work of nature, it may be put down as one of her strangest doings. Had it not been accidentally discovered we should not have made the descent without great labour, if at all.

Some of the waggons needing repairs, and our present encampment affording every facility for that purpose, it was resolved to remain here until General M'Leod should arrive, and with him the additional cattle for our subsistence. On the afternoon of the 8th we were all overjoyed to see the expected party winding their way down the singular natural road which we had travelled two days previous. General M'Leod now resumed the command, and ordered us to make every preparation for an early start on the following morning. Our course, up to this time, had been north, varying a little to the east, perhaps, as the broken and hilly country intervened. The object of Mr. Howland, our guide, was to cross the Brazos at the nearest practicable point, and follow up between the waters of that stream and the Trinity.

After travelling some sixteen miles on the ninth, to gain certainly not more than half that distance, we were fortunate in reaching a small spring of water. Our progress had been considerably impeded and made devious and tiresome by deep gullies and runs. The ensuing night we encamped upon the banks of a small creek of fresh water, emptying into the Brazos. This latter stream was now but a few miles to our right, its rich and fertile bottoms, flanked by a heavy growth of timber, being plainly visible.

Our route on the 11th of July, was along a chain of rough hills which separate the valley of the Brazos from the prairies. During the day, several waggons were in some way broken and injured, and it was only after a tedious and toilsome march that we were enabled to reach a cool and delicious spring of water, and find good pasturage for our jaded horses and oxen. Here we found grass in great abundance, and as many of the waggons were again in need of repairs, we remained until the 14th.

The location upon which we were encamped, being in the edge of the timber, with rich prairie directly in front of us, was one of the finest we had yet met on our route. The valley of the Brazos at this place abounded with every species of timber known in Texas; grapes, plums, and other fruit were found in profusion; honey could be obtained in almost every hollow tree; trout and other fish were plentiful in the small creeks in the neighbourhood, and the woods and prairies about us not only afforded excellent grazing for our cattle and horses, but teemed with every species of game—elk, deer, bears, wild turkeys, and, at the proper season, buffalo and mustang. No fresh Indian "sign" was discovered, but the year previous a large body of Cherokees or Wacoes had evidently made the neighbourhood their home, old tent poles being found still standing near our camping-ground, as well as corn-fields which had been cultivated the year before.

As I have said, we were encamped by a cool and delicious spring of never-failing water. Some half a mile distant, in an eastern direction, the Brazos meandered along, whose salt and brackish waters, although unpalatable for man, were swallowed with avidity by both horses and cattle. Indeed, so fond were the latter of this water that they drank incredible quantities of it, and could hardly be induced to leave the stream the first time they were taken to it. At certain periods of the year the prairie Indians visit the salt streams of Texas, considering the waters highly beneficial to their stock.

We crossed the stream on the 14th, after much difficulty from the quicksands and high banks. The waggons all over, we stopped for an hour or two under the shade of some oaks that skirted the border of the valley, and here, for the first time, I saw the magnificent spectacle of a prairie on fire. It was purely accidental, and caused us little damage; but had the wind been in a different direction it would have swept the whole face of the country for miles and miles in advance. The dry grass flashed up like powder, and the fire spread over the prairie with alarming speed. At first an attempt was made to extinguish it, by means of switches made of green boughs and bushes; but those who exerted themselves in this way returned from the task with singed whiskers, eyebrows, and hair, and without having effected anything.

We pursued our journey in the afternoon, and reached a mud-hole—for it could not be called anything else—where we encamped. All night the long and bright line of fire, which was sweeping across the prairie to our left, was plainly seen, and the next morning it was climbing the narrow chain of low hills which divided the prairie from the bottoms of the Brazos.

With a single exception of one day and night, we had suffered little from want of water up to the 15th of July. After a tortuous and tedious march, over a dry prairie ridge, we were finally obliged to encamp without water. Of course we suffered most intolerably ourselves, after having travelled all day in a hot sun; but the cattle and horses felt it even more seriously. At night the guard found great difficulty in herding and keeping them together, so anxious were they to start off in search of water, and the next morning the horses had a wild expression about the eyes, combined with an uneasiness and fretfulness, which forcibly told their suffering.

Our start in the morning was early, and eagerly did we press forward with the hope of finding water. No breakfast had been cooked, as eating only tended to increase a thirst which was already distressing. Late in the afternoon, and when we had almost despaired of finding water, one of the spies returned with the joyful intelligence that a large and cool spring had been discovered but a little way off our course. The line of march was now instantly broken; for those who had good horses dashed madly forward, while the drivers bestowed heavy blows, and imprecations if possible more horrible than ever, upon their tired cattle, to press them onward. In small straggling parties we reached the goal of our hopes. A ledge of rocks, from which cool and limpid water was gushing in all directions, formed the head of the spring, and a few yards below the different branches fell into a common basin some twenty yards in width, and filled to the depth of eight or ten feet with the transparent element. A purling stream was here formed, which carried the surplus waters of the beautiful reservoir to mingle with the brackish current of the Brazos—a base and most unnatural union.

Our thirst was slaked at the very fountain-head—the basin was converted into an immense bathing-tub, where all hands enjoyed the invigorating luxury of a bath. My ancle was still much swollen, and so sore that I was unable to use it in the least; but I made out to hobble to the basin on one foot, and gained great strength by lying at the edge and allowing one of the cool streams from above to fall upon the lame part. The next morning, after enjoying another bath, we left this delicious spring with regret, and pursued our journey with no prospect of water before us. We were fortunate enough, however, to reach a small branch of running water at nightfall, upon which we encamped.

Our camp was hardly formed before Captain Caldwell, or "Old Paint,"* as he was generally called, returned with the spy company, and reported that he had fallen

* Captain Caldwell received the *soubriquet* of "Old Paint," from the fact of his naturally dark hair, whiskers, and beard being covered with large white spots. In Texas, and some of our Southern States, a horse or other animal which is spotted is called a "paint." Captain C. was an old backwoodsman, had been engaged in conflicts almost innumerable with the Mexicans and Indians, and was what is termed in Texas an excellent "rough fighter" and hunter. He was one of the signers of the Declaration of Independence of Taxes, and many of his daring achievements are often recounted in that country. He was released, with the other Texan prisoners, and returned to his family at Gonzales; but on the invasion of Texas in 1842, by General Woll, he recruited a company and defeated that officer at the Salado. The following winter he died, much regretted by all who knew him.

in with an Indian camp which apparently had been deserted but a few hours. The duties of the spy company, I might here add, were to keep one day in advance of the main body, for the purpose of picking out the best road for the waggons, finding water, and keeping a look-out for Indians. Captain C. brought in a number of roasting ears, and stated that he found many unripe melons and pumpkins among the corn. While on Little River a report had been sent to General M'Leod that a large party of Cherokees, Caddoes, and individuals of other tribes, all hostile to Texas, had planted themselves in a large and fertile bend of the Brazos above the Camanche Peak, and that they had extensive and well-cultivated fields, besides a large number of horses and mules. At first it was determined to go somewhat out of our way and attack this party in their stronghold, for it is was said that they were well fortified; but upon after thought it was feared the detention would be too great, and the adventure was given up. It was now evident enough that we were in the vicinity of these hostiles, and at night strict orders were given the guard to be on the alert to prevent a surprise, or our horses and oxen from being *stampeded* and driven off.

The next day we made but five or six miles on our journey, and encamped near several mineral springs, the waters of which were strongly impregnated with iron and sulphur. The scull of a white woman, but recently killed, was found in the vicinity, and large and fresh Indian trails were discovered running in the direction of the Brazos. We also passed through a recently-deserted Indian camp upon the march, the bark wigwams still standing, and many of the implements generally seen in an Indian village remaining precisely as the frightened inhabitants had left them.

Some ingenious wag had left our camp early in the morning alone, and happened to be the first to discover this village. The fellow played off a fine trick upon some of us in the manner following: the interiors of some of the wigwams were lined with smooth bark, and choosing one of the larger domiciles, he covered the bark with rough but tolerably well-drawn figures of men, horses, and buffalo. He must have been a rapid sketcher, as the entire ceiling, if I may so call it, was in this way decorated. Underneath a group of figures stood out, in bold relief and in good Roman characters, the crack-jaw name of some Indian brave, leading us to suppose, at once, that this was the artist who had executed the work above. Not suspecting, for a moment, that any such hoax had been played, and never imagining that any of our men had gone a-head and alone, we could not but come to the conclusion that some erratic white genius had domesticated himself among the Indians, or that one of the wild sons of the woods and the prairies had cultivated, in some way, a taste for the fine arts. The author of the hoax, however, thinking the joke too good to be lost, finally divulged the secret.

Our next day's march was along the high ridge of prairies which divides the waters of what was thought to be Noland's river from those of the Brazos. The prospect on both sides was romantic in a high degree. To the east, for miles, the prairie gently sloped, hardly presenting a bush to relieve the eye. In the distance, the green skirting of woods, which fringed either border of a large stream, softened down the view. Occasionally a deer would jump suddenly from his noon-day rest, and scamper off across the prairie, but other than this no game was seen. The few deer we saw were exceedingly wild, from the fact of there being so many Indians in the vicinity; while the buffalo had evidently all been driven to the south.

To the west of the ridge, the immediate vicinity was even more desolate, but the fertile bottoms of the Brazos, with their luxuriant growth of timber, were still visible, and the Camanche Peak, rising high above the other hills, gave grandeur and sublimity to a scene which would otherwise have been far from monotonous. This peak is celebrated as a looking-out point for the Camanches, commanding, as it does, a complete view of the country around as far as the eye can reach—and hence its name.

Late in the afternoon we reached a small spring of water where we encamped, and the grass being excellent in the vicinity, we remained nearly all the next day to rest the jaded cattle and repair the ricketty waggons. Many of the latter were half worn out when we started, and the rough road over which we had travelled was far from improving them. An afternoon's march brought us to a noble spring in a grove of post oaks—a grove which turned out to be one of the outskirts of the celebrated Cross Timbers.

Up to the 21st of July, one month from the time when we left the Brushy, our course had been nearly north, the country we traversed principally fertile and rolling prairies, destitute of timber, except the bottoms of the different streams we had crossed. Our road in the mean time, although we had considered it very bad, was a perfect macadamized turnpike in comparison with what we were shortly to meet. There is a cant expression, *"I've seen the elephant,"* in very common use in Texas, although I had never heard it until we entered the Cross Timbers, or rather the first evening after we had encamped in that noted strip of forest land. I had already seen "sights" of almost every kind, animals of almost every species, reptiles until I was more than satisfied with the number and variety, and felt ready and willing to believe almost anything I might hear as to what I was yet to see; but I knew very well that we were not in an elephant range, and when I first heard one of our men say that he had seen the animal in question, I was utterly at a loss to fathom his meaning. I knew that the phrase had some conventional signification, but farther I was ignorant. A youngster, however, was "caught" by the expression, and quite a laugh was raised round a camp fire at his expense.

A small party of us were half-sitting, half-reclining around some blazing fagots, telling stories of the past, and speculating upon our prospects for the future, when an old member of the spy company entered our circle and quietly took a seat upon the ground. After a long breath, and a preparatory clearing of his throat, the veteran hunter exclaimed, "Well, I've seen the elephant."

"The *what?*" said a youngster close by, partially turning round so as to get a view of the speaker's face, and then giving him a look which was made up in equal parts of incredulity and inquiry.

"I've seen the elephant," coolly replied the old campaigner.

"But not a real sure-enough elephant, have you?"

queried the younger speaker, with that look and tone which indicate the existence of a doubt and the wish to have it promptly and plainly removed.

This was too much; for all within hearing, many of whom understood and could fully appreciate the joke, burst out in an inordinate fit of laughter as they saw how easily the young man had walked into a trap, which, although not set for that purpose, had fairly caught him; and I, too, joined in the merry outbreak, yet in all frankness I must say that I did not fully understand what I was laughing at. The meaning of the expression I will explain. When a man is disappointed in anything he undertakes, when he has seen enough, when he gets sick and tired of any job he may have set himself about, he has "*seen the elephant.*" We had been buffetting about during the day, cutting away trees, crossing deep ravines and gullies, and turning and twisting some fifteen or twenty miles to gain five—we had finally to encamp by a mud-hole of miserable water, and the spies had been unable to find any beyond—this combination of ills induced the old hunter to remark "I've seen the elephant,"—and upon the same principle I will here state that I had by this time obtained something more than a glimpse of the animal myself.

We were now fairly within the limits of the Cross Timbers, a singular strip of wooded country, a description of which may not prove uninteresting.*

The immense western prairies are bordered, for hun-

* My own opinion is, that we entered the Timbers near the southern extremity. What distance this singular forest extends north I am unable to say, but I believe it terminates not far from the Canadian or Arkansas. It probably reaches no farther south than a point near the junction of Noland's River with the Brazos.

dreds of miles on their eastern side, by a narrow belt of forest land, well known to hunters and trappers under the above name. The course of this range is nearly north and south, with a width ranging from thirty to fifty miles. The growth of timber is principally small gnarled, post oaks and black jacks, and in many places the traveller will find an almost impenetrable undergrowth of brier and other thorny bushes. Here and there he will also find a small valley where the timber is large and the land rich and fertile, and occasionally a small prairie intervenes; but the general face of the country is broken and hilly, and the soil thin. On the eastern side of the Cross Timbers the country is varied by small prairies and clumps of woodland, while on the western all is a perfect ocean of prairie. The belt, therefore, for whatever purpose it may have been fashioned by the Great Creator of all things, appears to be an immense natural hedge dividing the woodlands of the settled portions of the United States from the open prairies which have ever been the home and hunting-ground of the red man. To use another figure, it may be looked upon as the western side of the frame of an immense landscape painting, the United States forming the subject. The Gulf of Mexico may be considered the frame on the southern side, the Atlantic on the east, while the great lakes which divide the picture from Canada must serve for the northern side.

In that portion through which we passed, and we spent nearly a fortnight in the Cross Timbers, we found the face of the country broken, and full of deep and almost impassable gullies. These, in the rainy season, carry off the waters from the hills to the larger streams outside the woods, but in July we found them all dry. Had we been able to travel directly west we should have materially shortened our journey; but the country was such that we were compelled to pursue a diagonal course, subjecting men, cattle, and horses to great privation and suffering, to say nothing of the vexations of our slow and toilsome march.

Bear and deer are found in the Cross Timbers and the vicinity, and small gangs of buffalo take shelter in them when scattered and driven from the prairies by Indians. In many of the trees swarms of wild bees are found, affording delicious honey—a great luxury to those who are engaged in a border life, for it is well known that the absence of breadstuffs increases the appetite for sweets of every description. Often, while living upon nothing but poor beef, and not half enough of that, did fallacious pictures of confectionary-stores and cake-shops pass before my dreaming fancies—the shadows of pies, puffs, and patties, of comfits, candies, and creams were there, but the substance was far away.

For two or three days we journeyed through the middle of the belt, every attempt to find a passage out proving futile. On one or two occasions, distant fires were seen upon the hills at night, but we were unable to get a sight of the Indians who were encamped by them.

On the night of the 23rd we reached Noland's River.* As many of our oxen were much travel-worn, and some of our horses needed shoeing, we encamped upon this

* Some of our men thought it was one of the forks of the Trinity. I am inclined to believe they were wrong in their surmises, although far from confident.

stream until the 26th. At this camp the officers of the expedition held a consultation to devise means for more rapid progress. While upon the prairies, it was evident that the waggons were too heavily loaded, and now that we were in a much rougher country it was deemed imperatively necessary that they should in some way be lightened. The first step towards effecting this desirable object was the throwing away a large portion of the dry beef we had brought from Austin, much of which was found to be spoiled. This meat had been provided as a last resort in case the Indians should deprive us of our cattle; but to carry it farther was considered unwise, and such portions of it as were fit for use were immediately served out to the men instead of green beef, but half the weight of the latter being given. It was also resolved to deprive us of one of our greatest comforts—the tents. There were many of them new, well made, and easily pitched—but that there should be no repining, nor ill-feelings engendered in the camp, all the poles were burned, as well those of the officers, commissaries, and merchants, as of the men. But one was saved—the hospital tent, for the use of such as might be sick—and we had now nothing to protect us from the rain or cold but our blankets and the sky. During the three days we passed on the western side of Noland's River the waggons received a thorough repairing. The fatigue-men also dug away the steep banks of the stream, and cut a road through the heavy timber of the bottoms.

By the 26th of July everything was in readiness for resuming the toilsome journey, and after crossing the river without accident we were enabled to travel some ten miles before we encamped. The road was through a stony and hilly country, interspersed with an occasional grove of black jacks and post oaks. To the right of our line of march we saw the ruins of what had been a large Indian village, many of the wigwams being still in a partial state of preservation.

The next day we reached a small grove of timber, bounded on all sides by a level and beautiful prairie—an island, it would almost appear, in the heart of the Cross Timbers. The water and grass being good at this place, and the country beyond appearing rough and our farther advance almost impossible, it was determined to remain until the spies had found some outlet from the labyrinth of difficulties in which we were entangled.

At this camp, for the first time, the latitude and longitude were taken by Mr. Falconer and Lieutenant Hull, the latter of whom had been an officer in the English navy and fully understood the use of the quadrant. According to their calculation, we were upward of two hundred miles in a course nearly north from Austin, and the distance to Santa Fé was close upon five hundred miles, the direction a little north of west. The exact latitude and longitude I made a memorandum of in my note-book, together with a description of the country through which we passed, the course each day, and the number of miles we travelled. This book is now in the hands of the Mexicans, and as a matter of course I am compelled to depend upon memory. Circumstances difficult to forget, however, occurred every few days, the dates of which were so strongly impressed upon me that I still retain them, and the events of the intervening time I am obliged to fill up, as I have said before, from memory.

The spies returned in the evening and reported that they had found a route through the timber in a northwesterly direction — the only one in which we could travel. They stated the distance to be about twenty miles, the country covered with brush and post oaks, cut up by ravines, and without water: but it was believed that by sending a large fatigue party in advance with shovels and axes, and by making a very early start, we could cut our way through in one day—at all events it was determined to attempt it. Mr. Navarro, although extremely lame, would not trust himself in the little Jersey waggon, but mounted a horse and left me the only passenger. Fitzgerald volunteered to drive the mules for this day only. His style of handling the reins was peculiarly of the break-neck order, but as we had to travel over a break-neck road the driving may be set down as in perfect keeping.

The morning was pleasant, but the bright July sun gave promise of an unusually hot day, and did not disappoint us. At the first gully we crossed, which was not more than half-a-mile from out starting-point, two of the foremost waggons upset. The labour of righting them and repacking their heavy loads occupied some two hours, and thus it was near the middle of the day before we had made one quarter of our day's march. In the mean time, the road grew worse and worse as we advanced, the weather was unusually hot and sultry, our stock of water was soon exhausted, and with that went our patience and good temper. One difficulty was no sooner passed, than even a worse stared us in the face. The narrow passage cut for the the waggons was stumpy and stony, cut up every two or three hundred yards by deep gullies, or the dry beds of what had been running streams. The ground was covered with a heavy undergrowth of briers and thorn-bushes, impenetrable even by mules, and these, with the black jacks and post oaks which thickly studded the broken surface, had to be cut away, their removal only showing, in bolder relief, the rough and jagged surface of the soil which had given them existence and nourishment.

Night finally overtook us, when we were but half way through our toilsome march. By this time fatigue-men and drivers were worn down, hungry, half choked with thirst, and completely dispirited; the oxen were jaded, unwilling or unable to draw, as well as suffering for want of water, and the imprecations bestowed upon them were louder, deeper, and more disgustingly blasphemous than ever. Several waggons had been upset, broken to pieces, and left by the roadside, while the command was scattered for miles through the woods, every one eagerly pressing forward for water, uncontrolled and uncontrollable. To make the matter worse for Fitzgerald and myself, we had fallen in the rear of the long train of waggons, with the hope of finding a better road, and it was impossible to pass them. Had we started with the party in advance, we might have pressed forward in our light waggon, and thus have reached water; as it was, we were compelled to keep the position we had originally taken in the cumbrous and gloomy procession.

To make our situation still more desperate, a dark and cloudy night followed a clear and hot day. How fervently we wished it might rain, that it might descend in torrents, and thus enable us to slake a thirst which was almost intolerable ; yet while the muttering thunder plainly told us that heavy showers were passing around us, a few drops only fell to our share—the clouds but made our march more difficult and dangerous.

Midnight came, finding us in the midst, I might say in the very thickest of our troubles. The extended train of waggons made an unusually long stop, and while we were peering through the gloom and wondering what had caused the delay, word was passed along the line that the artillery-carriage had stuck fast in a gully some half a mile a-head, that most of the fatigue-men had mounted their horses and started off in search of water, and what was more annoying than all, that we must remain where we were through the night! Here was a climax to a day and night of horrors. Had I been in possession of the use of my limbs I would have started at once for water; as it was I was compelled to bear my sufferings as best I could. Fitzgerald merely unhitched the mules from the waggon, and without taking off the harness made them fast to a neighbouring black jack with the reins. He then betook himself to the ground under our carriage, while I took an inside seat, or rather couch. Thirsty and hungry as I was, I soon fell asleep, and never woke up till morning. It must have been sheer exhaustion that induced this sleep, for my mind was certainly attuned to anything else.

When the morning light enabled us to see the surronnding objects, we discovered that our mules had broken their fastenings, and started off, probably in search of water. Here was a prospect of another annoying delay, for we could form no opinion as to the time when the mules had left or the course they had taken. After a long search, however, they were found, led back to the waggon, and a few minutes saw us again on our journey. About the middle of the day we finally emerged from the Cross Timbers, and a short ride across a smooth prairie brought us to our companions, who were comfortably encamped on the banks of a running spring of fresh water. Those, and those only, who have passed twenty-four hours without water, half the time under a hot broiling sun, and in circumstances of feverish excitement, can judge of our feelings and sufferings—are alone able to appreciate the perfect happiness experienced as the parched lips and swollen tongue first touched the precious element. But our march of the previous day and night—never can I forget that march. I had previously travelled many weary miles, over the worst roads, and by the worst conveyances; I had *thought* my sufferings great during these different journeyings; but to alter a remark of the facetious and renowned Sancho Panza, all those sufferings were cakes and gingerbread compared with what I experienced the last day and night we passed in the Cross Timbers.

We were hungry as well as dry on reaching our encampment; so, after having slaked our thirst, we sat down to a most delicious repast. And what was this repast? the gentle reader may ask: simply a piece of ordinary beef, cooked before a fire on a ramrod; but keen appetites supplied bread, vegetables, and seasoning, and a heartier meal I never enjoyed. I thought, while eating, of the *gourmands* of cities, men who spend half their time in getting up an appetite to relish the delicacies placed before them—I pitied them, and ate on.

It was not until a late hour in the evening that the broken waggons and scattered oxen were safely brought into camp; if my memory serves me aright, several of the latter had strayed so far away that they were never found. The blacksmith's forge was, in the mean time, put in operation, the greatest exertions being made so to patch up the injured waggons that they would be in condition to resume the journey early on the morrow.

Now that we had made the dreaded passage of the Cross Timbers, we were sanguine in believing our troubles and difficulties over. As far as the eye could reach in a west-northwest direction, which was the course resolved upon by our guide, Mr. Howland, nothing could be seen but a succession of smooth, gently-undulating prairies. From several hills in our vicinity, known to many hunters who were among us, it was evident that we were within twenty miles of Red River: in fact, the distant timber which skirts the borders of that stream was now supposed to be in sight. It was also known that we were but a short distance from an old Towish Village, a noted camping-ground for the Pawnees and other prairie Indians in their annual excursions south in quest of buffalo.

By going directly to the banks of Red River, and attempting to follow it too closely, it was feared that we should meet with many of the deep gullies through which the waters falling during the rainy season pour themselves into that stream, and should find none but the river water for use, which in the dry months, is characteristically brackish and unpalatable. By keeping farther out, it was thought we should not only find fresh water in greater abundance, but a far better road than by a route nearer the stream. Unfortunately for us this was the course adopted. Mr. Howland formed his plans with much judgment and deliberation; that we afterward encountered and followed a stream mistaking it for Red River, was one of those unfortunate errors against which no human foresight or prudence could have guarded. The fate of the expedition might have been altogether different had we adopted the repudiated plan, keeping on until we had reached the above stream, and then followed it so closely that there would have been no possibility of loosing it.

Another important error, in the opinion of many, was the crossing of the Brazos. Had we kept directly along the ridge which divides that stream from the Colorado, we should certainly have avoided the toilsome and tedious passage of the Cross Timbers, and it may be have suffered as little from scarcity of water. This route would certainly have been much nearer, as we could have travelled almost a direct course; but to oppose it, different objections were raised. By some it was said that we should be obliged to cross large prairies abounding with salt lakes, where no fresh water could be procured; others, again, prudently contended that the country in that direction was much of it unexplored, and consequently unknown, while by crossing the Brazos, a short distance below the Camanche Peak, we were almost certain of finding fresh water every day, and a country over which the waggons could be taken. Perhaps it was better that we took the course we did:

> "There's a divinity that shapes our ends,
> Rough-hew them how we will;"

and until more is known of the country between the head waters of the Brazos and Colorado, it is folly to indulge in idle regrets that we did not take that course.

CHAPTER VII.

Trail of the Chihuahua Traders.—Causes of the Failure of that Enterprise. —A fresh Indian "Burn."—Dr. Whittaker lost. Indian Dogs.—Their forlorn Appearance.—Exciting Scene.—An Indian Buffalo Chase—Well rid of annoying Visitors.—Buffalo Meat for Dinner.—Pack of miserable Curs.—A recently-deserted Indian Camp.—Dr. Whittaker again among us.—A White Flag sent out.—Beautiful Camping-ground.—An Eclipse. —Once more on Horseback.—Singular Chase.—Both Parties mistaken. —A Soaking.—Carlos, a Mexican, joins the Spy Company.—Plausibility of his Stories.—The supposed Red River.—Parley with a Party of Wacoes.—Their Insolence.—Arrival at a Waco Village.—Its desertion by the Inhabitants.—Beautiful Location of the Town.—Its Houses and Corn-fields.—An Indian Musical Instrument.—Speculations upon Love. —High State of Civilization of the Wacoes.—Causes of the Hostility of the Wacoes to the Texans.—Departure from the village.—Brackish Water.—Fear of the Prairie Indians of Artillery.—Origin of this Fear.

We left our camp, near the western margin of the Cross Timbers, late on the morning of the last day of July, and, such was the excellence of the travelling on the prairies, were able to make twelve miles on our journey. During the forenoon we crossed the great trail made the year before by the Chihuahua traders. A company of American merchants, residents of Chihuahua, had conceived the project of opening a direct trade with the United States by way of the prairies, in lieu of the circuitous and expensive route through St. Louis, Santa Fé, and El Paso del Norte.

Thinking that, by crossing the Rio Grande at a point not far from the latter town, and then taking a course nearly east, they could reach Red River near Jonesboro', they visited the United States with the intention of testing its feasibility by experiment. Having purchased and loaded some eighty waggons, they left the western borders of Arkansas early in the spring of 1840. No less than five months were these men employed in cutting their way through the Cross Timbers, while the heavy bottoms, and the dismal bogs and fens of Red River, were rendered thrice dreadful by constant rains. After they had passed these disheartening obstacles, and reached the open prairies, they were still three months upon the road, making eight in all. So great was the expense, and so much time was lost in crossing the prairies, that the enterprise proved a losing speculation, and has not been repeated. A company of American equestrians, with all their horses, canvass, and circus appointments generally, crossed the prairies with the traders, and afterward performed in many of the towns and cities of Mexico with various success.

We had scarcely crossed the Chihuahua trail before we found ourselves upon a "burn," or place where the prairie grass had been lately consumed by fire. During the day we also noticed fresh Indian "sign," consisting of recent trails; and other more subtle evidences, cognisable only by the instincts of old campaigners, convinced us that we were not far from a body of savages. We passed a small creek of sluggish water during the day, but at night were obliged to encamp without any. Scarcely had the guard-fire been kindled, and the sentinels posted, before it was discovered that Dr. Whittaker, our surgeon, was missing, and no one could give the least clew to his mysterious disappearance. The band was immediately ordered out to play at different commanding points, fires were kindled on the highest rolls of the prairie around us during the night, and the cannon was fired the next morning, with the hope of attracting his attention; but he came not, and we were obliged to continue our march without him.

We had not gone more than three miles when a mean, sneaking, scurvy-looking dog came crouching and whining among us, and soon two others made their appearance. They were poor, miserable curs, half wolf apparently, and their homeless, half-starved, and forlorn condition would have protected them from the operation of any code of dog laws in Christendom. Their appearance created a good deal of speculation among us. That they were Indian dogs, and that their owners were not far distant, we were well satisfied; but why they came crying around us and seeking our protection it was difficult to conceive, for the dog of the red man usually avoids the whites.

But a far more exciting incident than the appearance of these worthless curs took place during this day's march. Our animals had had no water the night before, and this circumstance made all anxious to press forward to a small stream which had been discovered by the spies. As a consequence, such as had good horses left the ranks —for when there is no water there is no subordination— the advance-guard left the waggons to take care of themselves, the drivers pressed their oxen forward, in the vain hope of keeping up with the mounted men, and in this way the command soon became scattered for miles along the undulating prairie, the different parties not being even within sight of each other.

Mr. Navarro, who had only mounted his horse the last day we were in the Cross Timbers, had now resumed his seat in the little waggon, Fitzgerald was still driving, when we suddenly found ourselves out of sight of any of our friends. This circumstance did not in the least alarm us, as we anticipated no immediate danger, and the trail of the advance-guard was so plainly visible on the grass that we could follow it at a rapid pace.

While jogging briskly along at the foot of a prairie ridge, the roll running nearly parallel with our course, a buffalo cow came dashing madly past, and within but a few yards of us. Her tongue was out and curved inward, while her tail was carried aloft, showing that she was running in hot haste, and apparently for very life.

One of the waggon-curtains had at first prevented us from seeing aught in the rear of the buffalo; but as she swiftly sped past us, a pursuer, in the shape of an Indian, who could not be more than ten yards behind her, appeared in full view. The savage was mounted on a small but beautifully-formed bay horse, of short, quick stride, yet fine and powerful action. He was armed with a long lance, which he held poised in his hand, while a bow and quiver were strapped to his back. His dress was a buckskin shirt, with leggins of the same material, while his long, black hair, although partially confined by a yellow band about his head, was waving in the breeze created by his rapid course along the prairie. He had scarcely got clear of the curtain, which confined our view to objects only in advance of the waggon, when another Indian was discovered following immediately in his steps.

"Los Indios! Los Indios!" said Mr. Navarro, with consternation depicted on his countenance, while he was eagerly feeling about in the bottom of the waggon for his rifle.

"Camanches!" shouted Fitz, at the same time pummelling and kicking the mules into a break-neck gallop, in the hope of soon coming up with the advance-guard, which now could not be far a-head.

"The whole tribe!" I could not help exclaiming, as I now looked out at the hinder end of the waggon, and saw still another well-mounted Indian dashing down the roll of the prairie with the speed of the wind, and to appearance, making directly for us.

This whole scene was enacted in a few seconds, and in our lame and unprotected situation our minds were but ill at ease on the score of an attack. The appearance of the last Indian, and the reasonable supposition that a large body might be following him, induced Fitz to kick and beat the mules more zealously than before, and at such a rate of speed did they go, that the race between us and the formost Indian swas close, and for a short distance well contested; while the buffalo led her wild pursuers along directly by our side, and so near that the very earth, thrown from their horses' hoofs, rattled against the curtains of our waggons. The savages, though they must have been aware of our proximity, did not appear to bestow a single glance upon an object so strange as a Jersey waggon must have been to them, but kept their eyes steadily bent upon their prey.

With mad eagerness this strange race went on, the Indians using every endeavour to overtake and lance the unfortunate cow, while we were even more anxious to gain the protection of our friends. I had noticed, not a little to our relief, that the hindmost Indian wheeled his horse suddenly on seeing our waggon, and retraced his steps over the roll of the prairie; but the other two never deviated from their course. In a race of half a mile they had gained, perhaps a hundred yards on us. An abrupt turn in the prairie ridge now concealed them from our sight, and before we had reached this point the sharp reports of several rifles, in quick succession, convinced us that our unexpected neighbours had been seen by the advance-guard, and that succour was near if needed.

From the time when the Indians were first in sight, until they were lost to view by a roll of the prairie, could not be more than five minutes, yet there was an ordinary lifetime of excitement in the scene. Had we known that there were but three, or even three times that number, and had we been in possession of our limbs, with our rifles fresh loaded and in readiness, we should have taken their sudden advent with less trepidation; but neither Mr. Navarro nor myself could more than hop about on one foot, and our rifles were in the very bottom of the waggon, where, in our over haste, we could not get at them. We even found, on reaching camp, that our arms were not loaded: a pleasant situation, truly, for one to find himself in on being attacked by prairie Indians, whose movements are characterized by a startling rapidity, and who must be met with the utmost promptness—yet so it was. We took special care, however, not to be caught in like predicament again.

On arriving at our encampment, which was hardly a mile from the point where the Indians had passed our waggon, we found that all was hurry and excitement. A small but well-mounted party had already set off in pursuit, and General M'Leod had detailed another party who were on the eve of mounting. The savages had driven the buffalo directly into the lines, the rifle-shots we had heard turning the course of the pursuers, but not that of the pursued. The cow was shot with a musket by one of our officers, Lieutenant Scott, and found to be young, and exceedingly fat and delicious.

Our encampment was a beautiful grove of timber, and near a small stream of warm, turbid water. A few yards below was a large Indian camp, apparently but just deserted, some twenty or thirty half-starved curs still lingering about, which seemed too weak to follow their masters. From the appearance of the closely-picked fish, snake, terrapin, and pole-cat bones which were scattered about, the late occupants of the camp had suffered much from want of food, and the dogs might be supposed to have eaten nothing for weeks. The Indians who had driven the buffalo into our lines, evidently belonged to this camp. The desperation of their hunger was such as to overcome any astonishment or intimidation the appearance of our waggon might have caused, and they never gave up their chase until their prey was in our very jaws.

After enjoying the hearty dinner which had thus accidentally been thrown in our way, preparations were made for an evening march. The spies had discovered a larger stream some six miles distant, with excellent grazing in the vicinity. Before starting, General M'Leod sent out two or three parties, in different directions, in quest of the Indians. Each party carried a white flag, strong hopes being entertained, notwithstanding the unfriendly reception given to the Indians who had driven the buffalo into our camp, that some of the company might be induced to come in on amicable terms. Guides were wanted, not only to inform us of our present position, but to lead or direct us onward by the best and easiest route. Not an Indian could be found, however, but one of the parties went as far as the large river north of us. The waters were described as brackish and of a brownish colour, agreeing, in every way, with the description of Red River. The stream was running nearly, east, and our west-northwest course had by this time brought us within some ten miles of it.

As the command was on the eve of resuming the march, we were all rejoiced by the arrival of Dr. Whittaker, for whose safety, now that Indians had been seen almost in our very midst, the liveliest apprehensions were felt. Our worthy surgeon told us that he had halted a short distance from the line of march on the previous day, for the purpose of enjoying a short rest under a small shade tree; that he had fallen into a sleep from which he did not awake for two or three hours, and that on rising he felt that he was "turned round," or in other words, that he was completely lost, and uncertain as to the direction in which the command had come or gone. In this state of doubt he had taken a course which he supposed to be the right one, and when night came he hid himself in a quiet hollow, until daylight should allow him to continue the uncertain task of finding his companions. Fresh Indian sign he had seen in every direction, and during the night his horse, the end of whose rope he had made fast to one of his arms, gave well-known indications that an enemy was lurking in the immediate neighbourhood. With the early dawn the doctor continued his hap-hazard search. He had a good horse and rifle, with some twenty rounds of powder and ball, but he was far from being a skilful woodsman. Fortunately, I might say providentially, he came upon our trail, although at the time he was in doubt which direction we had taken. An examination of the foot-prints, however, gave him the course, and two hours' hard riding brought him in safety to our camp.*

Having crossed the sluggish stream upon which the Indian camp was situated, we journeyed on some two hours until we reached the new quarters found for us by our spies. This situation was in a beautiful cove of the prairie, nearly surrounding a skirting of timber. Our camp was upon the banks of what appeared to be a large stream in the rainy season, though now there was but little water in its bed. Its course was nearly north-east, and those among us who pretended to know anything about the country at once concluded that it was the Wichita,† a stream that was said to empty into Red River high up, and about which but little was known except by trappers and Indians. Unfortunately for us we had none of these in our company. Finding excellent grass, water, and timber upon the banks of this stream, we remained the next day to recruit our cattle and repair some of the waggons. The spies were sent out, in the mean time, to examine the country and find a good route.

* Dr. Whittaker has since paid the debt of nature. He was liberated at the city of Mexico with the rest of the Santa Fé prisoners, but died at Puente Nacionel, of yellow fever, on his way home. He was a generous-hearted and brave man, and left many warm friends.

† On some of the maps the reader will find this river put down as the *Big Washita*. I believe the correct spelling and pronunciation to be *Wichita*, but the general course of the stream has been wrongly laid down.

At night we had an eclipse of the moon, without any one knowing that such an occurrence was to take place; the next morning many and queer were the speculations, especially among the guard, as to what caused the singular appearance of the heavens.

Although still unable to bear much weight upon my foot, or walk without great pain, I made out to mount my horse, with assistance, on the 3rd of August, and bade farewell to the old Jersey waggon in which I had journeyed nearly six weeks. Scarcely had we gone three miles that morning, before a small herd of buffalo was seen quietly feeding in a valley to the right. It was the first opportunity that had been offered me of enjoying the excitement of a chase, and I immediately dashed after them; but the hard gait of my horse over the rough prairie pained my ankle so much that I was obliged to give it up.

Another chase came off, however, on the same day, which, for excitement, fairly went beyond anything in the way of horse-racing. One of the volunteers had set out in search of water by himself, and a short time after, without knowing that he had gone, Major Howard left the command on the same errand. By accident they came suddenly upon each other in a little valley, and the man, mistaking Major H. for an Indian, set off at full speed. The latter, also thinking the other an Indian, gave chase with a yell, and away they bounded across the prairies as fast as their horses would carry them. The first part of the chase was plainly seen by many of us, and created the greatest interest. The Major was by far the best mounted of the two, and was also a bold and dashing rider; but he was a much heavier man than the pursued, and this gave the latter an advantage. The chase continued until both were out of sight, Major H. slowly gaining upon the supposed Indian by his superior riding. On one or two occasions the former raised a pistol to shoot the other, and nothing prevented it but a desire to bring him into camp alive. Finally he came up with the chase, both horses nearly broken down, when the frightened volunteer turned his pale face imploringly around, and recognised, in his pursuer, the well-known major, with a pistol cocked in his right hand.

"Wh—wh—why, major," he exclaimed, stammering from fright—"Why, major, is that *you?* D—d—don't shoot me. Is it really you, major?"

"Certainly it is, and I'm not going to shoot you; but what, in the name of common sense, did you take me for, and what induced you to run so fast?"

"I—I—I—thought you was an Indian—indeed I did," replied the man, still pale and trembling from his recent terror.

"Well," continued the major, "I thought you an Indian too, and you ought to consider yourself lucky that I did not shoot you for one."

In the course of an hour Major Howard rode into camp with his prisoner, who was really half frightened to death. In fact, the man afterward died on the road, and those who knew him best, said that he never got over the "scare." It may appear singular that two white men could mistake each other for Indians; but it should be recollected that we were in an Indian range, and the small parties that went out were in constant expectation of meeting gangs of them. It should also be borne in mind that the dresses we wore were anything and everything that came handy, and conduced most to our comfort while upon the solitary prairies. After being out two months upon a campaign, any man will regard his personal convenience more than his personal appearance, and hence we all more resembled Indians in dress than civilized men. The hot sun and winds of the prairies had also imbrowned our faces to a light mahogany colour, while our hair, allowed to remain uncut, in every case where it was black, made the resemblance to the red man still more close and striking.

On arriving at camp that evening, it was found that Frank Combs was missing, and with him young Curtis Caldwell, son of the old captain of the spy company. Knowing as we did that so many enemies were in our neighbourhood, their absence caused great solicitude; but they came in shortly after our guard fires had been kindled.

About nine o'clock at night we had a tremendous shower, which continued until near daylight. When the water first came trickling through my blanket, I thought of snug rooms, clean bed, moscheto bars, and all that sort of thing; but while thinking of them I fell asleep, and never had a better night's rest in my life, although I awoke at daybreak wet to the skin. The heavier part of the shower was over when we crawled from our soaked blankets; there was yet a misty, drizzling rain, however, and we were compelled to continue the march that morning in wet clothes.

From the higher rolls of the prairies we could now distinctly see, to the right and in a northern direction, the dim outline of a belt of timber running nearly parallel with our course, supposed by all to be the skirting of Red River. A Mexican named Carlos, a native of Taos, in new Mexico, who was attached to one of the companies, now for the first time said that he had trapped up and down Red River, and knew every part of it; that the country around us resembled in every respect the vicinity of that stream, and that he had no doubt we were now close upon the Red River bottoms. So plausible were his stories, and his knowledge of the country appeared so extensive, that he was immediately transferred to the spy company; and here I might add, that Carlos had been employed as mail-carrier between Austin and San Antonio for several years, and had always been found an honest and trustworthy fellow. This circumstance was related when his claims as a person entitled to credit were canvassed in camp, and went far to establish for him a character for probity which few of his countrymen of the same class receive or deserve.

As we desired neither to cross the river to our right, nor approach too near its wooded bottoms, our course was now altered a point or two—perhaps more, as I noticed we were frequently travelling a little south of west. The fog, clouds, and drizzling rain of the early morning had dispersed before the middle of the forenoon, the sun coming out intorerably hot. Some two hours after meridian, the advance-guard, with which I was now in company, came up with the spies, comfortably encamped in a small grove of timber on the margin of a dry creek, where they were anxiously awaiting our approach.

On the arrival of General M'Leod, the spies had an exciting adventure to relate. They had met and held a parley with a body of Indian warriors, about their own number, all well armed and mounted, many of them upon large and powerful American horses which had evidently been stolen. They were large, athletic men, sat boldly and proudly upon their fat and well-trained steeds; and while many of them had American rifles in their hands, and were far better dressed than the Camanches, Caygüas, and other prairie Indians, their manner was stately and overbearing. Their quick and experienced eyes, as they ran over the jaded and travel-worn animals of the spies, at once convinced them that they could outrun, if not outfight them, and hence their daring and insolent behaviour.

Not one of the Indians could speak English; but there were two or three of them who had picked up a smattering of Spanish, and Carlos, from the affinity their language bore to the Camanche, which he partially understood, was enabled to carry on a conversation. They frankly declared that they had been watching our movements three or four days, and with cool effrontery asked the spies whether we had come for peace or war. The answer was, that our intentions were peaceful; that we were journeying towards Santa Fé with merchandize, and had many waggons and a large force a short distance in the rear. The Indians retorted by saying that they knew all this well enough —they had seen and measured our entire strength. They were next asked if they could direct us on our journey by the best route which would afford the most grass and water; all the Texans wanted was to cultivate a peaceful understanding with these men, and to obtain their assistance in furthering us on our journey.* The questions of the spies were answered in a sullen swaggering manner, so much so that Captain Caldwell —than whom no man in Texas better understood the treacherous and uncertain "ways" of every tribe upon its borders—at once remarked to his men, in a low tone and in English, that "these fellows looked *ugly* and *fighty*, and that they must all keep an eye upon their rifles, and be ready to give them a volley should he make a signal." It was thought by many of the spies that some one of the Indians could understand English, as a movement towards examining the flints and caps upon the rifles of the former was met by a corresponding movement on the part of the red men.

Captain Caldwell next asked his new acquaintances to what tribe they belonged. They told him they were Wacoes, and volunteered the information that a party of two hundred Camanches had been residing near them for some little time, but that they had recently left for the more western prairies. In addition, they said that they themselves were now out on a hunting expedition, and that their village was a long way off. Captain C. now requested them to remain with him until our commander arrived, as the latter was extremely anxious to see and have a friendly talk with them. A few muttered sentences passed between them in their own language at this request, when the principal chief replied that he would return at night and visit our

* General M'Leod was really anxious to encourage friendly relations with these savages: but they appeared to be far from disposed to reciprocate, probably distrusting his motives.

camp and its leader. The fellows then went off at a brisk gallop, and were soon lost to sight by an undulation of the prairie.

Anxious to ascertain the movements of these Indians, Captain Caldwell, the moment they had disappeared, sent out Tom Hancock and another trusty spy to watch them. They returned in an hour, and said that they had discovered a large village some five miles distant in a northern direction, situated upon the banks of a stream, and that, from the general appearance of the country, we should be compelled to pass, with our waggons, directly through the town. Our officers now held a short and hurried consultation, at which it was determined to despatch fifty of our best-mounted men directly to the village. A flag of truce was taken, so that an amicable understanding might be brought about, if possible, with fellows who could make themselves exceedingly troublesome if they felt so disposed, and at the same time the party examined well their arms, to be ready in case the Indians should receive them in a hostile manner. As I was now able to ride, and felt anxious to be among the first to enter the village, I mounted my horse and accompanied the party. The advance-guard under General M'Leod followed at a convenient distance, ready to support us should hostilities ensue.

When within a couple of miles of the Indian village a beautiful spectacle suddenly presented itself. Before us was a large and delightful valley, through which a river coursed along, with just trees enough to relieve the eye without concealing any of the beauties. In a large bend of the stream the village was situated, and all around were the corn-fields, pumpkin and melon patches of the inhabitants. In the distance, on the other side, the prairie rose gently, without a tree or bush to destroy the uniformity of the rich carpetting of green with which it was covered; in a western and south-western direction, exactly on our course should we not cross the river, the country appeared rugged and broken, and offering the greatest difficulty to our progress with the waggons.

As we descended the long wave of the prairies which overlooked the valley, we could see that all was bustle and commotion in the village, now scarce a mile distant. Suddenly a considerable party was seen, dashing off to the southwest, accompanied by a large troop of horses. We were not near enough to distinguish with certainty, but saw enough to convince us that this party was composed of the women and children, as well as old men of the tribe, and that with these they were despatching all their superfluous horses. This seemed to indicate that our own reception would be anything but pacific, as the warriors always send off their families and movable property when they themselves make a stand; but our party kept steadily on. Some of the older Indian fighters cast glances back, to measure the amount of support we might receive from the command in case we should be attacked, while all looked well to their powder-horns and bullet-pouches, and examined their flints and percussion-caps, to see that all was right. In low and hurried tones one volunteer would ask another for a few caps or ball patches, or for a spare flint, and the whole face of things began to assume an aspect decidedly belligerent, when suddenly another party was seen dashing from the village, and following directly in the footsteps of the former and larger throng. We were now within less than half a mile, and it was evident enough that the latter party was composed of warriors only, or grown men. Before we had reached the river, which bounded the village on its southern side, still another party was seen flying off in a northern direction, ascending the undulating prairie on the opposite side of the town.

From these movements it now appeared evident that the Indians were deserting their heretofore peaceful home; yet thinking there might still be some of the tribe remaining, Van Ness and Carlos were sent forward with the white flag. As they entered the village a solitary Indian, the last of his tribe that had remained to this time, was seen emerging from the opposite side and dashing off at lightning speed on the trail of his brothers. Thus, in certainly less than half an hour, was the Wacoe village deserted by all its inhabitants, and in even less time not one of them could be seen in any direction upon the prairies.

A small party of us crossed the river and entered the deserted town. Everything gave evidence of the hasty departure of the inhabitants. Fires were still burning in the vicinity of every lodge or wigwam, and earthen pots were found, in which pumpkins were still boiling. Deer, antelope, and wolf skins, sewed up and full of corn, were left in their haste, and everything betokened the unexpectedness of our approach, and the suddenness of their flight. Not having time to examine everything as closely as I wished, I recrossed the river, with the intention of visiting the village at an early hour in the morning.

The command had arrived, and a camping-ground been chosen by the time I reached the opposite side of the stream. The site of this camp was near a corn-field, the position rendered strong by a grove of heavy timber immediately in our rear. The river would have been crossed had there been a sufficiency of grass on the opposite side for our animals. Strict orders were given not to touch or molest anything belonging to the Indians, and at the same time, fearing lest they might undertake a night surprise, every preparation was made to guard against such uncertain neighbours. We reasonably anticipated that the Wacoes would at least make an attempt to *stampede* and steal some of our horses and cattle; yet the guard were not disturbed, and the night passed off quietly.

Early in the morning I visited the village on the other side of the river. The water of this stream was slightly brackish, enough to make it unpalatable as a beverage, but for boiling meat or making coffee it answered very well. We felt confident that the Indians must have a supply of fresh water near, but were unable to find the springs from which they procured it. The village itself was situated at the western extremity of a large bend in the river, and although the bend must have been some five or six miles in length, by nearly two in breadth in the wider parts, every portion of it appeared to be under cultivation, and the land was extremely fertile. The purlieus of the village appeared to be kept clean, which can be said of few Indian towns.

The wigwams—or houses, rather, for they really deserve that name—appeared to be built in rows, and had an air of neatness and regularity about them such as I had never observed before in an Indian village. They were of conical shape, some twenty or twenty-five feet in height, and of about the same diameter on the floor, the materials used in their construction being poles, buffalo hides, and rushes. The poles were stuck in the ground, and after running up perpendicularly some ten feet, were bent over so as to converge to a point at the top, thus giving a regular dome-like slope to carry off the rains. Over these, buffalo hides in some instances were made fast, and these again were covered with long rushes—thus making thatched cottages, impervious to dust or rain.

Within many of the houses, at an elevation of four or five feet from the ground, was a row of berths extending nearly the whole circuit, and very neatly got up. The bottom of these berths appeared to be of rough basket work, the frame which supported them being of large poles. As all the cooking for the family was done out of doors, their lodges had neither fireplaces nor chimneys. The inhabitants had carried off the principal part of their furniture, but had still left enough, from the haste with which they departed, to convince us that for Indians they lived in much comfort, and not a little style. Attached to each residence, and immediately in the rear, was another building of smaller dimensions, the lower part of which was evidently used as a corn-crib and storehouse. In these buildings we found a quantity of corn and pumpkins, besides finely cured venison, antelope, and buffalo meat. Above the corn-crib was a species of balcony, although without a railing, and this led into a small room in the second story, if I may so call it. One of the company said that this room was the sleeping apartment of the young and marriageable squaws of the family, and that their mother kept a ladder by which they climbed up to it at night and were let down in the morning. This story may be true and may be not—I tell it as it was told me.

In one of the main buildings an instrument, evidently intended for musical purposes, was found. It was made of cane, and in some respects resembled a fife, although much longer. It had five holes for the fingers, besides a mouth-piece somewhat after the fashion of a clarionet. The notes of the instrument were nearly as soft as those of a flageolet, the workmanship extremely neat, and evincing not only ingenuity, but taste; and after hearing the story of the ladder, I could not help thinking that this same instrument had, perchance, while in the hands of some Indian Romeo, discoursed most eloquent music to a belle of the tribe, who, like Juliet, would step out on her balcony and pour forth her love and fealty to her soul's idol in return for this sweet token of his homage. He would then, very possibly tell of his flaming, burning, and inextinguishable passion—recount to her his perilous 'scapes in the chase—talk of buffalo hunts, mustangs, war-paths, bear-fights, corn dances, and scalps; while she eagerly devouring each word, would throw back volumes of tender affection—tell what she would do for him, where she would go for him, how she was willing to pack meat, make moccasins, hoe corn, dig potatoes, and do out-door work generally, besides sitting up of nights for his sake, and for no other persons' sake would she do a thing. He would then, as in duty bound, drop on one knee, lay down his lute, and conjure her to fly—instantly fly with him, on a chosen steed to the farthest prairies—fly any where, every where, so that she was with him, and only him. With beating heart and lip trembling with emotion, she would tell him that her mother had carried off the ladder, and that she dared not, even for his sake, run the risk of breaking her neck by jumping down. Such might have been a scene to which this humble instrument I now held in my hand had been a witness; and then, again, it might not.

Little skilled am I in the vocabulary of an Indian girl's pledges of love; but as in these affairs between parties in civilized life each make out as long a catalogue as possible of what he or she intends to do to make the other completely happy, it is more than probable that the case is the same among the uncivilized children of the prairies. Love is a very pretty theme for poets to dwell upon, and many of them have been known to *live* upon it in the absence of more substantial food; but there is far more of matter-of-fact even in this same love than your sentimentalists would make us believe, and occasionally those afflicted with it have a decided preference for mush, mutton, and safety over moonbeams, moss-banks, and incensed mothers—and hence the Indian girl's repugnance to leaping the balcony. This is all mere speculation—the reader may take it for what it is worth, while I return to my narrative.

We spent two or three hours in the pleasant village, examining the houses, implements, manner of cooking, cultivating the land, and other matters. I will not say that the Wacoes know as much of civilization as the Cherokees or Choctaws, who have had the opportunity of intercourse with the whites; have had their eyes opened somewhat to the plan of civil government by their treaty-dealings with the United States, and been made to know something of the system of the Christian religion by the pious zeal of missionaries. I have seen all these tribes, and while the Wacoes did not exhibit any of those fruits of civilization which too often mar the virgin leaf of those other nations, I confess that I saw evidence of a more elevated kind of humanity than I had supposed was to be found anywhere among the original Americans.

Near the centre of the village was a house of larger dimensions, and more elaborate workmanship than any of the other dwellings. This may have been the general council-house, or the abode of the medicine man of the tribe, or it may have been the residence of their principal chief, who must needs, as is the custom in more civilized nations, live in better quarters and more costly style than his subjects. Be this as it may, it was there, and afforded additional food for the mind to speculate upon.

The Wacoes, although not a numerous, are certainly a brave and warlike, and consequently a strong tribe when compared with the Pawnees and Camanches. Like the latter, they are said to be always on horseback, and equally well skilled in the uses of that noble animal; but here the comparison ends, for the Wacoes have comfortable houses, and corn-fields, and many luxuries to which their prairie neighbours are strangers. The Wacoes have never been corrupted by association with the whites, nor made weak and effeminate by the use of alcohol; and here again they enjoy advantages. In the early history of Texas they were at peace with the inhabitants of that Republic. Large hunting parties of the tribe were frequently seen within her limits, and every relation appeared to bring additional peace and harmony, until an unfortunate affray occurred which induced them to dig up the tomahawk, and since that time many have been the inroads they have committed along the northern frontiers of Texas.

I heard it stated that the whites were guilty of bringing on this war by some act of bad faith towards the Wacoes, and the wound they then received has never been healed. From the fact of their hurrying off their women and children, as well as their large *cavallada* of horses and mules, it was evident that they placed no reliance in our assertion that we came among them with pacific intentions—they had been deceived by our men once, and Indian-like, looked for another violation of our words.

The village we visited probably contained three or four hundred inhabitants, and there were others, both up and down the river, which we could see in the distance. A crossing of the river was effected about ten o'clock in the morning, and after winding slowly through the village, the command continued the journey along the fertile bottoms of the river, our course a little south of west. Carlos said confidently that it was the Red River, and no one doubted, for a moment, that we were upon the banks of that stream, some distance above Coffee's Upper Station. The latter is a well-known trading-house high up on Red River, and the place where the different Indian tribes rendezvous to barter off their skins for rifles, blankets, and ammunition.

At night we encamped upon the banks of the stream. Although the waters of the river, as I have before remarked, were brackish, a pure and fresh stream was discovered close by. This was used by the men, but the cattle and horses would not touch it when they could obtain the river water.

All the spoil we took from the Waco village consisted of a few pumpkins; the houses and everything about them were left untouched. Fine fish were now caught in the stream, which, with our regular rations of beef and the pumpkins we had procured in the morning, gave us a feast. Many of my readers may think this but a meagre feast—boiled beef, fried fish, and boiled pumpkins—but they should recollect that we had eaten no vegetable substance for nearly two months, and that even fried catfish was a rare dainty.

During the day, Indians were seen scouting about on the distant hills, watching our movements; but our position was a strong one, and although we anticipated, no one feared the consequences of a night attack, farther than the danger of having our horses run off.

The fact that the Indians did not make an attack upon us, or attempt to steal our horses, was probably owing to the circumstance that they had seen our six-pounder. It is well known that the Camanches and other prairie tribes have the greatest dread of cannon, and can never be induced to approach within a mile of them. The story is told that a large party of Camanches attacked, many years since, one of the early Missouri expeditions journeying with a small cannon, loaded with grapeshot and rifle-bullets.

So greatly did the savages outnumber the traders, that they felt confident of an easy and sudden victory, and impressed with this belief attacked them in a solid body, and with their usual yells. The traders calmly waited until they had approached within a few yards, when they let fly among them the unexpected shower of missiles. The gun was well directed, and sent a large number of the Indians tumbling to the ground. Those who escaped were so panic-striken at the strange discharge, which carried such fearful destruction to their ranks, that they instantly wheeled and fled, and could not be induced to renew the attack. Overrating, as they did, the power of a cannon from the effect of this well-directed and fortunate shot, from that day to the present no party of the tribe has ever dared attack openly any company fortunate enough to possess a fieldpiece. The fame of the big gun of the whites, so it is said, has spread from the Camanches to the neighbouring tribes, and to such an extent has the story of its powers been magnified, that it is difficult to get an Indian within its utmost range.

CHAPTER VIII.

Join the Spy Company.—Farther Speculations as regards Red River.—Advantages of travelling with the Spies.—Beautiful Streams and Cool Arbours.—Visit from Mustangs.—A dashing wild Horse.—Different Modes of catching Mustangs.—Indians in Sight.—Guarding against a night Attack.—Description of Country.—Rough Travelling.—Arrival at a Fresh-water Stream.—Carlos thinks Himself at Home.—General Joy in Camp.—Scanty Rations.—A Shower and a Stampede.—Cross the supposed Red River again.—Scarcity of "Sign." — Mountains a-head.—A Labyrinth of Difficulties.—Broken Country.—A hunting Adventure.—Get lost upon the Prairie.—Hopelessness of my Situation.—Ruminations upon the Horrors of being Lost.—Fortunate Escape from Difficulty.—A Ride through a Rattlesnake Region.—Once more among my Friends.—Unpleasant Dreams.—A Mesquit Prairie.—Carlos again "at Home."—Three of the Texans sent forward to the Settlements.—Carlos takes the Guidance of the Expedition.—A Buffalo Chase.—River seen to the South.—An Adventure with Deer.—Great Waste of Powder and Ball.—A severe Case of the "Buck Ague."—Symptoms and general Appearance of that singular Disease.

On the 6th of August I joined the spy company. By this time I was able to ride without pain, although I walked with much difficulty, and required assistance in mounting my horse.

The course of the stream we were upon was a little south of east—to follow it up was not the right direction to Santa Fé, but as every one supposed that we must be on Red River, there was no suspicion that we were not taking the true route in doing so. At times, as we journeyed along its fertile bottoms, some bend of the stream would bring us directly upon its banks, which were fringed with a few cotton-wood trees; again, the river would turn away abruptly, leaving us at a distance of several miles from its waters. It was now low, being fordable in many places. Its bed may have been sixty or seventy yards in width, its banks, in many places, high and steep, and giving evidence that in the rainy season there was depth of water sufficient to float the largest steamers.

There were two great advantages in marching with the spies: one was the opportunity of meeting with more exciting adventure, while the other was the brisk pace at which we travelled, being a steady trot, instead of the snail-like movement of the waggons. On the day when I joined them, after a pleasant ride of some ten miles, we arrived at a small creek of fresh and running water, a delicious treat on a hot prairie march. It was a beautiful stream, overhung with grape and other vines now in the full richness of summer verdure. In many places the vines had completely crossed the creek, thus forming a delightful natural arbour, and under this cool shade the restless waters swept along to mingle with the hot and brackish river, now some two or three miles to the south. After finding an easy crossing-place, a man was sent back to the command as a guide, while we unsaddled and turned our horses loose to graze, and then threw ourselves upon the green carpetting of grass under the shade-trees, to enjoy a quiet noonday siesta.

We scarcely had time to establish ourselves comfortably before three or four mustangs were seen approaching at a rapid gallop. Ever and anon they would halt for a moment, throw up their heads as if to scan us more closely, and then, as though not satisfied with the scrutiny, would again approach at the same rapid pace. It may be that they could not see us while reclining under the shade-trees, or mistook our animals for some of their own wild companions; be this as it may, they approached within a few hundred yards, wheeling and dashing about with all the joyousness of unrestrained freedom, and occasionally stopping to examine our encampment more closely. The leader was a bright bay, with long and glossy black tail and mane. With the most dashing and buoyant action he would trot around our camp, and throw aloft his beautifully-formed head, as if, after the manner of some ringleted school-girl, to toss the truant hair from his eyes. Then he would lash his silken tail, shake his flowing mane in pride, and eye us with looks that plainly told his confidence in his powers of flight should danger or treachery be lurking in our vicinity. I had formed a strong attachment for my own powerful bay, for he was gentle as a house-dog, and would run all day if necessity required it; yet I would instantly have "swapped" even him for this wild horse of the prairies, with no other knowledge of his qualities than what I could discover at the distance of a hundred and fifty or two hundred yards.

After gambolling about us for some little time, his bright eyes apparently gleaming with satisfaction, as if conscious that we were watching and admiring his showy points, he suddenly wheeled, and, in a canter, placed himself at a more prudent distance. Then he turned again to take another look, curved his beautiful neck, once more tossed his head, half timidly, half in sport, pawed the ground playfully, and again dashed off. Several times he turned to take still another look at our encampment, and even in the far distance we could distinguish his proud and expanded nostrils, his bright, flashing eyes, and the elastic movements of his symmetrical limbs as he playfully pranced and curvetted about. I watched him until he was but a speck upon the prairie, and then turned from gazing with regret that he was not mine.

The Indians and Mexicans have a way of capturing mustangs by running up on their fleetest and most untiring horses and noosing them with the *lariat*. The white hunters have also a method, which is often successful, of taking the wild horses. It is called *creasing*, and is done by shooting them with a rifle-ball upon a particular cord or tendon in the neck, immediately under the mane. If the ball takes effect precisely in the right spot the animal falls benumbed, and without the power to move for several minutes, when he is easily secured. Should it strike too low, the horse is still able to run off, but eventually dies. An attempt was made to *crease* the magnificent steed I have mentioned; but it was impossible to approach near enough to shoot with accuracy, and to endanger his life would have been a wanton act, which the most eager hunter among us would not have committed. When our provisions became scarce several of these animals were shot for their flesh. It seems repugnant to the feelings to eat horseflesh; but the meat is tender and finely flavoured, and a three-year-old mustang is really better food than either buffalo or common beef.

After the mustangs left us we passed two hours very agreeably in a shade which completely screened us from the hot, noonday sun. In the cool of the evening we once more saddled our horses and continued the march in close order. Deer and antelope were seen in every direction, but as they were at too great distance to be shot from the ranks, not one of them was killed. Our party was small, and as Indians were seen several times during the day, watching us from the different swells of the prairie, it was deemed prudent to keep close and in a body. The Indians seen were to the right of our line of march; that bodies of them were also watching us from the timber on the left was more than probable, as there they could find secure hiding-places. At nightfall we encamped upon the banks of the river, and were obliged to drink the brackish water or none, as no fresh spring could be found. An abundance of the finest catfish were caught in the stream, the bed of which was here nearly a hundred yards in width.

Again a strong position was chosen for our camp, and the guard had strict orders to keep a good lookout at night, to prevent a surprise from the Wacoes. It was evident that they were watching us at every turn, and while their fears prevented them from attacking us openly in a body, they were still, as is their custom, looking out for an opportunity to *stampede* our horses and cattle, or cut off any little straggling party that might wander from camp in search of water or to hunt. The night passed, however, without a visit from them, and the only inconvenience occasioned by their proximity fell upon our horses, for we were compelled to hobble them well, and stake them inside the lines of sentinels, where the grass was soon cropped close to the ground.

For three days after leaving the village of the Wacoes our route was along the wide and fertile bottoms of the river. Our course, as already mentioned, was a little south of west, but being confident that we were on the banks of Red River, it was thought from day to day that the stream would soon turn off more to the north.

On the opposite or south side of the river the country had been rugged and broken up by hills—on the side along which we were travelling, nothing could be seen but a boundless and unbroken prairie, with naught to destroy its sameness except here and there a light fringing of trees bordering the banks of the small creeks and rivulets, which, rising in the prairies to the north, found their way to the river after flowing many miles along cool and secluded courses. Rack fancy to the utmost, and it is still impossible to draw a picture of more enchanting, sylvan loveliness, than some of the beautiful arches formed over these murmuring streamlets. In many places the limbs of the trees which decked either bank would cross over as if to commune and shake hands, one with the other. Along these the wandering grapevines would creep, lock themselves, as it were, in each other's embrace on meeting, and thus form a cool and delicious harbour, so closely interwoven that not a solitary ray from the sun could reach the recess below. Under these natural arches the deer would while away the hot, mid-day hours, slaking his thirst from the gently-flowing waters which were gliding with sweet music at his feet; there, too, we saw the solitary white heron, standing tall and erect, like some elfin spirit. Our approach would frighten him from his secret place, only to seek some other lonely dell of equal beauty, coolness, and seclusion. Such scenes of rural beauty—of soft, pure, unsophisticated nature, are clearly, brightly painted upon my memory—but I am utterly wanting in the power to delineate them.

Our encampment on the banks of the river we left early in the morning, the spies starting some hour in advance in search of fresh water and the best route for the waggons. We had travelled but a few miles when the country before us appeared more rough and broken, and by mid-day the hills and gullies we encountered almost prevented the farther progress of the waggons. The spies finally were fortunate in finding a fresh-water river, running into the larger and brackish stream, and after much fatigue and trouble a crossing-place was discovered, which we were able to reach with our waggons. The banks, on the side at which we approached, were high and steep, offering serious obstacles; on the opposite side of the river, a gradual ascent from the water led to a pleasant valley. Carlos, the Mexican, at once pronounced it the Rio Utau, or Eutaw, a stream upon which he said he had often trapped; and to give his story greater plausibility, he said that at the very point where we made the passage the Mexican hunters had frequently crossed with carts laden with dry buffalo meat.

There really was every appearance of an old waggon road when we reached the opposite side of the river, and if any one had previously doubted the statements of Carlos, those doubts were now set at rest. He said that he was as well acquainted with the country in the vicinity as with his mother's door-yard, and spoke of the country beyond with a plausibility that convinced all of his being now "perfectly at home." He said that the *angosturas,* or narrows of Red River, were distant only some seventy miles, and that the same distance beyond would bring us to the Mexican *ranchos,* or farms, in the immediate vicinity of the frontier town of San Miguel.

Placing confidence as we did in his reports, it is needless to say that all was joy and congratulation in camp that evening. Our beef, the only thing we had in the shape of provision, was now becoming extremely poor from the fatiguing marches and want of grass and water. Our sugar was all gone, and although our coffee still held out, we were too near the end of that great luxury to expect that it would last much longer. Independent of this, many of us began to think, in earnest, that bread, if not *the* staff of life, offered at least a very comfortable support. We still had our regular allowance, three pounds of beef a day, but it was greatly inferior in comparison with the same allowance we had in the earlier stages of our journey, and this inferiority began to be felt seriously. Nevertheless, all was joy and gladness in camp at the good news of our near approach to settlements, and it was thought that twenty days, at farthest, would bring us to the rich wheat and corn-fields, as well as the sheepfolds of New Mexico. Far different would have been our feelings had we anticipated the sufferings yet in store for us.

Had we known that four or five hundred miles of dreary travelling were still before us, and that hunger and thirst were to weaken our frames and destroy our spirits; had we been aware that hostile Indians in great numbers were in our paths, and treacherous friends—if it is not a solecism—in our very midst, far different would have been our expectations and our feelings that night, on betaking ourselves to our earth, our blankets, and our sky.

Scarcely had we finished our scanty and homely supper, and quietly nestled ourselves each on the spot he had chosen for his lodging-ground, when a drizzling rain set in, which, before sleep had visited our eyelids, deepened into a heavy shower. Our encampment was in a grove of small timber, within some thirty yards of the river. A flock of hooting, screeching owls had engaged a cotton-wood tree, almost directly over our heads, for the purpose of giving a grand concert, while a pack of sneaking wolves were howling a horrible accompaniment in the edge of the prairie near us. In the very midst of this discord, our oxen, which had been quietly feeding in a neighbouring prairie, took a *stampede*, and came rushing madly towards us. The earth fairly trembled as they bounded along, many of them with their yokes still on, and all impelled by an indescribable panic. I took to a tree at once, or rather clambered up a small sapling hand over hand, to place myself out of harm's way, for I well knew that no human obstacle could check the onward career of a drove of fear-stricken oxen. Fortunately the steep bank of the river on the opposite side, or some other cause, stopped them in their headlong flight. The guard were unable to collect and herd them that night, yet they were all found without much trouble the next morning. What could have given them the "scare" no one could divine. The cattle-guard declared that they suddenly started off in a body, as if impressed by a common fear, and that in the hurry-scurry they had no time except to look to their own personal safety. Some of the old campaigners hinted that the cries of owls and wolves, heard a short time before the stampede, were but imitations of these birds and beasts by Indians in the vicinity, and that some lurking savage had frightened the oxen. Whatever the cause, I knew the effect well enongh; and in my half-asleep, half-awake condition, felt well satisfied that I had not been run over and trodden under foot.

Our start on the ensuing morning was late, several hours having been occupied in drying our blankets and collecting the scattered beeves. We had marched but a short distance before it was evident to all that the stream that we had been following up—the same we had crossed at the Waco village — now bore more to the northward, and that from the appearance of the country before us we should be compelled to recross it. This troublesome labour was effected in the afternoon with no little difficulty, and night found us once more encamped near its banks, with no other than its brackish waters to drink.

By this time both buffalo and Indian "sign" had become extremely scarce, and the little seen appeared to be months old. The general impression among our older hunters, whose opinions we all looked upon as law and gospel, was that the buffalo had all gone north, and the Indians with them; for, although natural enemies, they are seldom seen except in company.

The next day we made but six or seven miles, the country in every direction becoming more and more broken. A-head we saw nothing but chains of steep and rugged mountains; low, but of sufficient height to render our farther advance extremely problematical, at least in the right course. At night we found a small spring of fresh water within a mile of the river, and in the luxury of a cool sweet draught forgot the hardships and privations of the previous twenty-four hours.

Carlos still insisted that he was acquainted with the country, and that he could extricate us, in a day or two, from the labyrinth of difficulties by which we were surrounded. An early start was made the next morning, and near half the day was spent in climbing steep and abrupt hills, so rocky that the feet of the oxen suffered severely, and many of them had to be unyoked and turned loose. I thought I had previously seen a country in a state of nature, but this was the roughest part of "out doors" it had ever been my unfortunate lot to traverse. It appeared to have been just *got out* rough hewn, without a single finishing stroke in any quarter. Rough and mis-shapen hills, formed of rocks and sand, were piled up here and there without system or order, and not a bush or blade of grass could be found upon them to relieve their desolate appearance.

By noon we had partially extricated ourselves from the mate of hills on which our feet had been stumbling during that morning's march. Seeing what appeared to be a level and grassy prairie, a mile or a mile and a half to the left of our line of march, which seemed as though it might afford pasturage for a stray deer or antelope, myself and "Old Paint" rode off in that direction. As the old hunter expected, we quickly saw a drove of some fifteen deer; but they happened to see us first, and set off on a run. My companion was well enough versed in their "ways" not to think of following them; for after having once seen an enemy, the deer seldom allows him to come within gunshot.*

My experience, in comparison with that of the veteran borderer, was limited, and I was simple enough not to resist the temptation of following the herd over a roll of the prairie, in the vain hope of obtaining a shot. They halted, as I supposed they would, but were on the look-out, and before I was within three hundred yards again bounded off across the prairie. Hope induced me to give one more trial, which terminated like the first. I now reluctantly gave up the chase and cast my eyes about for my fellow-hunter, but he was nowhere in sight. I tried hurriedly to ascertain the direction in which I had left him; but the result of my reflections convinced me that I was, to use a common expression, thoroughly "turned round"—lost. I put spurs to my horse and galloped to the highest roll of the prairie, with the hope of obtaining a sight of my companion or companions, but without success.

A sickening feeling of loneliness came over me on *finding* myself in that worst of all situations upon a prairie—*lost!* The sun was still high in the heavens, and I could not tell which was north or which south. I had my rifle and pistols with me, was well mounted, and had a sufficiency of ammunition, but I was not well enough acquainted with a prairie life to steer a course, even if I had known what course to start upon, neither was I hunter enough to feel confident that I could kill a sufficiency of meat in case I should be unsuccessful in

* It appears to be a point of honour with an old hunter never to follow a deer after the animal has once discovered him.

finding my companions. Another thing, I had already found out what every hunter knows, that the more hungry a man grows upon the prairies the more unlikely he is to find game, and the more difficult it is to shoot it. There, then, I was, without a companion and without experience—starvation staring me in the face, or even if I was fortunate in obtaining meat, I still was almost certain to be killed and scalped by the Indians, or end my days in vain efforts to reach the settlements. I thought of home, and made up my mind firmly that if ever I was fortunate enough to reach it, I should be in no particular hurry to leave it again.

I dashed off to what appeared a still higher prairie swell than the one I now stood upon—nothing could I see except a solitary wolf, trotting stealthily along in the hollow below me: I even envied this most contemptible of the brute creation, for he knew where he was. I strained my eyes as though to penetrate beyond the limits of human vision; but all was a waste, a blank. I leaped from my horse and sat upon the ground for a moment; it was only for a moment, for in my uneasiness I could not remain motionless. I tried to reflect, to reason; but so fast did thoughts of starvation and of Indian perils crowd on my mind, that I could come to no definite conclusion as to my present position with reference to that of my companions. I tried to follow my own trail back to the point where I had so foolishly left "Old Paint," but the ground was so hard that my horse's hoofs had made little or no indentation, and I was too impatient to examine the face of the prairie with that searching scrutiny which might have resulted in success.

Yet I resolved to make one desperate effort, at least, to find the command. I knew enough of my situation to feel convinced that by circling about, from prairie roll to prairie roll, I might gallop my horse for hours, and at last find myself at the point I started from, "with confusion worse confounded"—travelling in a straight line alone might save me. Here was another difficulty; for the course I might adopt, even were I successful in keeping it, might leave me at a still greater distance from my friends. How I wished for the presence of Tom Hancock—the presence even of the greatest dullard in the command would have assisted in removing the mountain of torturing uncertainty that pressed upon my mind. Man never knows the full weight of *hopelessness* until he is made to bear it alone, with no human intelligence near from whose resources he can hope to draw something for his relief when he is too consciously aware that his own are exhausted. Even sympathy imparts something of hope. I felt that even my horse was some company to me: I patted him kindly on the neck and told him so, aloud.

"But," the reader will perchance inquire, "why did you not give your horse the reins and trust to his natural instinct for regaining his and your companions?" And again, "Why did you not wait until the sun was low in the western heavens, then reflect, for one moment, in what direction the command was travelling and the side on which you had left it? You knew that the sun would set in the west, and that as you faced it, north was to the right and south to the left—surely you could then steer a course, even if you could not while the sun was vertical."

Gentle reader, you have never been lost on a wide ocean of prairies, unskilled in border life, and little gifted with the power of first adopting a course to follow and then not deviating from it. You must recollect that there, as on the wide ocean, you find no trees, no friendly land-marks, to guide you—all is a wide waste of eternal sameness. *To be lost,* as I and others have experienced, has a complex and fearful meaning. It is not merely to stray from your friends, your path, but from yourself. With your way you lose your presence of mind. You attempt to reason, but the rudder and compass of your reflective faculties are gone. Self-confidence, too, is lost—in a word all is lost, except a maniacal impulse to despair, that is peculiar and indescribable.

In my case, fate, fortune, good luck, call it by what name you may—stepped into my assistance. While upon one of the highest rolls of the prairie I resolved to proceed in a certain direction, and, if possible to keep it without variation. Whether I did so or not I am unable to say—I only know that after travelling at a rapid pace, it may be some five miles, I suddenly found myself upon the brow of a high and steep declivity, overlooking a narrow but beautiful valley, through which a small creek was winding. I had examined the prairies in every direction, during my short ride, until my eyes ached from overstraining, yet had not for a moment allowed my horse to slacken his pace. I now paused to examine the valley before me. The reader may judge my feelings when, after an hasty glance I discovered the white tops of the waggons, far off in the distance to the right, slowly winding their way down a gentle slope into the valley. Never was the sight of friendly sail more welcome to the eye of a shipwrecked mariner than was the appearance of these waggons to me, and I fairly laughed aloud at my good fortune.

Immediately in front of the spot where I had made this truly fortunate discovery the declivity was steep, amounting almost to a precipice, with craggy rocks jutting out in every direction. A few steps beyond, the descent, although rough, appeared less steep, and in such haste was I once more to reach the command that I put spurs to my horse and dashed headlong down. Scarcely had I proceeded twenty steps ere my horse snorted and jumped furiously aside, frightened by a rattlesnake lying almost directly in the path. Blind at the time, in all probability, it being in August, the snake did not give the well-known and frightful alarm until the feet of my horse were close upon him. Numbers of these poisonous reptiles, coiled among the rocks immediately around, soon joined in the alarm, and at the same time emitted an odour which was disagreeable in the extreme.* If I had been frightened while lost upon the prairies, it was now my horse's turn to share a panic with me. With quick yet tremulous leaps he dashed down the craggy steep, and I was unable to restrain or check him until he had reached the smooth grassy bottom in safety. How many snakes there were in this immediate neighbourhood is more than I can tell—I did not stop to count or calculate; but if the lot had been purchased at five hundred, I honestly think the buyer never

* Every animal, with the single exception of the hog, has an instinctive fear of the rattlesnake, can scent them easily, and will fly at their approach with terror. The hog cares nothing for the reptiles, but on the contrary has been known to attack, kill, and devour them with avidity and impunity.

would have had reason to find fault with the reckoning. On looking back, I discovered a large hole or cave among the rocks, and near the path I had taken, which I had not seen before. This was probably the den or dwelling-place of the reptiles, and at the time when I passed along they were all out airing themselves in the sun. Half an hour's brisk trot brought me up with the command, which I found my companion had already rejoined. He did not know even that I had been lost until I informed him of my adventure. I said little about it, but inly resolved never to be caught out of sight of the command again.

Two or three rattlesnakes had been killed that night within our lines, stragglers, probably, from the den I had passed, and belated, or else too blind to find their way back. After falling asleep at night my dreams partook of anything but the agreeable. At one time I thought myself, like Mazeppa, beset on every side by ravenous wolves, grinning and snapping at me at every step. Next, I was suffering horribly from both hunger and thirst—my powder had all become spoiled by rain, and the clouds gave down no other than bitter water. Soon I was chased by a gang of bloodthirsty Indians, and to increase my fright my faithful horse suddenly lost half his speed. Anon, the prairie was covered in every direction with rattlesnakes, and at the next moment it was on fire, myself standing on a small unburned knoll, the flames rapidly approaching me in every direction. From these dreams I would awake with a start, the horrors of the night even exceeding those of the day which had preceeded it. Right glad was I when morning at length came to dissipate the annoying dreams.

After proceeding a short distance on your journey that morning, we encountered even a worse road than any over which we had travelled, if my memory serves me. We boxed the compass for several hours, going some ten or twelve miles to gain three on our course, but were finally fortunate enough to reach a high piece of table-land where the *mesquit** grass was fresh, and far better than any we had previously found. To this spot Carlos said the Mexicans frequently brought their sheep, on account of the superiority of the pasturage, and he also pointed in the direction of a large spring and creek of fresh water, which he said emptied into Red River a few miles to the north. Although no sign could be seen indicating water in the direction he assigned, his assertion proved correct; for after a travel of five or six miles a spring was found in the precise situation which he had described. More singular than this, he had frequently informed the men where plum-patches

* Whether this is a Mexican or Indian name for a particular kind of grass, found in great abundance on the great prairies of the West, I am unable to say. Cattle and horses are extremely fond of it, and it is very nourishing. There is a small, brambly bush of the same name, and also a tree about the size of a cherry or peach tree. The latter bears a pod containing beans, which are greedily devoured by horses and cattle, and are said to fatten them as well as grain. The Camanches make a species of meal from the beans, very palatable and nutritious, and the Mexicans also use them in making beer as well as sugar. When our provisions and coffee fell short, the men ate them raw in immense quantities, and also either roasted or boiled them. The wood makes the best of charcoal, throws out a great heat, and lasts a long time. The tree, as well as the small bush, has a long sharp thorn. I have spelled the word *mesquit*, believing that to be the Spanish mode—it is pronounced *meskeet*. West of San Antonio there are immense groves of mesquit-trees, and the grass is also found there in several varieties.

were to be found in the vicinity of our journey, and he was almost invariably correct. With all these corroborating circumstances, it cannot be wondered at that we all thought we were within a few days' march of the frontier Mexican settlements.

On encamping at night, fully convinced as the commissioners were of the truth of the statements made by Carlos, who said that San Miguel was not more than seventy-five or eighty miles distant, they determined upon sending Messrs. Howland, Baker, and Rosenberry forward to procure sugar, coffee, and breadstuffs, and consult with the inhabitants, more particularly with some of the principal men, as to the reception the expedition would probably meet. Howland had lived several years in Santa Fé and the vicinity, spoke Spanish fluently, and was well acquainted with all the leading inhabitants. He was a man of great intelligence, brave, and at the same time cautious. The party took with them but three days' provisions, and as large numbers of hostile Indians were known to infest the borders of New Mexico, they were to travel only by night, lying concealed during the day.

Had it not been for this circumstance alone, I should most certainly have accompanied this party; but I had a pack-mule with no inconsiderable wardrobe to take along, and to travel through an Indian country with such an encumbrance was deemed not only unsafe, but impracticable. So anxious was I to hasten my journey, that I was almost tempted to leave my mule, and take such articles only as I could carry on my horse; but my friends so strongly advised me to continue with the command that I relinquished the idea of accompanying them much against my wishes. After circumstances proved, almost beyond a doubt, that the fact of my being compelled to remain with the command saved my life.* I was particularly anxious to hasten forward on more than one account. In the first place, the season was becoming far advanced, and I was in no little anxiety to prosecute my journey through the interior of Mexico, so as to reach the United States by the early part of winter; in the next place, I had passed about time enough, I will not say *lived,* on weak coffee without sugar, and a rather short allowance of beef, anything but good; and I was extremely solicitous to change my diet. To sum up all, "*I had seen the elephant.*"

The whole of August 11th we remained in camp, partly to repair some of the waggons, but principally to rest the oxen, many of their feet having been worn to the quick by the rough and stony roads. In the evening, Howland and his unfortunate friends left for the settlements, and were never seen again save by four of us. On the ensuing morning we made an early start, under the guidance of Carlos, who now was stationed with the advance-guard, as the spy company had been broken up. The day was extremely hot and sultry; yet our guide found a smooth and level prairie, and we were enabled to make some twelve miles in a north-west course before the middle of the afternoon. The advance-guard had by this time arrived at the brow of a small hill, overlooking a cool and shady dell, when a fine buffalo

* Afterward I saw Howland and Baker shot, like dogs, in the *plaza* at San Miguel. Rosenberry was also killed, although I was not present at his death. My fate would, in all human probability, have been the same had I accompanied them.

cow was seen lying under a large mesquit-tree, and apparently fast asleep.

One of our party immediately dismounted with the intention of creeping up within gunshot of the animal, while two of us disencumbered our horses of saddle-bags and all superfluous articles, handed our rifles to some of the men, with a request that they would take charge of them, and then closely examined our pistols to see that they were in order. My comrade's name was Torry, and we felt determined on giving the buffalo a hard chase should the first hunter not succeed in killing her.

He was successful in creeping within sixty yards of the unconscious animal, but unfortunately his rifle hung fire, throwing the ball wide of the mark. The buffalo rose at the report, and turned her head until her eye caught a glance of us, when she immediately set off in a westerly direction and at a lumbering gallop. Myself and companion were instantly in pursuit at a brisk canter, not intending to push our horses to the utmost until we were close upon our prey. After climbing the acclivity, on the opposite side from where the buffalo was first seen lying, we had a level plain before us, miles in extent, and presenting no other obstacles to a fair race than an occasional patch of small and tangled mesquit bushes. As we were some little distance from the hunter when he fired, the buffalo had a good half mile the start of us; yet before we had been two miles in chase, we were within fifty yards of her. With full confidence that we should soon be alongside, we now spurred our horses to their utmost speed. At almost every stride a deer would start in affright from his covert under the larger mesquit-trees,* and with a few jumps place himself out of harm's way. Never have I seen the deer so plentiful as they were during that exciting chase, and so close did we come to them before they started, that we could easily have shot them with our pistols.

We were almost up to the buffalo as we neared a large patch of the smaller mesquits, and had already cocked our pistols, when the affrighted animal dashed directly into the thickest part of the matted thicket. Many of the bushes were dry, yet breaking and crashing through, she rushed madly on, utterly regardless of the long and sharp thorns with which they were covered. Not so with our horses; their chests and shoulders were not shielded by the long shaggy hair found upon the buffalo, and as the thorns entered the flesh, they shied, bolted, and ran so unkindly that we could hardly spur them through. This gave the cow every advantage, and enabled her to gain some fifty yards while going twice that distance; but on emerging from the thicket the race was our own again. Once more we were nearly up with the flank of the huge and unwieldy animal, and about to discharge our pistols, when another tangled thicket intervened to cut us off. A third and a fourth time we were nearly up with our prey, and considered her in our very hands; but just in the very nick of time another tangled patch would present itself as a shelter and protection to the hunted beast. In this way the

* It should be understood that the larger class of these trees, and the only one which afford a shade on the prairies, never grow close together, but are generally found fifteen or twenty feet apart. At a short distance, a grove of them resembles a peach orchard.

race continued some five or six miles, and until our nags gave manifest symptoms of distress. Had the prairie been smooth and clear of thickets, we should have at least discharged every pistol we had, and in all probability brought our noble game to the ground; as it was, with jaded animals and every prospect of farther obstacles a-head, we reined in and gave up the chase—reluctantly enough on my part.

We immediately dismounted from our horses to give them an opportunity of recovering their wind and resting, and in the mean time watched the still retreating animal we had vainly endeavoured to kill. She never appeared to check her heavy, lumbering gallop, until lost to view on the distant prairie. The ridge upon which the chase had taken place ran nearly east and west, on the side along which the buffalo led us there appearing to be a slight gradual slope towards the south. In that direction, and running parallel with the ridge, we could see the dim outline of what appeared to be a heavy belt of timber—the bottoms, as we then thought, of a large river. Having noted well the points from which this timber could be seen, we once more mounted our horses, and slowly retraced our steps. The deer, which, as we sped along after the buffalo, had jumped almost from under the very feet of our horses, were now nowhere to be seen—gone with our hopes of a meal of the fat cow, and affording another specimen of the luck of hungry hunters.

We found the command encamped near the spot where we had first seen the buffalo, although there was barely water enough for the men, and our animals stood in the utmost need. We mentioned the circumstance of our having seen a long line of timber to the southward, with every appearance of a large stream in that direction; but Carlos said that such could not be the case, and he spoke with a confidence that gained belief even over the testimony of our senses. He admitted, however, that there might be a creek or small stream, but thought it could not run in a parallel course with the river north of us, the bottoms of which we could see on every day's march. Here, for a time, the matter of a southern watercourse rested.

With the result of our buffalo hunt I was far from satisfied. I had fully made up my mind to have a meal of wild meat that night; and now that visions of the cow, with her delicious marrow-mones had faded, my mind was led to investigate the chances of obtaining at least a fat buck for our mess. We had seen enough during our hard chase to convince us that they were not only exceedingly numerous, but very tame. The main body of those we had frightened from their noonday rest, as we galloped along, had gone in the direction of a beautiful valley scarcely a mile from our camp. Confident that I could find some of these feeding in this valley, I shouldered my rifle and hobbled off, as well as my lame ankle would allow me, in that direction.

The sun was just setting as I crossed a little roll which overlooked this retreat. So far from being disappointed in my expectations of finding deer in the quiet dell, I was agreeably surprised on seeing a large drove of them feeding upon the short, sweet grass. They saw me, too, for they lifted their heads on high, gave the well-known whistle, and stared with their mild, large eyes directly towards the spot where I was standing; but instead of leaping hurriedly away, as is their wont when worried and hunted by either whites or Indians, they soon bent their heads to the ground again, and unconcernedly resumed their evening meal.

I could have shot the nearest, from the spot where I first discovered them, and without, to borrow one of the comedian Hackett's expressions, running any great risk of straining my rifle; but they were so exceedingly tame that I thought I would creep directly into their very midst, where I could have my choice of the largest and fattest buck. It seemed hardly necessary, so little did the naturally timid animals regard my approach, to seek the cover afforded by some scattering mesquit-trees; yet I made use of them, and in five minutes was in a position where I could make my selection from among at least fifty, and the farthest was not seventy yards from me. I soon selected a victim, a noble buck, whose plumpness and lightish blue colour betokened an exceeding degree of fatness. Sitting upon the ground, I raised my rifle across my knee as a half rest, took a sight which I thought close and deliberate, and "blazed away." The light blue smoke curled slowly upward in fleecy wreaths upon the still evening air, and as it partially dispersed I saw my deer staring me full in the face, somewhat astonished, perhaps, but far from frightened at the report of my rifle. He hoisted his tail, made five or six bounds, and then stopped to give another inquiring look in the direction where I was sitting. Supposing, of course, that I had given him a mortal wound, I quietly began to reload my rifle with the intention of sacrificing another buck, for not one of the gang had moved ten steps; but what was my astonishment, after having driven well home a bullet and put on a percussion cap, to see the buck I had shot at absolutely nipping the grass with as good a relish as any of the herd. I *knew* that I had hit him—I could not, by any possibility, miss him at so short a distance ; but there he stood, a living witness that if I had hit I had at least not hurt him much.

I could easily, from the spot where I was sitting, have selected a victim for my second shot much nearer than was my first love by this time ; but having certain misgivings that he *might* not have received a mortal wound, I determined upon paying my respects to him a second time—it was my duty to "put him out of his misery" as quickly as possible. With these intentions I again rested my rifle across my knee, again pulled the trigger, again the rifle went off with a good, sharp, and, as I thought killing, crack, and again the deer went off, too, some half a dozen jumps across the prairie. If I thought I had given a mortal wound the first time, I was *sure* of it now—it could not be otherwise—there was no such thing as missing a vital part twice at a distance which was absolutely short enough for putting out a squirrel's eye without spoiling his skin.

But to be ready for another, I again commenced re-loading. Once or twice, while handling the powder and lead, I cast a glance at the buck to which I had already dedicated two shots, every moment expecting to see him totter—to see his legs give way—yet there he stood, as firm on his pins as ever, and what was stranger than all, again commenced a supper from which he had been twice interrupted. Still there was no necessity of wasting more lead upon him—he could not get away—and I therefore commenced a survey of the herd for the next biggist. There was no difficulty in making a choice, for by the time my rifle was ready for a third discharge another large buck had fed along until he was within forty steps of me. I waited until he presented a fair broadside, and then fired. The result was precisely the same as on the first two discharges—the buck I had last shot at jumped off as did the first; his bounds may have been a trifle longer, and there may have been a few more of them. That he was a dead or dying deer there was no question.

Once more I commenced loading my rifle. Some of the deer, in my more immediate vicinity, had, after the three shots, placed a few yards more of ground between us; but others had taken their places, and I was still within half rifle-shot of at least twenty of them. By the time I had reloaded, and was ready to renew the destruction I had commenced, the dark shades of evening had fallen upon the more distant prairie swells, yet it was still light enough for me to see distinctly every object in my neighbourhood. Deeply did I regret the lateness of the hour, as with a little more light I was sanguine in the belief that I could strew the prairie with trophies of my skill as a hunter. Often, while in the settlements, had I remained patiently at a stand, hour after hour, watching for a pack of hounds to drive some affrighted deer within gunshot, and had even considered myself in some way rewarded if, during a long day's hunt, I had a glimpse of a buck dashing madly through the bushes at a distance of three or four hundred yards, and had heard the exciting bay of the hounds while in hot pursuit. If, by any chance—and such accidents had happened two or three times in my life—I was fortunate enough to bring down a deer, the exploit would furnish me with food for thought and speech for a twelvemonth—now, look in what direction I would, the animals were staring me in the face within a stone's throw, and seemed coaxingly to ask me to shoot at them: surely, never before were deer seen so tame.

Anxious to make the most of my time before it was yet too dark, I drew up my rifle a fourth time and discharged it at still another buck. He followed in the footsteps of his shot-at predecessors, evincing astonishment or alarm no otherwise than by bounding off a few jumps, and then stopping to gaze at me. Of the two I was probably the most astonished—astonished that he did not fall instantly to the ground.

What was the matter? It might be that may rifle, "sighted" for a distance of one hundred and twenty-five yards, carried too high at forty or fifty. But then, if I did not shoot them directly through the heart, the ball could not have passed far above it—the animals must be badly if not mortally wounded.

After having poured a charge of powder into my rifle, I found that I had but a single ball left—for not anticipating such luck I had started with only five. The confidence I at first felt, that the deer I had shot at must soon fall, was now sensibly diminishing, although lingering hopes were still harboured in my mind that the more tender portions of some one of them, at least, would furnish the raw material for my supper. I had finished loading, and on looking over the little valley I noticed that the deer, with the daylight, had become scarce. There was one buck, however, close by me—

not sixty yards distant. Determined to make sure of this one, if the others were really unhurt, I crept up until I verily believe he was not thirty steps from me. The motion of placing my rifle across my knee, for I made each shot sitting upon the ground, attracted the animal's attention so much that he absolutely advanced several steps towards me. He fairly seemed bent upon his own destruction — to meet me half way in my desire to make my last shot certain.

The dimness of night by this time rendered it impossible to "draw a fine bead," in hunter's parlance; but then at a distance at which I could have killed him with a brickbat, what was the necessity of being too particular about my aim? I fired.

The buck did not bound off as the others had done, but, on the contrary, advanced towards me with looks of inquiry. I knew that the severest and most motal wounds are frequently unattended with pain or a sense of injury—I must have given the buck one of this description. I jumped from the ground and hobbled towards him as fast as my lameness would permit. He turned and scampered off after his comrades. By a fair mathematical calculation the animal went at least twenty yards while I went one; yet I continued the pursuit with the hope that his race would soon be run. Until his broad white tail was lost in the dim twilight of evening did I press forward, and only gave up the chase when I could see nothing to pursue.

Thus ends a long but veritable account of an adventure with a herd of deer on the Western prairies. To account for their exceeding tameness and approachability, I can offer no other solution than that they had never before met either the white or red man. The narrow space of country which afforded them food was bounded by sterile wastes, and their natural enemies, the red men, had never visited their peaceful dell.

I slowly picked my way back to camp, out of humour and out of conceit with myself, my rifle, my powder, and more especially my bullets. On reaching my comrades, I ascertained that Tom Hancock had shot three noble bucks, and had gone out some time after me. Nothing, he said, save the want of light, had prevented him from killing twenty. I was asked if I had seen any deer. I merely remarked that I had seen several, and here the conversation dropped. I was not disposed to be communicative.

And what, the reader will probably ask, was the reason of my want of success? In all frankness, and with a desire to answer his question fairly, and to the best of my knowledge, belief, and ability, I will here state that there is a very common disease prevalent among young and inexperienced hunters in Texas, which is known as the "*buck ague*." It manifests itself whenever the subject is suddenly brought in close proximity with game of the larger class, and more difficult to kill, and its effects are to give a hurriedness of action, a tremulousness of the nerves, and an unwonted excitableness to the feelings generally. It strikes me forcibly, and I have little doubt the reader's impressions are closely akin to mine, that I underwent a severe attack of the "buck ague" while on the little hunting excursion of which I have just given a description—in plain English, that I was too nervous even to hit a barn door at twenty steps.

CHAPTER IX.

Brackish Water.—Los Cuervos, or The Crows.—Carlos and his speculations.—Stream on our left visited.—Opinion of "Old Paint."—Startling Surmises.—No Water.—Endurance of the Mule.—Singular Valley.—Water seen in the distance—Perilous Descent of a Bluff.—Arrival at the River.—More Brackish Water.—An Alarm.—Fire in Camp.—Terrific Spread of the Flames.—Explosion of Cartridges.—Night Ascent of the Bluffs.—Ravages of the Fire.—Extent of our Loss.—Magnificent Night Scene.—Our Camp by Daylight.—Coffee too much Burned.—Compelled to fall back upon First Principles.—Again on the March.—Intolerable Suffering from Thirst.—A Beautiful Camp.—Disappearance of Carlos and Brignoli.—Horrors of our Situation.—Lost, and without a Guide upon the Prairies.—Shower on the Espy Principle.—Party sent out to Explore.—Rough Travelling.—Gloomy Prospects.—Return to Camp.—Ten Miles for a Draught of Water.—"Doing" our Washing.—Company of Spies sent out.—Death of Doctor Brashear.—Bitter Water.—Rations reduced.—Sufferings now commencing.—Return of one of the Spies.—Again on the March.—Visit to a Commonwealth of Prairie Dogs.—Description of these singular Animals.

The 13th of August was an eventful day with us—one which few of the party can ever forget. The night previous we encamped without water for our cattle or horses, and the little we obtained for our own use was of the worst quality, and swallowed only to ally the intolerable thirst brought on by a long day's march under the hot sun. The hard buffalo chase had jaded my horse severely, and at such a time I well knew he needed water more than ever; but not a drop could I procure for him.

We had proceeded but a short distance, on the morning of the 13th, before the blue tops of several mountains were seen, far in the distance to the west. Carlos was the first to discover them, and remarked that they were *Los Cuervos*, or *The Crows*, three high mountains in the chain through which the supposed Red River has cut its way. The place where the stream winds its course through the mountains is called the *Angosturas*, or Narrows, and the Crows stand out in bold relief to guide the distant traveller to that point.

Our route, at the present time, was along a high prairie which appeared to be a dividing ridge between two large streams. During the morning, Captain Caldwell visited the stream which my companion and I had discovered the day previous, while chasing the buffalo. On returning, about noon, he said that the stream was a large one, and that he believed it to be the Brazos! This river was supposed by all to be a long distance to the south. Captain C. also, for the first time, declared his conviction that the stream we had been following up from the Waco village was the *Wichita*, and that the Red River was some seventy-five or a hundred miles to the north. All were startled at this report; but still, so strong was the reliance placed in the assertions of Carlos, few could be induced to give it credit.

We continued our journey until the middle of the afternoon, altering our course somewhat to the north to avoid the bad travelling we found more immediately on our route. Small parties of men were out in every direction in search of water, but they met with no success. By this time the want of the reviving element was plainly seen in our horses; their wild and glaring eyes, with their broken nervous, and unsteady action, showing the intensity of their suffering. The mules, too, suffered much from the want of water, but nothing in comparison with the horses and oxen. The endurance of the mule is never so well tested as on a journey where both water and grass are scarce.

I have said that we continued our journey until the middle of the afternoon. About that time, and without seeing any sign a-head that could lead us to expect there was so great a change in the face of the country, we suddenly reached the brow of a precipitous bluff, some two or three hundred feet in height, which overlooked a large valley of broken and rugged appearance. This valley was four or five miles in width, a ridge of rough hills bounding it on the northern side, and not only the descent to the valley from the bluff on which we stood, but the whole surface below, was covered by dry cedars, apparently killed the previous year by fire. The spot upon which we stood was a level plain, covered with rank and coarse grass several feet in height. This grass, no rain having fallen for weeks, had become as dry as tinder. While consulting as to what course we should pursue, some one of our party discovered water at a distance of three or four miles across the valley below, a turn in the river bringing it to view. We immediately determined, if possible, to effect the descent of the steep and ragged bluff before us, and at least give our suffering animals a chance to quench their thirst, even if the water should prove too brackish for our own use.

Some thirty-five or forty of the advance-guard instantly determined upon undertaking the toilsome and dangerous descent, and, to give my horse the earliest turn at the water, I accompanied this party. After winding and picking our way for a full hour, pitching down precipices that were nearly perpendicular, and narrowly escaping frightful chasms and fissures of the rocks, we were all enabled to reach the valley with whole bones; but to do this we were frequently obliged to dismount from our horses, and in some places fairly to push them over abrupt descents which they never would have attempted without force. I have said that this bluff was some two or three hundred feet in height—we travelled at least a mile to gain this short distance, so devious and difficult was our path. The side of the bluff was formed of rough, sharp-pointed rocks, many of them of large size, and every little spot of earth had, in former years, given nourishment and support to some scraggy cedar, now left leafless and desolate by fire. Shoots of young cedars, however, where springing up wherever they could find root-hold; but they were not destined to attain the rank and standing of their sires.

After reaching the valley, we soon found the sandy bed of what had been a running stream in the rainy season. Immediately on striking it, our tired nags raised their heads, pricked up their ears, and set off at a brisk trot, instinctively knowing that water was in the vicinity. The horse scents water at an incredible distance, and frequently travellers upon the prairies are enabled to find it by simply turning their horses or mules loose.

A tiresome ride of three or four miles now brought us to the river. On reaching its banks, nothing could restrain our nags from dashing headlong down. Equally thirsty ourselves, we had fondly hoped that the waters might prove fresh and sweet; but they were even more brackish than any we had yet tasted. Repulsive as it was, however, we swallowed enough to moisten our parched lips and throats, and ten minutes after were even more thirsty than before. Our horses, more fond of this water than any other, drank until apparently they could swallow no more.

While some of our party were digging into the sand at the edge of the stream, with the hope of finding water more fresh, and others were enjoying the cooling luxury of a bath, a loud report, as of a cannon, was heard in the direction of the camp, and a dark smoke was seen suddenly to arise.

"An Indian attack!" was the startling cry on all sides, and instantly we commenced huddling on our clothes and bridling our horses. One by one, as fast as we could get ready, we set off for what we supposed to be a scene of conflict. As we neared the camping-ground it became plainly evident that the prairie was on fire in all directions. When within a mile of the steep bluff, which cut off the prairie above from the valley, the bright flames were seen flashing among the dry cedars, and a dense volume of black smoke, rising above all, gave a painful sublimity to the scene.

On approaching nearer we were met by some of our companions, who were hurriedly seeking a passage up the steep. They had heard, from those on the prairie above, that the high grass had caught fire by accident, and that with such velocity had it spread that several of the waggons, and among them that of the commissioners, had been consumed. This waggon contained, in addition to a large number of cartridges, all the trunks and valuables of the mess to which I was attached, making me doubly anxious to gain the scene of destruction and learn the worst. It afterward proved that the explosion of the cartridges in the waggon was what we had mistaken for the report of our six-pounder.

With redoubled exertions we now pushed forward towards the camp, but before we could reach the base of the high and rugged bluff the flames were dashing down its sides with frightful rapidity, leaping and flashing across the gullies and around the hideous cliffs, and roaring in the deep, yawning chasms with the wild and appalling noise of a tornado. As the flames would strike the dry tops of the cedars, reports, resembling those of the musket, would be heard; and in such quick succession did these reports follow each other, that I can compare them to nothing save the irregular discharge of infantry—a strange accompaniment to the wild roar of the devouring element.

The wind was blowing fresh from the west when the prairie was first ignited, carrying the flames, with a speed absolutely astounding, over the very ground on which we had travelled during the day. The wind lulled as the sun went down behind the mountains in the west, and now the fire began to spread slowly in that direction. The difficult passage by which we had descended was cut off by the fire, and night found our party still in the valley, unable to discover any other road to the table-land above. Our situation was a dangerous one, too; for had the wind sprung up and veered into the east, we should have found much difficulty in escaping, with such velocity did the flames extend.

If the scene had been grand previous to the going down of the sun, its magnificence was increased tenfold as night in vain attempted to throw its dark mantle over the earth. The light from acres and acres, I might say miles and miles, of inflammable and blazing cedars, illuminated earth and sky with a radiance even more lustrous and dazzling than that of the noonday sun. Ever and anon, as some one of our comrades would approach the brow of the high bluff above us, he appeared not like an inhabitant of this earth. A lurid and most unnatural glow, reflected upon his countenance from the valley of burning cedars, seemed to render still more haggard and toilsome his burned and blackened features.

I was fortunate enough, about nine o'clock, to meet one of our men, who directed me to a passage up the steep ascent. He had just left the bluff above, and gave me a piteous recital of our situation. He was endeavouring to find water, after several hours of unceasing toil, and I left him with slight hopes that his search would be rewarded. By this time I was alone, not one of the companions who had started with me from the river being in sight or hearing. One by one they had dropped off, each searching for some path by which he might climb to the table-land above.

The first person I met, after reaching the prairie, was Mr. Falconer, standing with the blackened remnant of a blanket in his hand, and watching lest the fire should break out on the western side of the camp; for in that direction the exertions of the men, aided by a strong westerly wind, had prevented the devouring element from spreading. Mr. F. directed me to the spot where our mess was quartered. I found them sitting upon such articles as had been saved from the waggon, their gloomy countenances rendered more desponding by the reflection from the now distant fire. I was too much worn down by fatigue and deep anxiety to make many inquiries as to the extent of our loss; but hungry, and almost choked with thirst, I threw myself upon the blackened ground and sought forgetfulness in sleep. It was hours, however, before sleep visited my eyelids. From the spot on which I was lying, a broad sheet of flame could still be seen, miles and miles in width, the heavens in that direction so brilliantly lit up that they resembled a sea of molten gold. In the west, a wall of impenetrable blackness appeared to be thrown up as the spectator suddenly turned from viewing the conflagration in the opposite direction. The subdued yet deep roar of the element could still be plainly heard as it sped on as with the wings of lightning across the prairies, while in the valleys far below, the flames were flashing and leaping among the dry cedars, and shooting and circling about in manner closely resembling a magnificent pyrotechnic display—the general combination forming a scene of grandeur and sublimity which the pen shrinks from describing, and to which the power of words is wholly unequal.

Daylight the next morning disclosed a melancholy scene of desolation and destruction. North, south, and east, as far as the eye could reach, the rough and broken country was blackened by the fire, and the removal of the earth's shaggy covering of cedars and tall grass, but laid bare, in painful distinctness, the awful chasms and rents in the steep hillside before us, as well as the valley spreading far and wide below. Afar off, in the distance, a dense black smoke was seen rising, denoting that the course of the devastating element was still onward. Two of our waggons only had been entirely consumed, but nearly all had suffered. A part of the baggage in the commissioners' waggon had been saved by the extraordinary exertions of some of the men, and just as they had relinquished the work the explosion of cartridges, which had first alarmed the party in the valley, scattered the burning fragments of the waggon in every direction. My friend Falconer was so disfigured that I hardly knew him. His hair and eyebrows were scorched completely off, his face was in a perfect blister, his clothes burned from his back, and, without a hat, he seemed as though some insurance office had met with a heavy loss. Object of pity, however, as he appeared to be, I still could not help smiling at the sad and wo-be-gone figure he presented. Among the few trunks saved I fortunately found mine, containing nearly all my money, clothing, watch, and other valuables. The loss of a carpet bag, which contained my boots and the rough articles I wore upon the road, was all I had to regret in the way of private property. Not so with the mess to which I was attached. The remnant of coffee we still had left was *burned* entirely too much; our pots pans, and kettles, knives and forks, were converted into old iron—everything was gone. We had nothing to eat, however, except half rations of miserably poor beef, and the necessity of falling back upon first principles, or, in other words, eating with our fingers, annoyed us but little.

The waggon of the commissioners contained, besides our private baggage, a quantity of jewelry, blankets, cartridges, rifles, muskets, &c. These were all destroyed. The other waggon which was consumed was loaded with goods, and from this nothing was saved. At one time the ammunition waggon, containing a large quantity of powder, was on fire, and only saved by the daring exertions of some of our men. It may appear singular to some of my readers that so much damage could be caused by the burning of grass alone, for on the spot where the waggons were drawn up there was nothing else; but it should be remembered that this grass was very high, had been killed by dry weather, and flashed up and spread almost with the rapidity of a train of powder on being ignited. It is very easy, when a fire upon the prairies is seen coming towards a party, to escape its dangers by kindling the grass immediately about and taking possession of the newly-burned ground before the distant flames come up: but in this instance the fire commenced on the windward side, and with a frightful rapidity flashed directly along our line of waggons. The only wonder at the time was, how anything had been saved from the furious elements that roared and crackled around.

We packed up and arranged our baggage as well as we could, hunted up and drove in our cattle, and late in the forenoon made a start. Our course was nearly west, and along the level prairie that overlooked the large valley upon our right. The mountains that we had seen the day previous gradually opened to the view, and as they became more visible, did not so well answer the description Carlos had given of *The Crows.* But few, however, felt disposed to doubt the man's words. We are slow in giving credence to any story, however plausible, that runs counter to our desires and hopes.

Our road was a good one this day, and we journeyed on with unusual rapidity. The men suffered incredibly from thirst, and were constantly seen eating the pods from the mesquit-trees, drawing the little moisture they possessed to relieve their parched tongues and throats. A bullet has considerable virtue in relieving thirst, and a piece of raw hide imparts much moisture to the mouth, as I have proved by sad experience.

At night we encamped in a beautiful dell, covered with the larger mesquit-trees and excellent grass. This encampment appeared to be near the termination of the valley of cedars, and the face of the country onwards was now entirely changed, being broken and mountainous. The only water we could find in the vicinity of this camp, which would otherwise have been one of the finest on our route, was entirely too brackish for use. The cattle and horses were fond of it; the men, however, could not swallow it without great nausea, and it did not in the least quench their thirst. That evening Carlos left camp, in company with an Italian, named Brignoli, as they said, in search of water and the best route for our waggons on the ensuing day. Late at night they returned, Brignoli showing some specimens of quicksilver he had found, which were said to be very rich by those who pretended to any knowledge on the subject. He had joined the expedition as a volunteer, but was known to be constantly in search of precious minerals.

In the mean time every one in camp who spoke Spanish was questioning Carlos as to our position and prospects. Those who doubted his knowledge or mistrusted his faith did not hesitate to declare their misgivings aloud. No threats were offered, but Carlos understood just enough of English to know that they were talking of him, and not saying anything complimentary either to his knowledge of the country or his honesty. The next morning early he was missing, and, on looking about the camp, Brignoli, too, was found absent. This crcumstance created the greatest excitement among all; yet Carlos had many believers and friends—and they still insisted that he had only left the camp for a short time, to hunt. The oxen were yoked and hitched to the waggons, and every preparation made for resuming our journey, but Carlos was yet missing.

It is impossible, either to be placed or imagined, in a worse and more pitiable situation than the one in which we now found ourselves. The hope that we were within some sixty miles of the frontier settlements vanished with Carlos, for we knew that he would not have left so long as there was a probability of his leading us safely through the difficulties in which we were involved. He had been offered inducements too strong for him thus to desert us, unless he himself was lost and feared the consequences of leading us farther astray. We were suffering, too, from the want of fresh water, and knew full well that there was none on the road we had come short of three days' march over a prairie rendered desolate by the great fire. Our only hope was in going a-head, and when nine o'clock came we pushed on without rudder or compass, the melancholy truth plainly visible in almost every face that we were lost among the wilderness prairies of the West.

As we pursued our melancholy journey, there were

still a few among us who thought that Carlos would come up and honestly account for his absence. They even declared their belief that we had now arrived within sight of the Angosturas, or Narrows of Red River, and that if Carlos had really left us it was because he feared that some of the leading men in New Mexico, inimical to the Texans, might blame him for guiding us directly to their homesteads. About noon we were fortunate enough to find a cool and delicious spring of fresh water, and near it a pond large enough to water all our horses and cattle. After drinking deeply at the fountain-head, and fervently hoping for a continuance of such good fortune, we filled our gourds and canteens, and resumed our march. Whenever we looked back we could see an immense smoke in the east, plainly denoting that the prairie fire which had broken out two days previous was still raging. Early in the afternoon a heavy, black cloud was noticed directly over the spot, from which rain was descending apparently in torrents; beyond, and in fact all around this cloud, the sky was clear and without a speck. Here was a shower got up on the Espy principle, although at a heavy cost to our party.

Our course was now nearly west. On our left, and running in nearly a northwest and southeast direction, a range of mountains was plainly visible—the chain which, it was now evident enough, Carlos had mistaken for *The Crows*. I say mistaken, for up to the morning of his departure I believe the fellow's intentions were honest, and that he really supposed the party to be on Red River. The water in the Wichita, for that the river we were on undoubtedly was, resembled in every way that of the former, while the country around here the same appearance; and as Carlos had trapped on both streams, probably without noticing either carefully, and knew but little of them even as low down as Coffee's Station, and was unacquainted with the American name of the river, the mistake might easily occur.

I have mentioned the appearance of the country to the left; on our right it was much broken, and evidently impassable for waggons. A party of some thirty of us, all well mounted, left the command to explore thoroughly this latter section, and our leader, Captain Caldwell, declared that he would not return until he had satisfactorily ascertained whether we were in the neighbourhood of the Narrows or not. Captain C. was the first man to suggest that the stream up which we had been so long journeying was not the Red River, and also to express doubts whether Carlos really knew as much of the country as he pretended.

After working our way through a succession of rugged hills, cedar-brakes, and ravines, for a distance of some ten miles, we at length reached the stream upon our right. It had dwindled down to a small brook, and the head spring was evidently somewhere in the mountains in our vicinity.* The water was extremely salt, and unfit for use. Several trails were found leading along the banks, made by Indians and mustangs, and in one place mule and horse tracks were seen, together with the print of a white man's shoe in the sand, evidently made either by Carlos or his companion, or by one of Howland's men. Being satisfied that we were not in the neighbourhood of the Narrows, and that it was impossible

* I have little doubt that we were now among the Wichita Mountains. They have never, I believe, been laid down upon any map, but old trappers and campaigners often speak of them.

to take the waggons by the road we had travelled, we started back for the spring we had found in the morning, and arrived there at sunset, ourselves and horses completely worn down with fatigue.

Captain Caldwell had shot a fat buck during the day, which had been dressed, and by the side of the cool spring we made a delicious meal. At dark we re-saddled our horses, and after finding the trail of the waggons with some difficulty, pushed on and reached the command about ten o'clock, encamped without water, and extremely solicitous for our return.

Early the next morning spies were sent forward to seek water and a passage through the mountains, myself, with three or four companions, going back to the spring, a distance of some ten miles, for a draught of water! It may seem a long distance, ten miles, to go for a draught of fresh water, but at that time I would have gone fifty. After allowing our horses a rest of two or three hours, and *doing* our washing—for at this time every man was his own washer-*woman*—we set off to rejoin the command. It may not be amiss to say that our washing was very light, consisting only of a checked shirt and a pair of coarse stockings or socks.

Late in the afternoon we reached the camping-place of the previous night, and found that the command had moved forward. A brisk trot brought us up with our companions at dark, encamped by a small spring and creek of bitter water, strongly impregnated, to judge from the taste, with copperas and magnesia. Whatever the substances held in solution by this water may have been, it operated as a powerful cathartic; but the men, unable to find any other, partook of it in large quantities.

On the following morning a council of officers was held, at which it was determined to send a party of fifty of our best-mounted men in a northerly direction, with orders not to return until they had found Red River. Orders were also given to the commander of the party, Captain Caldwell, to send guides back from day to day, as a good waggon road could be found, in order that the expedition might get on as fast as possible.

The party left on the 17th of August, and on the same day Doctor Brashear, our assistant surgeon, died of a liver complaint, and was buried with military honours. He was a native, if I recollect right, of Kentucky, much respected by all who knew him.

Another council was held after the spies had left, and at this meeting it was resolved to reduce our rations of beef. Where we were was problematical: our distance from the settlements no one could even calculate, and as we might still be months in reaching them, it was evident enough that our beef would not hold out. The regular ration of three pounds a-day to each man was cut down to one pound and a half, and this at a time when the beef had become extremely poor and destitute of nutriment, and more than the former rations was really required to support men worn down and exhausted by long and fatiguing marches, and weakened by the effects of bad weather and no water at all. Prudence justified this reduction, however, and the men submitted to it with a cheerfulness that showed they felt the necessity of the course. In the mean time regular hunting parties were detailed for the purpose of adding to our scanty stock of provisions as much as possible; yet, although deer and antelope were far from scarce, nothing like a sufficiency of meat could be procured for our wants. Buffalo were seldom seen, only one being killed during the four days we passed at the camp of the bitter waters.

Much to our joy, a guide returned on the evening of the 20th, and reported that a passage had been found through the mountains. Many of us were unwell and extremely weak from the effect of the strong purgative waters; but the news that we were again to be on the move was of the most welcome kind, and every preparation was made for an early start the next morning.

Learning, from the guide who had returned, that there was a large city or commonwealth of prairie dogs directly on the route the command would take, with two companions I went on to visit these neighbours. We were induced by a double object—first, by a desire to examine one of the republics about which prairie travellers have said so much; and secondly to obtain something to eat, for the flesh of these animals was said to be excellent.

Our road wound up the sides of a gently-ascending mountain for some six or seven miles. On arriving at the summit we found a beautiful table-land spread out before us, reaching miles in every direction. The soil appeared to be uncommonly rich, and was covered with a luxurious growth of mesquit-trees. The grass was of the curly mesquit species, the sweetest and most nutritious of all the different kinds of that grass, and it was told me that the dogs seldom establish their towns and cities unless on sites where this grass is found in abundance.

We had proceeded but a short distance, after reaching

this beautiful prairie, before we came upon the outskirts of the commonwealth. A few scattering dogs were seen scampering in, their short, sharp yelps giving a general alarm to the whole community.

The first brief cry of danger from the outskirts was soon taken up in the centre of the city, and now nothing was to be heard or seen in any direction but a barking, dashing, and scampering of the mercurial and excitable denizens of the place, each to his burrow. Far as the eye could reach the city extended, and all over it the scene was the same.

We rode leisurely along until we had reached the more thickly-settled portion of the place. Here we halted, and after taking the bridles from our horses to allow them to graze, we prepared for a regular attack upon the inhabitants. The burrows were not more than ten or fifteen yards apart, with well-trodden paths leading in different directions, and I even fancied I could discover something like regularity in the laying out of the streets.

We sat down upon a bank under the shade of a mesquit, and leisurely surveyed the scene before us. Our approach had driven every one to his home in our immediate vicinity, but at the distance of some hundred yards the small mound of earth in front of each burrow was occupied by a dog, sitting erect on his hinder legs and coolly looking about for the cause of the recent commotion, every now and then some citizen, more adventurous than his neighbour, would leave his lodgings on a flying visit to a friend, apparently exchange a few words, and then scamper back as fast as his legs would carry him.

By-and-by, as we kept perfectly still, some of our near neighbours were seen cautiously poking their heads from out their holes, and looking craftily, and, at the same time inquisitively about them. Gradually a citizen would emerge from the entrance of his domicile, come out upon his observatory, perk his head cunningly, and then commence yelping somewhat after the manner of a young puppy—a quick jerk of the tail accompanying each yelp. It is this short bark alone that has given them the name of dogs, as they bear no more resemblance to that animal, either in appearance, action, or manner of living, than they do to the hyena.

We were armed, one with a double-barrelled shot-gun, and another with one of Colt's repeating rifles of small bore, while I had my short, heavy rifle, throwing a large ball, and acknowledged by all to be the best weapon in the command. It would drive a ball completely through a buffalo at the distance of a hundred and fifty yards, and there was no jumping off or running away by a deer when struck in the right place—to use a common expression, "he would never know what had hurt him."* Hit one of the dogs where we would, with a small ball, he would almost invariably turn a peculiar somerset, and get into his hole—but by a ball from my rifle, the entire head of the animal would be knocked off, and after this there was no escape. With the shot-gun, again, we could do nothing but waste ammunition. I fired it at one dog not ten steps off, having in a good charge of buckshot, and thought I must cut him into fragments—I wounded him severely, but with perhaps

* I trust the reader has forgotten my adventure with the large drove of deer, as related in the previous chapter.

three or four shot through him he was still able to wriggle and tumble into his hole.

For three hours we remained in this commonwealth, watching the movements of the inhabitants, and occasionally picking off one of the more unwary. No less than nine were got by the party, and one circumstance I would mention as singular in the extreme, and showing the social relationship which exists among these animals, as well as the kind regard they have one for another. One of them had perched himself upon the pile of earth in front of his pole, sitting up and exposing a fair mark, while a companion's head was seen poking out of the entrance, too timid, perhaps, to trust himself farther. A well-directed ball from my rifle carried away the entire top of the former's head, and knocked him some two or three feet from his post perfectly dead. While reloading, the other boldly came out, seized his companion by one of his legs, and before we could reach the hole had drawn him completely out of sight. There was a touch of feeling in the little incident—a something human, which raised the animals in my estimation, and ever after I did not attempt to kill one of them, except when driven by extreme hunger.

The prairie dog is about the size of the common wild rabbit of the United States, heavier, perhaps, more compact, and with much shorter legs. In appearance it closely resembles the woodchuck, or groundhog, of the Northern and Middle States, although not more than two-thirds as large. The colour is the same, being a dark, reddish brown, while the formation of the head and teeth is the same as in all the different species of squirrels, to which family it belongs. In their habits they are clannish, social, and extremely convivial, never living alone like other animals, but, on the contrary, always found in villages or large settlements. They are a wild, frolicsome, madcap set of fellows when undisturbed, uneasy and ever on the move, and appear to take especial delight in chattering away the time, and visiting from hole to hole to gossip and talk over each other's affairs—at least so their actions would indicate. When they find a good location for a village, and there is no water in the immediate vicinity, old hunters say, they dig a well to supply the wants of the community. On several occasions I crept close to their villages, without being observed, to watch their movements. Directly in the centre of one of them I particularly noticed a very large dog, sitting in front of the door or entrance to his burrow, and by his own actions and those of his neighbours it really seemed as though he was the president, mayor, or chief—at all events, he was the "big dog" of the place. For at least an hour I secretly watched the operations in this community. During that time the large dog I have mentioned received at least a dozen visits from his fellow-dogs, which would stop and chat with him a few moments, and then run off to their domiciles. All this while he never left his post for a moment, and I thought I could discover a gravity in his deportment not discernible in those by which he was surrounded. Far is it from me to say that the visits he received were upon business, or had anything to do with the local government of the village; but it certainly appeared so. If any animal has a system of laws regulating the body politic, it is certainly the prairie dog.

If a person is fortunate enough to gain the immediate

vicinity of one of the villages unobserved—a very difficult matter, for their sentinels are always on the alert—he will discover the inhabitants gambolling, frisking, and running about the well-trodden paths, occasionally stopping a moment as if to exchange a word with a neighbour, and then hurrying back to their own lodges. Should he chance to discover some quiet citizen, sitting gravely at his doorway, he has but to watch him for a short time ere he will notice some eccentricity of conduct. His manner of entering his hole will remind the spectator of the antics of Pantaloon in a pantomime; for, instead of walking quietly in, he does it with an eccentric bound and half somerset, his hind feet knocking together as he pitches headlong into the darkness below; and before the aforesaid spectator has yet fairly recovered from the half laugh caused by the drollery of the movement, he will see the dog slowly thrust his head from his burrow, and with a pert and impudent expression of countenance peer cunningly about, as if to ascertain the effect his recent antic had caused.

A singular species of owl is invariably found residing in and about the dog-towns. It has a longer body and smaller head than the common owl of the settlements, yet possesses all the gravity of deportment and solemnity of mien which distinguish the genus.

One would suppose that a constant intercourse with neighbours of such comic temperaments as the dogs possess would destroy his austerity of demeanour; yet the owl of the dog-village sits upon the earthen mound in front of the hole, and surveys the eccentricities of his friends without a change of countenance. He joins them not in any of their sports, yet still seems to be on the best of terms; and as he is frequently seen entering and emerging from the same hole, this singular bird may be looked upon as a member of the same family, or at least a retainer whose services are in some way, necessary to the comfort and well-being of the animal whose hospitality he shares.

Rattlesnakes, too, and of immense size, dwell in the same lodges with the dogs; but the idea that has been entertained of their living upon sociable terms of companionship is utterly without foundation. The snakes I look upon as loafers, not easily shaken off by the regular inhabitants, and they make use of the dwellings of the dogs as more comfortable quarters than they can find elsewhere. We killed one a short distance from a burrow, which had made a meal of a half-grown dog; and although I do not think they can master the larger animals, the latter are still compelled to let them pass in and out without molestation—a nuisance, like many in more elevated society, that cannot be got rid off.

The first town we visited was much the largest seen on the entire route, being some two or three miles in length by nearly a mile in width at the widest part. In the vicinity were smaller villages—suburbs of the larger town, to all appearance. After spending some three hours in the very heart of the settlements, and until not an inhabitant could be seen in any direction, we re-saddled our horses and set off in search of the command. Thus ended my first visit to one of the numerous prairie-dog commonwealths of the Far West.

CHAPTER X.

A Meal of Prairie Dogs.—Arrival at another brackish Water Camp.—Shower at Night, with Fresh Water in the Morning.—Return of the Spy Company.—A regular "Northeaster."—Report of the Spies.—Disagreeable Bivouac.—Indians in Camp.—Horses Stolen.—A bad Bargain.—Daring of the Indians.—Fine Weather again.—Once more on the Road.—Dog Towns.—Meeting with a Party of Indians.—Horse Meat far from being bad Eating.—Wolves about.—A Dreary Desert.—Delicious fresh-water Stream.—Latitude and Longitude again taken.—Pleasant Prospects.—Again encompassed with Difficulties.—A Passage out found.—Steppes.—Mesquit Prairie and Prairie Dogs.—Mountains in the Distance.—Singing Birds and Thoughts of Home.—Delusive Hopes.—More Horses Stolen.—Bed of Large River Crossed.—Arrival at the Quintufue.—Large Indian Camp Discovered.—Cayguas on all Sides.—Indian Provisions.—A Party sent out.—Farther advance Impossible.—A Night without Water.—Preparations for taking a back Track.—Exciting News.—Firing of Guns heard.—Lieutenant Hull and Four Men Killed by Cayguas.—A Chase after Indians.—Return to the Quintufue.—Determination to divide the Command.—Description of the Cayguas.

We had scarcely travelled three miles, after leaving the large dog-town, before we descried the white tops of our waggons at some distance in our rear. Finding a dry mesquit, we broke off some of the larger branches, kindled a fire, and cooked for each man a dog. The meat we found exceedingly sweet, tender, and juicy—resembling that of the squirrel, only that it was much fatter. Our meal over, we next wasted three or four hours in vainly endeavouring to shoot a deer or antelope. Numbers of them were seen, but the hunting parties had scoured their range, killed several of them, and rendered the animals unusually shy. Late in the afternoon we sought the trail of our waggons, and on finding it set off at a pace which brought us up with the command ere nightfall, encamped near a large reddish-coloured hill or mountain, and close by a small creek of brackish-water—a tributary, doubtless, of the Wichita, or else the main stream.

Scarcely had we finished a scanty supper of poor beef, and hastily rolled ourselves in our blankets, when it commenced raining in torrents—pouring down without intermission for hours, and drenching us completely. Little did we care for this, however, as we had the satisfaction in the morning of getting fresh and pure water in abundance—the first for a week.

After devouring the last of the prairie dogs we had killed the preceding day, wringing our blankets, and drying our clothes as well as we were able, we pursued our journey in a course nearly northwest. We had no little trouble in crossing the creek before us, swollen by the heavy rain of the night previous; but in a couple of hours waggons and all were safely on the opposite side.

After toiling across the soft and muddy prairie a distance of ten miles, we at length reached another running stream, the point at which our guide had left the spy company. Here we halted to await the return of the latter, or until another guide should be sent back. During the night the wind veered round into the north-east, bringing with it a cold, drizzling, and extremely disagreeable rain, which continued the next day. In the mean time the spy company returned, reporting that they had found a large stream to the north, which they confidently believed to be Red River, or one of its main tributaries.

Night came, the cold rain and raw wind still continuing. We were encamped immediately upon the stream, the banks of which were high, and flanked by a narrow skirting of timber. Under this bank I led my horse at dusk, and tied him fast to a small tree. Here he was protected from the piercing northern blasts, and to afford the same shelter, Doctor Brenham led thither his horse, a noble white animal of the best blood, and confined him to the same tree with mine.

Several of our horses were tied under this bank, the poorer animals being allowed to rough it upon the prairie in front of our encampment, hobbled, and many of them staked, to prevent the storm from driving them off during the night.

On awaking in the morning, it was ascertained that the horse of Doctor B. had been stolen by Indians. The *lariat* was cut, and part of it still fast to the tree. My horse was standing quietly where I had left him, his colour probably preventing the daring robbers from seeing him. Some half dozen horses were taken with Doctor B.'s, among them Mr. Falconer's. Generally the Indians selected the best horses in camp, dark as was the night; but they took themselves in in taking Mr. Falconer's, for he was continually performing some unseemly antics, had frequently caused much fright among our other horses, and was worth but little, even setting his tricks aside.

To show how daring the Indian horse-thieves were, I have but to mention that Doctor Brenham's horse was tied within six yards of the spot where we were sleeping; and after passing the guard, by no means an easy matter, the rascals were compelled to creep within a few feet of us before they could reach their prey. An Indian bow was found in the vicinity of our camp, which the thieves had left in their haste, and one of the artillery mules was shot through with an arrow, the animal probably not being able to move fast enough when the Indians withdrew from our vicinity.

As the day advanced the rain gradually ceased, and before ten o'clock the sun once more appeared. A happier set of men were never seen, for many of us had eaten, slept, and waked in wet clothes and blankets through the eight-and-forty previous hours. Some little time was occupied in filling up the creek with earth and logs, so as to secure a safe passage for the waggons, and about noon the whole expedition was once more on the road, travelling in a northwest direction. During the day we passed through a succession of dog-towns, scattered along every half-mile upon the route, as their favourite grass could be procured. Large numbers of the animals were killed by the men—killed for their meat alone.

At night we encamped in front of a small mot or clump of timber, and near a pond of fresh water. However much the rain of the two previous days had annoyed us, we now found that it had saved the expedition. Not a drop of water, save that which had recently fallen, could be found in any direction, and little doubt was entertained that we must inevitably have perished had it not been for the heavy storms.

A party of three hunters came in after we had encamped, and reported that they had fallen in with a party of nine

Indians during the day, and had held a "talk" with them. The fellows spoke Spanish, although badly, and were very insolent in their bearing. They did not dare attack our men, however, and finally rode off yelling across the prairie. They were doubtless Caygüas,* and belonged to the party that had stolen our horses the night before.

Another party of our men shortly after came in, their horses loaded down with deer, antelope, and other meat which they had killed during the day. The mess to which I was attached received a large ration of meat, which those who sent it said was young buffalo. It was fat, tender, and very juicy—the most delicious meat, I then thought, I had ever tasted—and what with some fine mushrooms we had found on the march, together with broiled antelope liver, we made a sumptuous meal. Not a little surprised were we afterward, when we ascertained that the meal we had partaken of so heartily, and praised so much, was the flesh of a *mustang!*

After having tied our horses close at hand, many of them to the waggons, and taken up our quarters in their immediate vicinity, we stretched ourselves upon the ground, and slept soundly, without a visit from Indians or disturbance of any kind, until near morning, when a pack of wolves, drawn to our camp by the smell of fresh meat, set up a dismal howling. A heavy dew, the first we had noticed since our departure from Austin, had fallen during the night, and the day broke with difficulty through a heavy fog: but it about eight

* Mr. Navarro, who was well acquainted with the different tribes south of Red River, told me they were *Cayguas*, and gave the name this spelling. It is pronounced *Kiwaa*, yet it is generally written *Kioway*.

o'clock the sun made his appearance, dispersing fog, wolves, dew, and all.

Our course of the previous day, northwest, which was considered the right one, we were still enabled to keep, with an excellent road for the first five miles of our morning's march. About noon we reached a singular tract, unlike anything we had previously seen. North and south, as far as the eye could reach, nothing could be seen but a sandy plain, covered with scrub-oak bushes, two or three feet high, upon which were found innumerable acorns of a large size. This desert, although the wheels of the waggons sank several inches in the sand, we were obliged to cross. Night set in before the passage was made—horses, cattle, and drivers alike tired out with the excessive fatigues of the day. We were fortunate, however, in finding a cool and pure stream of fresh running water just on the western edge of the waste. On the opposite side, the prairie had been recently burned, the fresh grass just springing up, and here we encamped.

At this camp the latitude and longitude were taken by Lieutenant Hull. The result of the observation, which, from the instruments not being in order, could not be depended upon, I inserted in my note-book, but have now forgotten. Lieutenant H. said that we could not be more than a hundred miles from the settlements, that we could easily reach them in ten days, and expressed himself highly pleased with the prospect before us. Little did he then anticipate the horrible fate that was soon to befall himself, or the many gloomy days of travel, of starvation, and of uncertainty in store for those whose spirits he had elevated by anticipations of soon reaching the settlement.

On starting the next morning after this observation was made, and ascending a high ridge of hills in the vicinity, the country before us was found extremely rough and broken. We pushed forward, however, some one way, some another—buffeting, turning, and twisting, about, without order or system, until nearly dark. Long and tiresome marches, bad water, and not half enough of even the worst provisions, had combined to weaken and dispirit the men, render them impatient of control, and inclined to disobey all orders. The consequence was, that one party would go in this direction in quest of grapes or plums, another in that, hunting for game, or water, and nearly all discipline was lost. It is difficult, and requires a most efficient officer to keep even regular soldiers under subjection, when half starved and broken down by fatigue—nothing can restrain volunteers under such circumstances.

After crossing and re-crossing deep gullies, our progress in one direction impeded by steep hills, and in another by yawning ravines, we finally encamped at night not two miles from where we began our day's march, although we had really travelled fifteen. Large plum patches had been found during the day, and such an inordinate craving had our men for almost any species of vegetable, that the country for miles in every direction was scoured, midnight coming before all the different parties arrived in camp.

A passage out of our difficulties was found next morning, and after winding about until noon among the hills, we at length reached a beautiful table-land covered with mesquit-trees.

So suddenly did we leave the rough and uneven surface of the valley, and so striking was the transition, that the scenic world of the theatre—and particularly the change from the humble cottage of the dancing girl to the Hindoo paradise in "La Bayadere"—was brought forcibly to the mind.

On starting in the morning, nothing was to be seen but a rough and rugged succession of hills before us—piled one upon another, each succeeding hill rising above its neighbour. At the summit of the highest of these hills the beautiful and fertile plain opened suddenly to view, giving scope to our vision and hopes that was unanticipated and thrice welcome. The country between the Cross Timbers and the Rocky Mountains rises by high *steppes*, for the different lines of hills can be called by no other name. As the traveller journeys westward, he meets, at long intervals, ridges of hills and montains, running nearly north and south, presenting the most serious barriers to his farther advance. As he ascends these, he anticipates a corresponding descent on the opposite side; but in a majority of instances, on reaching the summits, he finds nothing before him but a level and fertile prairie.

We halted an hour or two, on reaching the beautiful table-land, to rest our weary cattle and give our horses an opportunity to graze. Little villages of prairie dogs were scattered about upon the prairie, and numbers were shot by the men, to help out their scanty rations. The fat of this animal, old hunters say, is an infallible remedy for the rheumatism. In the evening we resumed the march, and at sundown encamped upon the banks of a running stream of fresh water. The blue tops of three or four high mountains were discerned in the distance, which, such phases did hope ascribe to them, we thought answered the description Carlos had given of *The Crows*.

We were awakened early the next morning by the warbling of innumerable singing-birds, perched among the bushes along the borders of the stream. Among the notes I recognised those of the robin, the lark, and the blue-bird, and as it was the first time any of them had been heard since the commencement of our journey, thoughts of home and civilization came fresh to the heart here among the western wilds. How these birds ever strayed so far from their usual haunts, for they are seldom found except in the immediate vicinity of settlements, is more than I can imagine. There they were, however, telling us of scenes to which we had long been strangers, and giving us pleasing but fallacious promises of a speedy return to the abodes of at least semi-civilization. In our fond imaginings they typified the dove, telling us that the wilderness had been passed; but, alas! their song, like the siren's, was uttered but to deceive.

Inspiriting as was the singing of these birds, we were obliged to leave them in the middle of their matinal concert, and pursue our weary march. Throughout the day we had an excellent road, and when night came we had made something like twenty miles, still in a northwest direction, which was considered our true course. The mountains that had been seen the day before were now plainly visible, and well answered the description Carlos had given of the landmarks in the neighbourhood of the Narrows of Red River. The opinion advanced by many, that we were approaching the end of our journey, spread a general joy through camp; and this opinion received fresh strength upon the return of two small hunting parties after night, who reported that they had seen what appeared to be Mexican cart tracks upon the prairie. With thankful hearts we swallowed our scanty supper that night, and the burden of our dreams, after *retiring* to rest upon the ground, was of bread and butter, potatoes, and the other substantials of life—things that had long been strangers to our mouths, but were fresh in our memories.

Early the next morning it was ascertained that several horses and mules were missing, and although diligent search was made by their owners, they were never recovered. The night had been clear and bright, the guard neither seeing nor hearing aught to excite their suspicions; but the animals were stolen, doubtless, by a marauding party of Indians.

The march was once more resumed, several well-armed parties scouring the prairies in various directions in search of water, Indians, and our lost animals. About noon, after a toilsome journey through a hilly and broken country, the command crossed the bed of a stream which was evidently a large river during the rainy season. At this time but little water was found, and that so salt that it was impossible to drink it. Towards night we came to the banks of a clear and delicious fresh-water stream, called, as we afterwards ascertained, the Quintufue, the waters of which were bubbling along over a bed of golden sand. Running nearly north and south, at the distance of some six miles to our left, was the chains of hills I have mentioned, and rising above the rest were three peaks, which really deserved the name of mountains. We crossed the stream with our waggons, and encamped, close on the opposite side.

Scarcely had we unsaddled our horses and turned them loose before one of our hunting parties came in and reported that a large body of Indians were in our immediate vicinity, and that they had driven off an immense *cavallada* or drove of horses. Soon another party arrived, with information that they had met a small body of Indians, one of whom spoke Spanish. They said that they were Caygüas, and on being interrogated concerning the direction towards Santa Fé, gave equivocal answers. They pointed to the south-west, however, to what appeared a passage through the hills, and said that was the direction to Chihuahua. They pretended to know nothing about the Rio Colorado or Red River. These Indians were mounted on fine horses, dressed in buckskin, and armed with lances and bows and arrows.

The stream upon which we were now encamped appeared to have its source in the long chain of hills upon our left, and ran in nearly a northeast direction. A short distance above us, occupying a beautiful situation on the same stream, the main camp of the Indians in our neighbourhood was discovered. It had apparently been just deserted, the inhabitants, in their great haste to drive off and secure their horses, not having time even to *cache* * their other property. Tent poles, skins, numerous rough utensils, besides a quantity of dried buffalo, mustang, and deer meat, were found precisely as they had left them. The latter we appropriated to our own use, and, in our half-starving condition, was found extremely palatable.

Captain Strain, with a party of twenty or twenty-five men, was ordered out immediately, with orders to find and bring in some of the Indians, if possible, and at all events to ascertain their feelings and intentions. In the mean time the horses and cattle were herded close within the lines, a strong guard set, and the cannon placed in an advantageous position to guard against a night attack. The night passed off, however, without any alarm.

The journey was resumed early in the morning, our course being now nearly north to avoid the chain of hills on our left. By many it was thought that Red River came through a pass in this chain, and it was even conjectured that we should find that stream at the base of the farthest mountain in the ridge, so well did the region about us answer the description given by Carlos, before he left us, of the country in the immediate vicinity of the Narrows.

A party of some twenty or thirty had gone forward in the morning for the purpose of finding the best road, while the main body followed slowly on. While stopping

* This is a term used by the Rocky Mountain trappers and Western traders, and is equivalent to the English word *bury*. Furs and other valuables, when secreted in the ground, are called *cached*. The word is an obvious derivative from the French *cacher*, to hide.

to noon, near a small hole of muddy water, the last-mentioned party returned, and reported that they had encountered deep and impassable ravines in a northern direction—impassable even for mules. A halt for the night, although there was no water by this time even for the men, was now called, and a party of ten picked men, well mounted, sent out under Lieutenant Hann to scour the country in a northeast direction, in order, if possible, to find a road around the head of the gullies and ravines. At the time, it was considered impossible to cross, with the waggons, the high and rugged hills and mountains west of us, and our only course appeared to be by a road to the northeast.

In the mean time night overtook us, and still no tidings were received from Captain Strain, who had now been out more than twenty-four hours. The bright dreams of the night before vanished when we saw that our onward course was impeded by impassable barriers, and in their stead were forebodings of the gloomiest nature. When the mind is harassed by uncertainty, it is singular how trifling a thing can raise the spirits to the highest pitch of excitement or depress them to a state bordering on despair.

We passed another night sadly enough, yet without an alarm or loosing any of our horses; but the morning brought no news of Captain Strain. Our camp was in a small bend, protected in the rear by a skirting of cottonwood and hackberry trees which fringed the dry bed of a creek. The berries of the latter tree were ripe, and the limbs were completely stripped by our men, to satisfy a gnawing desire for food of a vegetable nature.

A report was raised, early in the morning, that fresh

water had been discovered two miles distant, in the direction of the mountains, and our suffering animals were driven there immediately; but at about eight o'clock they returned unsuccessful in their search. To endure the horrible sufferings we were experiencing seemed no longer possible, and, at a consultation held among the officers, it was resolved to fall back upon the stream we had left the previous morning, and there await the return of the scouting parties which had been sent out. The weather, I might here add, was insupportably hot, adding much to our suffering.

Our conjectures were anything but flattering, on account of the continued absence of Captain Strain and his party, now out more than thirty-six hours. It was known, however, that both he and Lieutenant Hann, as well as the parties of three and five who were out hunting for water on their own account, could easily find their way back to camp by following the trail of the waggons, and immediate preparations were accordingly made to retrace our steps to the old camp, or some point higher up on the same stream.

The horses and mules were driven up and saddled, the oxen were yoked, and the other preparatory work was in progress for our departure, when suddenly a young man came dashing into camp from the northward, evidently much agitated, and announced that a large body of Indians were pursuing a party of our men directly towards us. Scarcely had he finished speaking before a firing was heard but a few hundred yards distant, a slight roll of the prairie concealing the combatants from our sight. Fast as they could mount horses, a party of some fifty of our men dashed off towards the scene of strife, while the waggons were drawn up in square, the cattle and horses brought inside, and every preparation made to resist an attack, which was now considered certain. The first impression was, that the scouting-parties had been entirely cut off, and that these successes would induce the Indians to attack our main body.

Just as the party of our men, who had gone out to the relief of their companions, reached the spot, the Indians retreated; but their bloody work was done. Scattered about within the circumference of a few yards were the dead bodies of Lieutenant Hull and four of our men, stripped, scalped, and horribly mutilated, while the appearance of the ground gave strong evidence that manfully and with strong hearts they had resisted the attack of their adversaries. They had left camp but a short time previous, probably with the hope of finding water, and in returning had been thus cruelly murdered. But one look at their mangled bodies was sufficient to stir deep feelings of revenge in every heart, and madly did our men spur their horses in pursuit, with the vain hope of avenging the death of their companions. The Indians were at least four times their number, yet they retreated, and, being far better mounted, were able to keep out of the way. So near, however, were our men, that they could plainly see the dead bodies of several of the Indians, packed upon extra horses they had with them for that purpose. The prairie warriors always have horses trained especially to carry off their dead or wounded companions, which they take with them on going into action; and it is considered one of the greatest calamities that can befall them if they are compelled to leave one of their number in the hands of an enemy.

The pursuit of the bloodthirsty Caygüas, for such the Indians proved to be, was continued by our men until it was evident that they could not be overtaken, and then reluctantly given up. Several times during the chase, the Indians reined up their well-trained horses on the higher rolls of the prairies, and formed in line as if intending to give battle; but before our men could get within gunshot they were off again, with lightning speed, across the plain. On returning to the spot where our men had fallen, a closer examination showed how hard and desperate had been the struggle. Lieutenant Hull had received no less than thirty lance and arrow wounds before he fell, and the broken stock of one of Colt's rifles was still retained in the grasp of a stout man, named Mayby, plainly telling us that he had fought to the last, and that after discharging the piece he had still continued the combat. The heart of one of the men was cut out, and had not the Indians been driven off the other bodies would have been mutilated in the same way. Two of the horses of our unfortunate comrades were lanced close by—the others were probably in better condition and more able to run, and had been taken off as spoils by the savages. It was evident enough that Lieutenant Hull and his men had retreated from the Indians until they had found it impossible to elude them, and that they had then thrown themselves from their horses in a body and sold their lives at a fearful rate. The resistance they made had probably terrified their adversaries, and induced them to fly when they saw our party coming up, although they outnumbered the Texans at least as three to one.

A party of fifty well-armed men, taking with them

shovels, were sent out immediately on the melancholy errand of burying our murdered companions, while the main body retraced their steps towards the Quintufue, which is said to be a branch of the Palo Duro, or Hard Wood River. Scarcely had we started, before all were rejoiced by the appearance of Captain Strain with part of his men. He told us that he had scoured the prairies in almost every direction, but without success, having been unable to hold a parley with any of the Indians, although he had seen several small parties. He also reported that he had been unable to find either a road or water ; there was a route by which the ravines might be headed in a course a little north of east, but in no other direction. A part of his men had left him early in the morning, having gone back to the Quintufue for water.

About noon the main body of the command again reached the river, at a point somewhat higher up than the former camping-ground. Here, after drinking incredible quantities of the water, and allowing our suffering animals also to quench a thirst which their eyes and general appearance too plainly showed had nearly driven them mad, a strong position was chosen and we encamped.

In the evening a general consultation of all the officers was held. At this meeting it was resolved to despatch a party of one hundred chosen men, on the best horses in camp, with instructions not to return until the settlements of New Mexico were found. Although no hopes were entertained that a passage over the mountains could be effected by the waggons, it was still thought that mounted men would be able to accomplish it.

The distance to the nearest settlements was not supposed to be more than one hundred miles at farthest, and it was accordingly determined that the party should take five days' provisions, allowing but scanty rations. The course to be taken was north-west, and this course was to be kept, as near as circumstances would admit, until the party struck either the settlements near Santa Fé, the Rio Grande at a point below, or the trail of the St. Louis traders above. On reaching New Mexico, a party was immediately to be sent back to the command with guides and provisions.

However impolitic it may be considered to divide a command, in this instance such a course could not be avoided. We were completely lost, and without power of moving forward; our provisions, which had for weeks been scanty, were now almost entirely exhausted; the men were enfeebled by long marches, with only poor beef enough each day to support nature;* and in addition we were surrounded by a large and powerful tribe of well-mounted Indians, scouring our vicinity, and always on the look-out to pick off any small party that might be sent out to hunt, or for other purposes. All these reasons considered, it will at once be seen that but two courses offered—one, to destroy the waggons, and to retreat hastily towards Texas; the other, to divide the command, and send one party forward with orders not to return until the settlements were reached. I will not say that the wiser course was adopted; but in answer to any one who may blame the leaders of the expedition for dividing the command, I would remark that few men,

* It may not be amiss to state that every part of each ox killed was devoured; the blood, hide, entrails—nothing was lost.

under the circumstances, would have advised to the contrary.

So soon as a division of the command had been determined upon, several of the oxen were killed for the use of the party to be sent onward, and preparations were made to dry the meat on the ensuing morning. Night came, but with it came no news of Lieutenant Hann and his little party. On calling the roll it was also found that others besides those killed in the morning were missing, and with the full conviction that they had shared the fate of Lieutenant Hull and his men, we that night laid ourselves to rest. The next morning we were still without tidings of our absent comrades.

The party detailed by General M'Leod to march in advance, was placed under the command of Captain Sutton, an excellent officer. It consisted of eighty-seven officers and privates, with merchants, travellers and servants enough to swell the number to ninety-nine. Among the officers were Captain Lewis, and Lieutenants Lubbock, Munson, Brown, and Seavy,* the latter acting as adjutant: the civilians were Colonel Cooke, Mr. Brenham, Major Howard, Messrs. Van Ness, Fitzgerald, Frank Combs, and myself. We were all well armed and mounted on the best horses in camp, and deemed ourselves able to cut our way through any party of Indians that might dare to attack us. That we should be molested was considered more than probable, as it was impossible to leave the command without be-

* Lieutenant Seavy was educated at West Point, had seen much service, in Texas, and was one of the best officers connected with the Santa Fé expedition. He died of yellow fever at Puente Nacional, Mexico, much beloved by his brother officers as well as the common soldiers.

ing perceived by the scouting parties of Caygüas continually hovering about our camp, who could observe our every movement. In a fortified position we felt confident they would not attack the command; but now that we were divided they might be emboldened to attack the smaller party.

The Caygüas appear to be a powerful tribe, about whom, from their geographical position, little has been known. Their range is south of the line of travel of the Missouri traders, and north of such parts of the Camanche country as were known to the Texans, their hunting-grounds probably not having been visited by the whites previous to our march across them. In their customs and manner of living they resemble, in every way, the Camanches, and may be said to be a branch of that large and powerful tribe. They lead a roving life, esteem the whites as their natural enemies, and never give them quarter. Like the Camanches, they are expert on horseback to an extraordinary degree, leaping from one horse to another while at full speed, and performing many feats upon the prairies never undertaken even by the best equestrians of the circus. In their attacks upon an enemy they expose but a small portion of their persons, riding along in parallel lines with their enemies, their bodies lying on the opposite sides of their well-trained steeds, and in this position they discharge their arrows directly under their horse's necks. If they meet with an unfortunate party whom they outnumber, they charge openly, despatching all with their lances. While encamped, they live in tents constructed of poles and buffalo hides. These can be struck at a moment's warning, and the whole party will move off in an incredibly short space of time. They appear to be on terms of peace with the New Mexicans so far as it suits their interest and convenience—no farther; at one time trading and exchanging their skins in amity, and almost in the same breath making a descent upon the unprotected frontiers, plundering and frequently murdering the inhabitants. When we passed through their country a party of Mexican traders were among them bartering meal, blankets, and trinkets for buffalo and deer skins. Some of these Mexicans we afterwards saw, and from them learned that ten of their warriors, besides a principal chief, were killed by Lieutenant Hull and his brave companions before they were overpowered. The traders also gave us an account of their ceremonies on returning to camp with their scalps and trophies. A wild dance was executed by the braves in celebration of their victory, while the women tore their hair and faces, and ran naked through the prickly pear and thorn bushes, in token of their grief for the loss of their husbands and brothers. Whether they considered our visit as hostile or not it is impossible to say; they had shed blood, and we well knew they would not cease murdering any of our companions they might dare attack. They have but a small number of rifles among them, and these are ineffective and useless in their hands: the larger portion of them are armed with shields, lances, and bows and arrows, weapons they use with surprising dexterity. Such are the most obvious features of a tribe of Indians occupying the prairies near the head waters of the Wichita, Colorado, Brazos, and Red Rivers.

The morning of August 31st was occupied in partially

drying our meat over slow fires, and in making preparations for our departure. Horses were shod, bullets moulded, our rifles and pistols thoroughly examined, and nothing neglected in the way of that precaution our uncertain adventure demanded. We were placed in a position demanding some extraordinary effort. The repeated reverses that we had met with, the hunger and fatigue which we had undergone, and the impossibility of travelling further with the waggons in any direction that would bring us nearer the settlements, formed a combination of evils for which a retreat or the plan determined upon was the only remedy. The indefatigable *go-a-headity* which characterizes the Anglo-Saxon race, no matter where or under what circumstances placed, prevented the adoption of the former plan—the same spirit induced the officers of the expedition to adopt and carry out the latter. Almost every one appeared to rejoice when this course was determined upon. The harrassing uncertainties which now encompassed all would speedily be removed, and we should soon know *where we were*.

As the advance party were about starting, we were all rejoiced by the appearance of Lieutenant Hann and his men. He had met with several small parties of the Indians, and endeavoured to induce them to come in and hold a friendly talk; but they were sulky and disposed to fight, although not strong enough to engage him. Up to this time he knew nothing of the murder of Lieutenant Hull's party. The other men who were missing, as I have since been informed, never came in, but were undoubtedly killed by the Indians.

CHAPTER XI.

Departure of the Advance in search of the Settlements.—Summit of the Steppe gained.—Level Prairie before us.—A lovely Scene.—Speculations in relation to Red River.—A Bear Chase —Bruin noosed.—The March continued.—Sagacity of a mule.—Arrival at a singular Chasm.—Imposbility of crossing.—A heavy Prairie Shower.—Appearance of our Men.—Description of the Chasm.—A crossing found.—Loneliness of the Prairies.—Scarcity of Game.—Begin to suffer Hunger.—Arrival at another awful Abyss.—Farther Difficulty in Crossing—Hunger increasing.—Singular Birds.—Mustangs and Antelopes.—Their exceeding Shyness.—Curlews.—A Buffalo descried.—Preparations for a chase to the Death.—Tom Hancock and his Skill.—Endurance of Jim the Butcher.—Description of the Chase.—Poor Prospects of a Supper.

The sun had but a short hour to run, in order to finish his day's work on the 31st of August, when, in double file and closs order, our provisions for the march hanging at our saddle-skirts, we left our companions on the Quintufue and struck across the prairie on our journey in search of the settlements of New Mexico, Mr. Hunt, the engineer of the expedition, taking the guidance. A brisk trot of two hours brought us, as night was throwing its sable drapery over the scene, to the foot of the mountains, and here, after choosing a strong position, we encamped. No water could be found in our vicinity, but as we had filled our gourds and canteens before we left the main body, we suffered but little.—Early the next morning, after travelling a mile or two along the foot of the high range, we discovered what seemed to be an Indian trail, the marks where the tent-poles had been dragged over the ground being plainly visible, leading in a zigzag course up the sides of the mountains. This we followed, and towards noon found ourselves at the summit of the chain. Here we were again gratified by finding spread out before us a perfectly level prairie, extending as far as the eye could reach, and without a tree to break its complete monotony. We halted a few minutes to rest our horses, and occupied the time in surveying the calm and beautiful valley lying hundreds of feet below us.

It was a lovely scene, beheld from the point where we stood, and I could hardly believe that but a few hours previous a horrible tragedy had been enacted upon its fair surface. Softened down by the distance, there was a tranquillity about it which seemed as though it never had been broken. The deep green skirtings of the different watercourses relieved the eye as it fell upon the wide-extending plain. The silver waters of the Quintufue, now reduced apparently to a mere thread, were occasionally brought to view as some turn of the stream threw them in a line with us, and again they were lost to the sight under the rich foliage of the banks. The white tops of our waggons showed the present encampment of our main body, while the small black spots around gave us the pleasing assurance that the cattle and horses were still there, and that the camp had been unmolested. In other parts of the valley, too, small moving specks were seen—mustangs, or perhaps our Indian enemies prowling about—but other than these no living objects met our gaze. Almost the whole valley was bordered by the yawning chasms that had impeded the progress of our waggons, now brought more plainly to view by the elevation upon which we stood, and the whole scene forcibly reminded me of one of Salvator Rosa's beautiful landscapes, framed with rough, gnarled, and unfinished oak.

The elevated chain of hills or mountains we had ascended, if they really deserve that title, was but another *steppe* towards the high table-land which forms the base of the Rocky Mountains. Where, now, was Red River? If the large steam our guides and scouting parties had seen, while in the valley below us, and in a northeast direction from the spot where Lieutenant Hull was killed —if that stream was Red River, then its source must have been near the base of the high steppe upon which we now stood, and the wide and almost dry beds we had crossed within the few past days were but its tributaries. In springtime, when the prairie snows melt away and the early rains fall, these beds are doubtless full, and when joined in one common channel form the great stream which, after passing through the Cross Timbers, fertilizes the valley known as the Red River country. The Rocky Mountains may justly be considered the parents of most of the larger streams of North America; but I cannot think that they give birth to the river we had been so long seeking. On the contrary, I am bold in hazarding the opinion that the Rio Colorado or Red River of the United States, the Brazos de Dios, and the Rio Colorado or Red River of Texas, all take their rise in the centre of the prairies, at no great distance apart, and that the steppe we had now reached is their extreme western limit. Their waters are similar, being of a dirty, brownish red colour, and of a slightly salt and bitter taste, which goes far to prove their common origin.

From the hillsides, as was the case with the Palo Duro and Quintufue,* small streams of fresh and limpid water arise ; but both their purity of taste and virgin transparency of colour are lost the moment they strike the reddish clay of the lower praries, and they become adulterated by the copperas and sulphate of soda with which these plains appear to be impregnated. The Red River of the United States has been traced and is well known to a point west of Coffee's Upper Station, a noted Indian trading post above the mouth of the False Wachita ; beyond that, certainty loses itself in speculation, and the true stream, its courses and its sources, will never be known until it is explored to its fountain head—and this point will be found, I have little hesitation in saying, some two hundred and fifty or three hundred miles east-southeast of Santa Fé, and but a few miles from the *steppe* to which I have now brought my reader. In these conjectures I am borne out by the testimony of Albert Pike, now a well-known lawyer of Arkansas, and a poet and writer of great distinction.† This gentleman, in 1832, made a hazardous journey from Santa Fé to the western settlements of Arkansas. His general course, for the first three hundred miles, was nearly southeast, the last two hundred taking him directly across the immense plain called *Llano Estacado*

* These names we learned from the New Mexican traders, whom we afterward met.

† His "Hymns to the Gods," published several years since in Blackwood, are gems of rarest strength and beauty, and as such were highly lauded by Professor Wilson himself.

—Stake Prairie—by the New Mexicans. Mr. Pike had now reached the head waters of the Brazos, and in about the same longitude we had reached when Lieutenant Hull and his men were killed. He then continued down one of the forks of the Brazos some hundred and eighty miles, the stream running nearly southeast, and a part of the country being broken into rough and mis-shapen hills, resembling those we encountered on the stream which I have put down as the Wichita. The course of Mr. Pike was next northeast, some hundred and forty miles, until he struck the Red River of the United States. The point at which he reached this stream was probably a little to the east of the Waco village I have described, and below the mouth of the Wichita. From the appearance of Red River—the similarity of its waters, both in colour and taste, to those of the Brazos—Mr. Pike entertains little doubt that they both take their rise in the same section of country, and nearly in the same longitude—the former rising but a short distance to the north of the latter. But I am running before my narrative, and after promising other speculations in relation to Red River in a more befitting place, will re-conduct the reader to the summit of the high steppe upon which we now found ourselves.

After giving our animals half an hour's rest, for they were much jaded by the precipitous ascent up which they had clambered, we resumed our journey in a northwest direction. We had ridden but a short distance before a large black bear was seen some mile or thereabout to the left of us. Major Howard immediately set off with the intention of running him down, and after a short race succeeded in placing himself on the opposite side, so as to bring the animal directly between him and our line of march. The chase was now assuming an exciting character, the bear from the lateness of the season, being poor in flesh, and able to run nearly as fast as our fleetest horses. Onward they came, directly towards us, and when within a quarter of a mile I cocked a pistol and left the ranks with the intention of having a first shot at the animal. When within some twenty-five yards, I reined up my horse, and while taking deliberate aim, at not half that distance, I was surprised to see the bear turn a species of somerset, and commence kicking with his hind legs. Unseen by me, one of our Mexican servants had crept up close on the opposite side of my horse, and had noosed the animal with a *lariat* just as I was pulling the trigger of my pistol. Bruin soon loosed himself from his fastenings, and while running down the line was shot by Major Howard.

The journey was again resumed, and continued at a rapid pace until near the middle of the afternoon. A short halt was then called to rest our horses, at a place where no water was seen, but where the grass was excellent. The bridles were no sooner slipped from the heads of our animals than an elderly and sagacious mule, instead of beginning to nip the short grass, put off at a deliberate trot in a southwest direction. "That cunning old rascal scents water *sure*," said his owner, and sure enough he did; for he had not proceeded three hundred yards before we saw him stoop his head and commence drinking at a pond-hole which was concealed from our sight. The discovery of this water was very opportune; for we had drank but little in nearly twenty-four hours, and our animals had not swallowed a drop.

As soon as we had given our horses and mules a short rest, and made a light meal of our half-cured meat, we re-saddled and resumed our journey. We were going forward at a rapid pace, the prairies before us presenting no other appearance than a slightly undulating but smooth surface, when suddenly, and without previous sign or warning, we found ourselves upon the very brink of a vast and yawning chasm, or *canon*, as the Mexicans would call it, some two or three hundred yards across, and probably eight hundred feet in depth! As the front ranks suddenly checked their onward course, and diverged at right angles, the rear sections were utterly at a loss to account for a movement so irregular; they could not see even the edge of the fearful abyss at a distance of fifteen yards from its very brink. The banks at this place were almost perpendicular, and from the sides projected jagged and broken rocks, with here and there a stunted, scrubby cedar. There was some appearance of a zigzag and precipitous trail down the sides of the canon at the point where we first reached it, and Mr. Hunt and Dr. Brenham took it with the intention of reaching the bottom if possible: they continued their winding path until they seemed mere pigmies, and only stopped when their progress was arrested by high and perpendicular bluffs. On their return, after an absence of some half an hour, they said they had not advanced half way to the bottom, and that to attempt crossing at this, or any other point within sight, would be useless. We travelled a mile or two along the banks, but finding it impossible to discover a crossing-place, we finally encamped in a little hollow of the prairie near the edge of the ravine. Here, finding that a large portion of our badly-cured meat was spoiling, we cooked what could still be eaten, and threw much of it away for the wolves and buzzards.

Younk Frank Combs and myself sought a comfortable lodging in a little sandy gulley, which had been formed by the washing of previous rains. A fine bed it was, too, for about an hour; but just as we commenced dozing we were startled by a tremendous thunder-storm. In three minutes we were wet through, and in five found that we were fairly floating, our rifles and saddles, the latter of which we used for pillows, being completely under water. We snatched our rifles from the swift-running stream, took up our bed, and walked to higher ground amid the terrible storm. We found means, however, to set fire to a large dry cedar, once more rolled up in our blankets, and after thinking of home and its thousand comforts, fell asleep. Yet never shall I forget the early part of that awful night. The lightning appeared to be playing about in the chasm far below us, bringing out, in wild relief, its bold and craggy sides. Deafening peals of thunder seemed rising from the very bowels of the earth, and then muttered away in the distance, rejoicing, as it were, at their escape from confinement. The yawning abyss appeared to be a workshop for the manufacture of the storm, and there we were at the very doors when the Ruler of the elements sent forth a specimen of his grandest, his sublimest work.

When morning came, which was bright and cloudless, we crawled out from under our wet blankets, and I doubt whether a more miserable, wo-begone set of unfortunates, in appearance, have been since the passage of the Red Sea. Not a man among us who was not as wet as though he had been towed astern of a steamer from the Falls of St. Anthony to the Balize, and without the privilege of going ashore at any of the "intermediate landings." Of my own personal appearance I can say nothing, as among our scanty stock of furniture there was no such luxury as a looking-glass; but the unshaven faces of my companions resembled, to use a threadbare comparison, the title-pages of so many distress memorials, and I cannot flatter myself into the belief that I differed from them in any material respect. Each individual hair upon our heads was sticking out almost anywhere, and to suit its own convenience; our broad-brimmed hats were cocked up, lopped down, and knocked into, or rather out of, all manner of shape and comeliness; our caps were mashed; our scanty and ragged vestments, full of sand and water, stuck close to our persons or hung heavily and drooping downward like weeping willows; and to sum all up, I verily believe that we could not have "passed muster" even in the ragged and renowned regiment promiscuously pressed into service by one Sir John Falstaff years before the Santa Fé expedition was thought of. Wretched and forlorn as we seemed, however, chilly and miserable as we felt after our soaking, good-humoured jokes were cracked at each other's expense, and every one was offering consolation and pity to his neighbour with an assumed sincerity and gravity that would have drawn a horse-laugh from Werter in his most sorrowful moments.

Unwilling to load our horses with wet and heavy blankets, we employed some two hours in spreading and drying them as much as possible. In the mean time, a scanty breakfast of half-cooked, half-dried beef was swallowed, our rifles were discharged, cleaned, and reloaded, and our powder examined to see that all was right. To keep his powder dry is the first thing the prairie traveller thinks of when a rain comes on, and fortunately we found that ours was all in good order, although it seemed almost a miracle that much of it was not spoiled.

The immense chasm we were upon ran nearly north and south, and by watching the current of the stream far below us—a furious torrent raised by the heavy rain—it was seen that it ran towards the former point. This induced Mr. Hunt to seek a crossing to the southward, and after saddling our horses we set off in that direction. We had gone but a few miles when large buffalo or Indian trails were seen, running in a southwest course, and as we travelled on, others were noticed bearing more to the west. We were obliged to keep out some distance from the ravine, to avoid the small gullies emptying into it, and to cut off the numerous turns, and in this way we travelled until about noon, when we struck a large trail running directly west. This we followed, and on reaching the main chasm found that it led to the only place where there was any chance of crossing. Here, too, we found that innumerable trails centered, coming from every direction; proof conclusive that we must cross here or travel many weary miles out of our way.

Dismounting from our animals, we looked at the yawning abyss before us, and the impression upon all was that the passage was impossible. That buffalo, mustangs, and very probably Indians with their horses had crossed here was evident enough, for a zigzag path had been worn down the rocky and precipitous sides; but many of our horses were unused to sliding down precipices as well as climbing them, and drew back repulsively on being led to the brink of the chasm. After many unsuccessful attempts, a mule was started down the path, then another was induced to follow, while some of the horses were fairly forced, by dint of much shouting and pushing, to attempt the descent. In some places they went along the very verge of rocky and crumbling ledges, where a false step would have precipitated them hundreds of feet to instant death; in others they were compelled to slide down pitches nearly perpendicular. Many of them were much bruised, but after an hour's hard work we all gained the bottom without sustaining any serious injury. Finding a small patch of grass in the low and secluded dell at the bottom of the abyss, we halted for an hour or two to rest our weary animals and to seek the trail leading up the steep on the opposite side. This was finally discovered, and after the greatest exertions suceeded in clambering to the top, where we once more found ourselves upon a smooth and level prairie. I shuddered, on looking back, to see the frightful chasm we had so successfully passed, and at the time thought it almost a miracle that we had got safely across; but a few days afterward I was convinced that in comparison the undertaking we had just accomplished was as nothing.

After giving our animals another rest we resumed our journey across the loan and dreary prairie. Not a tree or bush, and hardly a weed could be seen in any direction. A green carpetting of short grass, which even at this season was studded with innumerable strange flowers and plants, was spread over the vas expanse, with nought else to relieve the eye. People may talk of the solitude of our immense American forests, but there is a company even in trees that one misses upon the prairie. There is food for thought too, in the ocean wave, not to be found in the unchangeable face of these great Western wastes, and nowhere else does one feel that sickly sensation of loneliness with which he is impressed when nothing but a boundless prairie is around him. There he feels as if *in* the world, but not *of* it—there he finds no sign or trace to tell him that there is something beyond, that millions of human beings are living and moving upon the very earth on which he stands. Shakspeare was in the woods when he found

> "—— tongues in trees, books in the running brooks,
> Sermons in stones, and good in everything."

Had he been on the immense prairie I am now speaking about, he would have found no such companionship.

We rode briskly forward until near sundown, and then encamped by the side of a small water-hole—the basin formed by a hollow in the prairie. Although we were only two days out, the rations of many of the men were nearly gone by this time, so much of the meat had been spoiled from having been improperly cured. Not a buffalo could be seen on the prairie, nor was any fresh "sign" visible. The mustangs, too, had left this part of the plain, as also the deer and antelope, driven off, doubtless, by the scarcity of water. Had it not been for the showers which fell while travelling this dreary waste, we should all most certainly have perished; for even the immense canons had no other water in them than that which had fallen after we left the Quintufue.

Scarcely had we rolled ourselves up in our blankets before we were again visited by a heavy shower; but this time we had chosen higher ground, and though thoroughly drenched, we were not washed from our fastenings, as on the night before.

The morning of September 3rd broke bright and cloudless, the sun rising from out the prairie in all his majesty. Singular as it may appear, nearly every shower, from the time we left Austin until we reached the settlements of New Mexico, fell during the night, generally commencing shortly after sundown. Again we were compelled to lose some two hours in spreading and drying our clothes and blankets, after which we saddled our animals and pursued our weary journey. Our course, as I have already observed, was northwest, and we were now enabled to keep it without difficulty.

We had scarcely proceeded six miles, after drying our blankets, when we suddenly came upon another immense rent or chasm in the earth, exceeding in depth the one we had so much difficulty in crossing the day before. No one was aware of its existence until we were immediately upon its brink, when a spectacle, exceeding in grandeur anything we had previously beheld, came suddenly in view. Not a tree or bush, no outline whatever, marked its position or course, and we were all lost in amazement as one by one we left the double-file ranks and rode up to the verge of the yawning abyss.

In depth it could not be less than eight hundred or a thousand feet, was from three to five hundred yards in width, and at the point where we first struck it the sides were nearly perpendicular. A sickly sensation of dizziness was felt by all as we looked down, as it were, into the very depths of the earth. In the dark and narrow valley below, an occasional spot of green relieved the eye, and a small stream of water, now rising to the view, then sinking beneath some huge rock, was bubbling and foaming along. Immense walls, columns, and in some places what appeared to be arches, were seen standing, modelled by the wear of the water, undoubtedly, yet so perfect in form that we could with difficulty be brought to believe that the hand of man had not fashioned them. The rains of centuries, falling upon an immense prairie, had here found a reservoir, and their workings upon the different veins of earth and stone had formed these strange and fanciful shapes.

Before reaching the chasm we had crossed numerous large trails, leading a little more to the west than we were travelling; and the experience of the previous day led us to suppose that they all terminated at a common crossing near by. In this conjecture we were not disappointed, for a trot of half an hour brought us into a large road, the thoroughfare along which millions of Indians, buffalo, and mustangs had evidently travelled for years. Perilous as the descent appeared, we well knew there was no other near. The leading mule was again urged forward, the steadier and older horses were next driven over the sides, and the more skittish and untractable brought up the rear. Once in the narrow path, which led circuitously down the descent, there was no turning back, and our half-maddened animals finally reached the bottom in safety. Several large stones were loosened from their fastenings by our men, during the frightful descent; these would leap, dash, and thunder down the precipitous sides, and strike against the bottom far below us with a terrific and reverberating crash.

We found a running stream on reaching the lower level of the chasm, on the opposite side of which was a romantic dell covered with short grass, and a few scattering cotton-woods. A large body of Indians had encamped on this very spot but a few days previous, the wilted limbs of the trees and other "sign" showing that they had made it a resting-place. We, too, halted a couple of hours, to give our horses an opportunity to graze and rest themselves. The trail which led up on the opposite side was discovered a short distance above us, to the south, winding up the steep and ragged sides of the acclivity.

As we journeyed along this dell all were again struck with admiration at the strange and fanciful figures made by the washing of the waters during the rainy season. In some places perfect walls, formed of reddish clay, were seen standing, and were they anywhere else it would be impossible to believe that other than the hand of man had formed them. The veins of which these walls were composed were of even thickness, very hard, and ran perpendicularly; and when the softer sand which had surrounded them was washed away, the veins still remained standing upright, in some places a hundred feet high, and three or four hundred in length. Columns, too, were there, and such was their appearance of architectural order, and so much of chaste grandeur was there about them, that we were lost in wonder and admiration. Sometimes the breastworks, as of forts, would be plainly visible; then, again, the frowning turrets of some castle of the olden time. Cumbrous pillars of some mighty pile, such as is dedicated to religion or royalty, were scattered about; regularity was strangely mingled with disorder and ruin, and nature had done it all. Niagara has been considered one of her wildest freaks, but Niagara sinks into insignificance when compared with the wild grandeur of this awful chasm — this deep, abyssmal solitude as Carlyle would call it. Imagination carried us back to Thebes, to Palmyra, and to ancient Athens, and we could not help thinking that we were now among their ruins.

Our passage out of this place was effected with the greatest difficulty. We were obliged to carry our rifles, holsters, and saddlebags in our hands, and in clambering up a steep pitch, one of the horses, striking his shoulder against a projecting rock, was precipitated some fifteen or twenty feet directly upon his back. All thought he must be killed by the fall; but strangely enough, he rose immediately, shook himself, and a second effort in climbing proved more successful—the animal had not received the slightest apparent injury!

By the middle of the afternoon we were all safely across, after passing five or six hours completely shut out from the world. Again we found ourselves upon the level prairie, and on looking back, after proceeding some hundred yards, not a sign of the immense chasm was visible. The plain we were then upon was at least one hundred and fifty miles in width, and the two chasms I have mentioned were the reservoirs of the heavy body of rain which falls during the wet season, and at the same time its conductors to the running streams. The prairie is undoubtedly the largest in the world, and the canons are in perfect keeping with the size of the prairie. Whether the waters which run into them sink into the earth, or find their way to the Canadian, is a matter of uncertainty—but I am inclined to believe the latter to be the fact.

At sundown we halted by the side of a water-hole, and encamped for the night. Many of the men were now entirely out of provisions, while those who still had a little beef left had saved it by stinting themselves on the previous days. The worst of our sufferings had commenced.

At an early hour on the ensuing morning our march was continued, the cravings of hunger by this time being sensibly felt by all. Small droves of deer and antelope were seen during the day, brought from the water-courses doubtless by the recent rains, and towards night a drove of mustangs was descried upon a roll of the prairie half a mile a-head of us. They were all extremely shy, however, and although many rifles were discharged, not a shot was successful—we could not get near enough to kill one of them. Flocks of small birds, about the size of and in many respects resembling the blackbird, travelled with us much of this day's march, hovering along in front and rear of the line, and so exceedingly tame that they would light on our hats and arms, and on the necks and heads of our horses, without manifesting the least sign of fear. One or two of these singular birds were caught and killed, and found to be fat and of good flavour. That night we encamped near a water-hole, covering an area of some twenty acres, but very shallow. Flocks of large curlews, one of the finest birds that fly, were hovering and lighting about on all sides. Had

I been in possession of a double-barrelled gun with small shot I would have had at least one good meal, but I had only a heavy rifle, and went to my lodgings on the ground, supperless.

About two o'clock the next morning we saddled our horses and resumed the march, journeying still in a northwest course by the stars. On leaving the main camp on the Quintufue it was thought by all that we could not be more than a hundred miles from San Miguel—we had now more than made that distance, and were still upon the immense prairie. To relieve ourselves from the horrible suspense we were in, to get *somewhere,* in short, was our eager aim, and hurriedly we pressed onward, in hope of finding relief. Our horses, in the meantime, had comparatively suffered less than ourselves, for the grazing of the prairie had been good; but the hurried marches and the difficult crossings of the immense chasms now began to tell upon them.

At sunrise we halted near a small pond of water to rest the animals and allow them an hour to feed. Large white cranes were standing about in the pond, and flocks of ducks were swimming upon the surface. While we were lounging on the ground, a large antelope was seen slowly approaching us—now stopping, then walking a few steps nearer—evidently inquisitive as to who, or rather what we were. His curiosity finally cost him his life; for although Captain Sutton the evening before had given orders that not another shot should be fired without his consent, one of our men could not resist the temptation of bringing the antelope down. The man was arrested and sent to the rear for this disobedience of orders, but I have little doubt the excellent meal he made more than compensated for the disgrace. The order of Captain S. that no rifle should be discharged, was an excellent one, as many shots had been wasted on the previous day; but the best officer in existence cannot restrain a half-starved man when he sees a hearty meal directly within his grasp. A number of antelopes were seen in the neighbourhood of the water-hole, but no farther attempt was made to shoot them.

Shortly after this incident of killing the antelope we again resumed our journey. The same dreary spectacle, a boundless prairie, was before us—not a sign was observable that we were nearing its edge. We journeyed rapidly on until near the middle of the afternoon, when a dark spot was noticed some mile or mile and a half directly in advance. At first it was thought to be a low bush, but as we gradually approached it had more the appearance of a rock, although nothing of the kind had been seen from the time of our first coming upon the prairie, except at the chasms.

"A buffalo!" cried one of the men, whose keen eye had penetrated the mystery: "a buffalo lying down and asleep!"

A spyglass in our possession proved the man's assertion. Here, then, was a chance for at least as much as we could all eat, and the temptation was too strong to be resisted. The Leather Stocking of the party, Tom Hancock, was deputed to go forward on foot with a rifle, in the hope that he might at least get near enough to wound the animal, while myself and three of my companions, who were better mounted than the rest, made every preparation for a chase to the death.

Disencumbering our animals of every pound of superfluous weight, we tied handkerchiefs over our heads and prepared for a sport rendered doubly exciting by our starving condition. Each of my comrades had a pair of heavy belt pistols, and in addition one of Colt's revolving pistols, with a cylinder containing five shots. In my holsters I had a heavy Harper's Ferry dragoon-pistol, throwing a large ball with great force and accuracy, besides a bell muzzled affair which was loaded with two or three balls and some twenty-five or thirty buckshot. With this I intended at least to give the buffalo a broadside which would bleed him freely. To complete my armament, I also had one of Colt's pistols, which I had borrowed from one of the officers for the occasion.

Beyond where the animal was quietly lying, in a western direction, the prairie rose very gradually for a mile—farther than that we knew nothing of the nature of the ground. Tom Hancock could creep closer to the smooth prairie and make less show than any man in the command—knew all the advantages of taking the wind, and was conversant with every species of strategy by which to make his game certain—but he still thought it more prudent to give the animal a shot when within a hundred and fifty yards, than to run the risk of crawling nearer. He had desired us not to move unless the buffalo started, hoping to have another shot; we therefore sat quietly upon our horses to watch the effect of his first discharge.

The buffalo, evidently struck though but slightly wounded, bounded from the ground, stretched himself as does the tame bull on first rising, whisked his tufted tail right and left, looked slowly and inquiringly about him, and then lay down again upon the ground. We did not stir, and Hancock quietly reloaded his rifle without rising from the prairie. Another shot now followed, and this time the huge animal again bounded up and lashed his tail; but no sooner had he turned his head in our direction, and discovered his enemies, than he wheeled and started off towards the west at the usual heavy, lumbering gallop. He had evidently been hit by the second shot as well as the first, and this time the wound was probably more severe.

At an easy canter our little party now dashed off in pursuit, not putting our horses to their speed at first from fear of blowing them too early in a chase which we determined should last to the death. We kept on in company until we had neared the top of the first prairie roll; here finding my horse in much the best condition, I left my companions, and at an increased speed continued the pursuit. I have said that the praire was smooth; by this the reader, who has never seen one of those immense grassy plains, must not imagine an even, hard, and well-trod common, resembling the spot, may-hap, where in boyhood he has kicked football or joined in the many sports incidental to his earlier years; on the contrary, the smoothest of our Western prairies have an uneven surface, and are filled with the holes of the mole and the field-mouse. Through the slight thickness of earth which covers these holes the feet of the horse frequently sink; and unless he has been brought up and trained on the prairies, he can never be taught to run upon them with that confidence which developes his full powers. When pursued, the buffalo chooses the roughest road he can find, and leads his pursuers down break-neck precipices, or up rough and broken steeps, inaccessible to other feet than his. Clumsy as he really is, his headlong obstinacy frequently carries him through difficulties at which even the more active and well-trained steed recoils with terror, and which the latter might overcome with greater ease did he but dare attempt them. But to the chase.

On reaching the summit of the prairie roll, some little distance in advance of my companions, I discovered the buffalo still galloping heavily and clumsily along, about five hundred yards before me. The descent of the prairie was here so gradual that I could see every object at least five miles distant, and the surface was much smoother than I had anticipated. I now put spurs to my horse, and dashed boldly down the gentle slope. Giving one look behind, I saw that one of my companions at the starting-place, Major Howard, had given up the chase, or rather his horse had given up. Lieutenant Lubbock and one of the men, the latter mounted on a mule which, if he could not get over the ground particularly fast, had at least the commendable quality of running all day, were still in hot pursuit.

The prairie, as I have said, was comparatively smooth; and although I could not spur my horse into his full, free, and open stride, I was soon up with the huge animal, which was now at his utmost speed. Occasionally as if to rest his legs on one side, he would roll over on the other, changing from side to side as his weight would tire him. This roll of the body must have been noticed by all who have chased these animals, and is a peculiar gait which I believe belongs to the buffalo alone. The one I was chasing was a bull of the largest and most powerful frame, his bright glaring eyeballs peering out from his shaggy frontlet of hair, showing plainly that he was maddened by his wounds and the close pursuit. It was with the greatest difficulty, so terrible was his aspect, that I could get my horse within twenty yards of him, and when I fired my first charge at that distance the ball did not take effect.

As the chase continued my horse came to his work more kindly, and soon appeared to take an interest in the exciting race; yet I was still unable to lay him up directly alongside the buffalo. I could approach him closely in the rear, but the affrighted steed sheered as soon as he lapped the mountain of scraggy hair and flesh. Finding it impossible to gain the position I so much wished, I dropped a few yards behind; then, by dashing my spurs furiously in his sides, I was enabled to bring my horse to charge upon the buffalo's quarters. As I neared the animal I raised my pistol, and when about passing him, in a diagonal line, fired at less than four yards' distance. The now infuriated buffalo shrank as the ball took effect just back of the long hair on his shoulders. Under such headway was I when I discharged my pistol that I was compelled to cut across directly in front of him and close to his head, and when safely on the opposite or right side I reined up and once more dropped behind for another charge. Again I put spurs to their work, and, as I fairly flew by, gave the buffalo another wound directly in his side. He was now foaming with rage and pain. His eyes resembled two deep-red balls of fire—his tongue was out, and curling inwardly—while his long and tufted tail was either carried high aloft or lashed madly against his sides—a wild, and, at the same time, magnificent picture of desperation.

By this time my horse was almost completely subject to my guidance. He no longer pricked his ears with fear or sheered off as I approached the monster we were pursuing, but ran directly up so that I could almost touch the animal with my pistol. I had still two shots left in the repeater, and after discharging them I intended to fall back upon the old Harper's Ferry, and, by a well-directed shot, make a finish of the business.

After firing my third shot I again crossed the path of the buffalo, and so near that my right foot nearly touched his horns. The wound I had given caused him to spring suddenly forward, thus bringing me in too close a contact to be either pleasing or prudent. On coming up with him a fourth time, and so near that the muzzle of my pistol was not two yards from his side, the barrel dropped off just as I was about to pull the trigger. As I dashed by the infuriated animal he vainly endeavoured to gore and overthrow my horse by suddenly turning his head and springing at me.

The chase was now up, so far as I was concerned, for the pistol was a borrowed one, and very valuable. I had checked my horse and dismounted to search for it, when Lieutenant Lubbock came up. His horse was completely broken down, and unable to reach the buffalo—in the hurry and excitement I told him to mount mine immediately and continue the pursuit. Soon he was up with the buffalo. By this time, so kindly had the horse taken to his work, that his rider was able to fire every shot without once passing the wounded animal.

The latter stuck the horse once with his left horn, but did not hurt him seriously.

The other pursuer with the mule still continued the chase, and as the pace of the buffalo slackened from loss of blood and weariness, the former gradually crept up. I stopped to gaze upon the exciting scene. Every minute or two a flash and smoke would be seen, and then the sharp report of the pistol would reach the spot where I stood.

In this way the chase was continued until Lieutenant L. had discharged his own arms, together with my holster pistols. He then pulled up, and the other pursuer mounted my horse and continued the chase. I could not help pitying the noble animal, which had by this time run at least six miles. In a very short time the new pursuer was up with the buffalo, and again I could see the smoke as each pistol was discharged; but by this time the space between us was too great for me to hear the reports. I gazed until both the pursued and pursuer were mere black specks upon the prairie, and never turned my eyes until they were completely lost in the distance.

CHAPTER XII.

A successful Search.—The Buffalo brought to Bay.—Appearance of my Horse after the Chase.—Prospects of another Shower.—Adventure with a Rattlesnake in the Dark.—Fortunate Escape.—The Shower upon us.—Buffalo found in the Morning.—March resumed.—Swimming our Animals. — Singular Method of Cooking. — Wolves in our Vicinity. — Encounter with a Drove of Mustangs.—Excitement among us.—Mountains discovered a-head.—Leave the grand Prairie.—Singular Hills.—Compelled to abandon our Course.—Chances becoming Desperate.—Suffering and Starvation. — Large fresh-water Stream discovered.—Speculations as to its Name.—Mexican "Sign" seen.—More Remarks in relation to Red River.—Plum Patches.—Carlos and Brignoli seen.—Their Sufferings.—The Texans driven to the greatest strait for Food.—An Anecdote.—Compelled to eat broken-down Horse Flesh.—A cold, raw Night.—Fairly among the Rocky Mountains. —A beautiful Valley.—A Feast of Catfish.—Arrival at the Angosturas.—Encounter with a Party of Mexicans.—Unwonted Excitement.—Matias sent back to the Command.—Advance towards the Settlements.—Farther Sufferings of the Texans.—Meet with an immense Herd of Sheep.—A Feast.—Dissertation on Starvation.—Mexican Shepherds and their Dogs.

A SEARCH of brief duration enabled me to find the lost barrel of my pistol; and when this was accomplished I went back alone to seek the main body. After travelling a short distance, I met several of our men, who had previously been concealed by a slight roll of the prairie, and were now coming out, eager to learn our success. The last man who had taken up the pursuit of the buffalo with my horse was soon seen cantering back. Half an hour brought him up, when he informed us that after firing all his pistols he had brought the buffalo to bay, and that he had left him with the blood running from his mouth—a sure sign that he had received his death wound. I gave him Lieutenant Lubbock's horse, and with a small party he went back in search of the wounded buffalo.

I found my own horse completely white with foam, and much distressed after the long and exciting chase. Without mounting I trotted him briskly to the camp, distant about five miles, arrived there just at dark, and immediately commenced rubbing him violently with tufts of grass. Nobly had he sustained his part in our attempt to procure food, and I was anxious that he should not suffer after his severe, his killing, race. While thus engaged, the heavens became suddenly overcast and a distant roll of thunder warned me that we were to have another visitation of rain. I robbed myself of one of my blankets to favour the poor animal, strapped it tightly upon his back, and set out to stake him fast before the rain commenced. I had a *lariat* about his neck, some twenty yards long, and attached to the other end was an iron spike, which, when driven its full length into the earth, could not be drawn out by a horizontal pull. By this time it was pitchy dark, and while I was in the act of stooping to thrust the spike into the ground with my right hand, a rattlesnake, of large size, judging from the sound of his rattles, struck me a violent blow immediately above the elbow, but fortunately without breaking the skin. It is needless to say that I left horse and everything, and took the longest kind of steps out of the neighbourhood—my feelings I will not pretend to describe. By the remains of a fire, which had now nearly gone out, I ascertained that I had received no scratch. I was dressed in a course Attakapas, cottonade short jacket, under which I had a red flannel and a linen shirt. Through the folds of all these the fangs of the serpent had not penetrated, although at the time I should hardly have known it had the venomous reptile bitten my arm half off. I can conceive of nothing more startling than to find one's self suddenly in contact with a rattlesnake in the dark—the deadly sound of their alarm-notes is terrifying to a degree that sends the blood rushing to the heart, paralyzes the faculties, and strikes a cold tremour through the system with the suddenness of an electric shock.

The party who had gone out to look for the buffalo returned after dark, unsuccessful in their search. As the direction the animal had taken was well known, however, it was determined to send out a party early in the morning to hunt for him. We knew that he must be so badly wounded as to be past running; our hopes were that he had not died in the early part of the night and been devoured by wolves.

Frank Combs and myself were still bedfellows, doubling our scanty covering on the wet, cold nights, so as to render both more comfortable. I had now scarcely crawled under the blankets he had spread upon the ground before the heavy drops which precede a prairie shower began falling, and before I had well tucked and nestled myself in a comfortable position, a perfect avalanche of rain was pouring upon me. Every one of my readers who has taken a cold bath, must recollect the hesitation, the shrugs, the shiverings and the chills with which he first entered the water—the difficulty of making up his mind to essay the dreaded plunge when he knows full well it is to be made: so it is with a bivouac upon the prairie during a heavy thunder-shower. The unfortunate wight, who is destined to undergo a soaking, at first attempts to keep himself dry when his better sense teaches him that all efforts of the kind must prove unavailing. As the cold stream first penetrates his blankets, and trickles down his sides, he screws his body inward or outward to avoid the chilling current. Anon, another stream finds its way, then another, until finally he feels that farther attempts to stay the flood from without are useless, and he then stretches himself in as favourable a position as he can, and composes himself to that sleep which tired nature is sure to exact. The shower which fell, on the occasion to which I have just alluded, was among the heaviest of the heavy. The lightning lit up the prairie in every direction, and the darkness which succeeded each flash appeared to me of more than common blackness—thick and impenetrable—a wall of gloom. The wind, too, howled and moaned around us, and struck a cold chill through our scanty covering. Tired and faint, however, from want of food and the unusual fatigues of the day, wet and cold as I was, I soon fell asleep.

The next morning, while we were drying our blankets, a party went out in search of the buffalo, and with success. They found him badly wounded and unable to run, and a single well-directed ball completed at length our work of the previous evening. On taking off his hide, it was found that more than thirty balls had struck him. They were mostly small, however, and not one of them had touched a vital part, although he must have died during the day from the wounds. Every pound of his poor and tough flesh, for he was an old and lean bull, was brought into camp, and after it had been equally divided among the different messes, preparations were made for our immediate departure.

Our encampment was on the bank of a small ravine, bordered by a flank of low hackberry and other trees. It was almost the only place we had yet seen on the immense upper prairie where a sufficiency of wood could be found for cooking purposes, even had we been in possession of anything to cook; now that we had meat we were compelled by circumstances to continue the march, hungry, as wolves, and with the raw material for at least a full breakfast hanging at our saddle-skirts.

We had scarcely proceeded a mile before we encountered a narrow but deep gully, running nearly north and south, filled to the top with water. Having no certainty of finding a fording-place near, we dashed boldly in and swam safely across. The passage made, the journey was resumed, and briskly we scoured across the desolate prairie. We hurried rapidly on, with the hope that before nightfall we might discover either trees or bushes of some kind with which to cook our buffalo meat, but the sun went down, and with it all our prospects of having a well-dressed supper.

We gathered a few buffalo chips* — excellent fuel when dry, and universally used for cooking purposes by

* This is the name given by Western traders to the immense quantity of buffalo odour found scattered over the surface of the prairie. When dry and ignited it gives out a strong heat, emits little offensive smell and answers the purpose of a wood fire very well. The hunter throws his meat upon the coals, or places it upon his gunstick and holds it over the fire—in either case it is well cooked.

all travellers upon the lone prairies—but in the present instance they had been made damp by he heavy night-showers, and it was with the greatest difficulty that we could ignite them at all. We made out, however, to *warm* our meat a little—I will not say that it was *cooked* —and voraciously did I swallow several pounds of the tough, unsavoury food.

That night, and for the first time since we had struck the grand prairie, we were serenaded by a pack of wolves, which skulked and howled for hours within a few yards of our outposts. The "sign" was considered highly favourable, as these animals are seldom found far from woods or settlements. An old backwoodsman remarked that we should find Indians, white people, or an end to the prairie, the next day.

On the following morning we made an early start, the prairie before us still presenting the same lone and dreary appearance. We had travelled but a few miles when a drove of horses, numbering some seventy-five, was discovered a short distance to our left. They were near enough for us to see plainly that they were horses, and if wild ones that they were uncommonly tame, while many of our party asserted that they could see human beings among them, resting quietly upon the ground or moving about. Some even said that they could see mounted men in the extreme distance, as though driving in the *cavalladra*; at all events, the different surmises and assertions created an unwonted excitement among us. If our neighbours were only mustangs, it was an evidence that we were near the edge of the gloomy prairie, for those animals are seldom seen in large numbers far from mesquits and watercourses; if they were Indians, we might obtain some information from them, as they could hardly be Caygüas; and again, if they were Mexicans, and we really thought they were, then our journey might almost be considered at an end—we could obtain information of the nearest route to the settlements, and very likely a supply of provisions for our immediate use. Our main party halted and formed, while three or four of us set off with the intention of taking a closer look at our neighbours. We hoisted a flag of truce, and a sorry flag it was. I was the owner and possessor of a handkerchief which, in its better days, had been white. It was now a miserable whity brown; but at the same time it came nearer a peaceful colour than anything we had, and was accordingly hoisted upon a ramrod and held aloft. As we gradually approached, there appeared to be no little commotion among the animals—a running hither and thither, as is the custom with wild horses. We had noticed three or four white spots among them, which, in the distance, we had taken for flags; a nearer approach convinced some of us that these spots were young colts. With this impression we returned to the main body, but even up to this time I more than half believe that they were tame animals, and that human beings were moving among them. Had we proceeded a short half mile farther towards them all doubts would have been set at rest, and possibly wemight have saved ourselves many miles of weary travel and many hours of starvation.*

About the middle of the day, and some ten miles from

* We afterward met with a party of Mexicans who said that, while encamped, they had seen us upon the great prairie, and that from our actions they thought we were about to approach them. Perhaps this was the same party.

the place where we had seen the horses, the deep-blue tops of a range of mountains were discerned, which, as we journeyed on, soon more plainly developed themselves. It may be readily conceived that this was a joyful sight to all. We had now been seven days upon the prairie, averaging at least thirty miles a day, and many began to despair of ever getting off the dreary waste. There was now a prospect of a change, and any change, we then thought, would be for the better.

We continued on until near three o'clock, when suddenly a beautiful valley, studded here and there with a clump of trees, appeared in sight. To the north, in the distance, there was every appearance of a large stream of water, and that, in our fond anticipations, we put down as the long-sought-for Red River. A halt was called in a pleasant little grove of cotton-woods, through which a small stream of fresh water was gently purling, and here we built a large fire of wood from a dry and fallen tree, cooked what was left of our tough buffalo meat, and dried our wet blankets and clothing. Two hours were spent at this comfortable camping-ground, after which we mounted and pursued our uncertain journey. Unable to continue our old course, northwest, on account of deep and abrupt ravines to the northward, we travelled west this afternoon, through narrow valleys encircled by high, conical, and singularly-formed hills. At sundown we reached a small spring among these hills, where we bivouacked at once. During this night there was a panic and half stampede among our animals, caused, in the opinion of the guard, by the appearance of a small drove of mustangs on the steep hills which overlooked our encampment.

Resuming the march early on the following morning, we soon became entangled among high, steep, and rugged hills, the passage over which was almost impossible. Such was the nature of this singular piece of country that we were compelled, although reluctantly, to abandon entirely the course we had so long travelled, and seek an outlet from the hills in a direction south of west. We were all anxious to visit the river on our right, to note its general appearance, taste its waters, and form some opinion as to the probabilities of its being Red River; but as well might we have undertaken the task of climbing the largest cotton-wood upon its banks on horseback as that of cutting our way through the natural obstacles which intervened between us and the stream. But go on in some direction we must; and, as there was no alternative, we set off in a southwest course—the nearest point we could possibly make to what was considered the right one.

Even the country over which we were now compelled to travel, much as it threw us out of our course, was exceedingly rough, and for the sake of our poor horses at least, we wished ourselves back upon the smooth and open prairie. Many of their shoes were torn off by the rocks, and, unused to go without them, their feet became so tender and sore that they could not move without difficulty. To this should be added our own catalogue of misfortunes—travelling, day after day, while enduring the sharpest pangs of hunger, and in a state of harassing uncertainty as to our present situation, even more annoying than starvation—with all these hardships to undergo, the reader can easily imagine that our chances were becoming desperate. We saw numbers of antelope and deer during the day, and passed through one or two prairie dog towns situate deep in the narrow and secluded valleys; the animals were all so shy, however, that it was impossible to get a shot at them. The prairie dogs, in particular, appeared to shun us with more than their ordinary prudence—giving their short yelps of alarm before we were within half a mile of them, then tumbling hurriedly into their holes, and not once showing their heads so long as we were in sight. At night we encamped at another spring among the hills, without having tasted food since our scanty meal of buffalo meat on the preceding day. We tightened our belts by taking up still another hole—a great relief when suffering from want of food—and then threw ourselves upon the ground to seek forgetfulness in sleep.

We made another early start on the following morning, winding our way among rough and steep hills, and slowly nearing the chain of mountains west of us. About the middle of the afternoon—it was the 8th of September; I can never forget the date—we got clear of the hills, and entered a narrow but fertile valley running nearly east and west. A light fringing of trees in advance convinced us that the valley was watered by a stream larger than any we had recently met with, and with excited feelings we pressed our jaded animals forward. Our anticipations of finding a fresh-water stream were more than realized—we came suddenly upon the banks of a beautiful river of most delicious water, running over a bed of yellow sand, and so low that we forded it with ease. In the vicinity we found stumps of trees which had evidently been cut down by Mexicans. Remnants of old cart-standards and wheels were also discovered: proof conclusive that the place had been visited by other than Indians. With gladdened hearts we scanned these evidences of civilization, and even the keen cravings of hunger were for the moment forgotten in the anticipations of soon reaching the settlements.

All was now inquiry and speculation as to the name of the stream we were upon. Some of our men, and they the wisest, too, contended that we had either crossed or headed Red River, and that we were now upon one of the southern forks of the Canadian. Others, again, said that if there was any such stream as Red River above the lower or middle priaries, this must be it, although its waters were entirely dissimilar in all respects to what existed in our received opinions as the general features and appearance of that stream. Then there were two or three men among us, old trappers and traders who had visited Santa Fé by way of St. Louis, who said that we were upon the Mora, and but a few miles from San Miguel. Of course, nothing certain can be known; but the more probable conjecture is, that we were now upon the waters of the Arkansas, and that we had headed the Red River of the United States. This cuts off some two or three hundred miles from the length of the latter stream, as laid down upon a majority of maps; but I am inclined to believe that it deserves this abbreviation.

If the Red River of the United States rises in the Rocky Mountains—the reader will bear in mind that I say *if*—how and where does it make its descent, from the high table-lands which form the base of those eminences, to the prairies beneath the main western steppe?

The descent can hardly be gradual, but on the contrary, the stream must tumble, in some places, hundreds of feet down the eminences which the traveller is obliged to ascend as he journeys westward from the Cross Timbers. These steppes grow higher and more abrupt, as they extend to the south, after leaving the valleys of the Canadian and Arkansas; in fact, I do not know that they extend north of the southern fork of the Canadian at all.

The New Mexicans have a Red River, rising in the mountains north of Santa Fé, but this is known to be but a branch of the Canadian. Farther south rises the Mora; this is another stream finding its way to the Canadian, and at this, although by this time the name may have been changed, I have little doubt we had now arrived. Its waters are as unlike those of the Red River as are those of the Croton unlike the Mississippi. A majority of the map-makers, by joining the Red River as far as known with some one of the rivers rising in the Rocky Mountains, have made a long and very pretty stream, as seen upon their charts: were they to journey along the line of their imaginary river, with the hope of finding the water they have traced, I am inclined to believe they would suffer much from thirst before they had crossed the boundless prairie spreading eastward from the outer spurs of the Rocky Mountains.

Not to tire my reader much farther with speculations in relation to Red River, I will here state my belief that it takes its rise at the base of the high steppe I have so often alluded to, and but a few miles north of the head waters of the Brazos and Colorado of Texas. On its southern side it receives the waters of the Quintufue and Palo Duro, rising from the sides of the high steppe,* with other short but wide streams, which in spring contain much water. We crossed them during the dry season, and at a time when their beds contained but little, and that brackish and standing in sluggish pools. Southeast of the steppe, at a distance of perhaps seventy-five miles, rises the Wichita, which, after running a course a little north of east, empties into the Red River some fifty or seventy miles west of the Cross Timbers. It may be recollected that in a previous chapter, and prior to the daparture of Carlos, we had noticed a large stream south of the Wichita, and running nearly parallel; that was undoubtedly the red fork of the Brazos.

It is certainly not a little amusing to examine the Red River of the different maps, and trace its most singular windings. On several of the maps now before me, I see that it rises north of Santa Fé, near latitude 38° north, and in longitude varying from 104 to 106° west of Greenwich. On one of these maps its general course, for some five hundred miles, is southwest; on another it only runs some three hundred in that direction, and then strikes off across the prairies north of east. The most correctly-laid-down course of the stream on any of the charts I have examined, may be found on Tanner's map of Mexico; but there it is somewhat too long, although the general eastern course he has given it is in the main correct. But I must leave speculation and return to the watercourse we had by this time reached.

* The Mexicans, who started with Albert Pike in his journey across the prairies, spoke of this steppe, and gave the name of *Las Cejas*, or the Eyebrows, to the singular range. Mr. P. appears to have passed to the south of the steppe, his Mexican companions returning before he reached the Brazos.

Our little party remained some half hour upon the banks of the stream, considering which route to pursue. The general course of the river, as I have before stated, was a little north of east, and to follow it up was finally decided upon. We proceeded along its northern banks, as that side afforded the best travelling, until dark, when we encamped in a corpse of cotton-woods. A dreary, rainy night, was followed by a day so cloudy that we could not steer a course; yet there was the river acting as guide, and we followed it. At times we were close in upon the narrow but fertile valley which skirted its borders; at others, some long bend in the stream would throw us out upon a succession of low, barren sand-hills, with little other vegetation gracing their sides than dwarf thorn, prickly pear, or plum bushes. The latter were not more than eighteen inches high, yet they appeared to thrive luxuriantly in the sand, and when we were among them they were loaded with plums of the largest size, and such as were ripe were of delicious flavour. Ripe or unripe, however, the bushes were stripped by our famished men, the fruit filling their stomachs for the time, but yielding no real nourishment. Some of the half-dried plums we found in the sand tasted like prunes. During the day we also found large quantities of small but well-flavoured grapes, which were devoured with an avidity that told our suffering. It was on this day that our runaway guide, Carlos, was seen by two of our men, who where out some distance from the main body in search of plums. He was still in company with the Italian, Brignoli, and both said that they had been lost, and half starved from the hour when they left us, at the same time begging earnestly for provisions. Their worn and haggard aspect told more forcibly than words that they had endured suffering the most intense. As they promised to come into our camp at night, our men left them without asking many questions, but they never came. Carlos probably feared that we might shoot him, and for that reason kept out of our way. Had any of our horses been in condition, the fugitives would probably have been pursued, and brought in—as it was, we saw no more of them until after we were taken prisoners.

From after circumstances I have little doubt that Carlos now knew where he was, but he was undoubtedly ignorant on that point and lost at the time when he left us. The fellow has trapped up and down the innumerable watercourses of the lower prairies without knowing the name of one of them, else how could he direct our men to plum-patches and springs a long distance in advance, and invariably with accuracy? On arrriving at the stream of fresh water which he called the Utau, he doubtless saw signs and landmarks closely resembling the features of a stream called by that name which really exists but a few days' ride from Santa Fé. As he guided us onward, in the course of some three or four days he found that he had not only deceived himself, but the command, and his fear of punishment induced him to leave us at the earliest opportunity that offered.

On the 10th of September, the day following that on which our whilom guide had been seen, we found what appeared to be an old cart road, and also a deserted Mexican camp. The road we followed until it was lost upon a sandy prairie destitute of vegetation. This day, three mountains were discovered in a southwest direction, and some fifteen miles distant, which bore the strongest resemblance to the description Carlos had often given us of *The Crows.* It seemed, too, as though we could discover a passage through the chain of smaller hills north of them--an opening resembling the *Angosturas* I have often before mentioned—but we had been so often deceived that few of us could now anticipate any such good fortune.

In the mean time, our men were driven nearly to desperation by hunger. Little or no order could be preserved by the officers, the volunteers scattering about in every direction, hunting for plums, grapes, and such game as might fall in their way. Few deer or antelope were seen, and they were so shy that it was impossible to shoot them; but in place of them every tortoise and snake, every living and creeping thing was seized upon and swallowed by our famished men with a rapacity that nothing but the direst hunger could induce. Occasionally a skunk or polecat would reward some one more fortunate than the rest; but seven out of every ten of us were compelled to journey on without a morsel of anything to appease our sufferings.

One amusing little anecdote I will here relate, to show, in the first place, the direful straits to which our men were driven, and in the second to give my readers an insight into the trickery of old campaigners. We had reached a camping-ground late one evening, where a sufficiency of wood was found to kindle good, substantial fires. While a knot of us were reclining around one of the fires, speculating as to our prospects, a youngster brought in a spotted-backed land tortoise, alive and kicking, which he had been fortunate enough to find upon the prairie. Throwing it upon the ground, and placing the end of his rifle upon the back of the animal to prevent its crawling off, he next asked an old hunter how to cook his prize. The answer was, that he must open the coals and throw the tortoise in, cover it over and allow it to remain for at least half an hour in the fire—a longer time would only serve to make the repast more savoury.

No sooner said than done; for in less than a minute the unfortunate tortoise was roasting alive beneath a bushel of coals. The countenance of the young man was lit with joy in anticipation of a meal, which, although at any other time it would have been revolting, he now coveted with that longing which starvation only can create. But it was a meal he was not destined to enjoy. The old campaigner, after telling him three or four times that his supper was not cooked, finally found means to withdraw the youngster's attention from the coals, and then to whip the animal out with his iron ramrod was but the work of a moment. Another moment, and the well-roasted terrapin was safe behind the back of the more elderly ranger, and where the younster could not see it.

"Don't you think he's nearly done?" inquired the latter, now turning his head and looking wistfully at the fast-expiring bed of coals.

"Pretty well cooked by this time—you can take him out," retorted the old borderer, while he quietly watched the first speaker as he eagerly raked open the embers.

The movements of the youngster, as he first commenced opening the coals, were slow and decided: by-and-by, as he neared the bottom of the mouldering heap, his action grew excited and hurried. The expression of his countenance may be easier imagined than described, as, after having dug to the hard ground itself, he turned to the author of his misfortune, and, in utter ignorance of the trick, exclaimed, "*He's gone!*"

"Gone!" slowly repeated the veteran borderer: "was he alive when you threw him in the fire?"

"Certainly—why?"

"*Why!*"

"Yes, *why?*"

"Because," continued the ranger, "you must have thought the terrapin mightily troubled with the simples if you supposed he would stay in the fire and be roasted alive, when he could easily crawl out and make tracks off!"

Gloomily the youngster dragged himself to his blanket supperless, while the old trickster quietly wended his way to a neighbouring fire to pick the scanty meat from his ill-got prize, and chuckle at his success in "doing" the green-horn out of his supper. To return to my narrative.

The road we had found and followed some distance in the morning we hunted for in vain in the afternoon: all the old wheel-marks had lost themselves in a barren, gravelly prairie. That we must find a passage through or over the mountains before us was considered certain, but where that passage was, no one could imagine. We were far from being aware of it at the time, but they proved to be outer and eastern spurs of the Rocky Mountains. As the sun gradually sank behind their lofty and ragged summits, a raw, chill breeze sprang up from their neighbourhood. It was the first cold weather we had experienced, and in our weak and exhausted condition the biting wind seemed to pierce directly through us.

We continued our march until we reached the dry bed of a mountain stream, upon the banks of which we encamped for the night. A flock of wild turkeys had taken shelter under the banks, running off as we approached their roost. Although contrary to strict orders, nothing could restrain our men from banging and blazing away at the turkeys as they sped across the prairie—fifty rifles and muskets being discharged at them before they were out of sight. Two or three only were killed by the volly and running fire which ensued, and they were but half grown, and so extremely poor that they did not furnish a meal for half-a-dozen men. To go farther without *something* to eat was now deemed impossible—the wild and haggard expression, the sunken eyes, and sallow, fleshless faces of the men too plainly showed that some means of sustenance must be speedily provided. A horse formerly belonging to Howland, which in the early part of the campaign had been one of the best animals in the command, was now found to be so poor and badly broken down that it was resolved to shoot him and divide his flesh among the different messes. As they led the once proud and gallant animal to execution, the words of an old nursery song came fresh to my mind—one that I had neither heard nor thought of for many, many years. The burden of the ballad was,

"Poor old horse! he must die!"

and I have only mentioned the circumstance to illustrate the well-known eccentricities of memory. A man is often placed in situations and becomes a witness of scenes which suddenly awaken and bring back the long-forgotten associations of his childhood.

But to return to the actual. The horse was killed, and in less time than it takes me to tell it his hide was off and his flesh distributed. I have before said that the flesh of a young mustang is excellent—but that of an old, broken-down horse is quite another affair. It was tough as India-rubber, and the more a piece of it was masticated the larger it became in the mouth. Poor as it was, however, and hard to swallow, I am confident that many a man in the party ate four or five pounds of it, half cooked and without salt—I know that I devoured my share. That I lost some of the good opinion I entertained of myself while eating this food I will not pretend to deny, and even a buzzard, that sat perched upon a dry limb of a cotton-wood overhead, appeared to look down upon us reproachfully as he saw us appropriating food that legitimately belonged to him. There was something, too, like honest indignation expressed in the countenance of a wolf, which sat quietly watching our operations from the adjoining prairie; but at the time we were hungry enough to make a meal even of him had he fallen into our hands. A man never knows what he will eat until driven by a week's starvation.

Our tough and most unsavoury meal over, we spread our blankets in the ravine, where we could be partially protected from the biting northeast wind; but the cutting blasts found their way through our scanty covering, chilling our weakened frames to such a degree as almost entirely to prevent sleep. With the ordinary stock of flesh and blood we should have been far better able to withstand the bitter wind; as it was, we could only shrug and shake, and pass a sleepless night.

Weak and unrefreshed, we arose in the morning—breakfastless and desponding, we mounted our horses, and once more resumed our gloomy march. Our course was southwest, and in the direction of what appeared to be a passage through the mountains; but after travelling some six or eight miles we found our farther progress cut off by high and precipitous ascents. To return was our only alternative, and at noon we again found ourselves near the point whence we had started in the morning.

A consultation was now held as to our future course. Running directly north was a high chain of mountains, extending as far as the eye could reach, and many contended that our best course would be to travel along the base of this chain until we either found a passage through or met with the trail of the St. Louis traders. Others, again, thought our wisest and safest plan would be to attempt crossing directly over the mountains where we then were, laborious as was the prospect. The latter party prevailed, and the attempt to cross was immediately made.

After incredible fatigue to both horses and men, for we were obliged to dismount and carry our arms and baggage in our hands, the ascent was finally achieved. Arrived at the summit, a beautiful prospect was before us. Below, a peaceful and lovely valley was spread out, through the centre of which the large stream we had left the previous day wound along. Innumerable brooks, taking their rise in the mountains around, meandered through this valley, and finally found their way to the larger stream. Their immediate borders were fringed with small trees and bushes of the deepest green, while the banks of the river were skirted with a narrow belt of timber of larger and more luxuriant growth.

The valley was hemmed in on all sides by mountains, whose frowning and precipitous fronts appeared to offer impassable barriers against all approach to the tranquil and beautiful scene lying far below us. At another time these ragged and dangerous steeps might have stayed our farther advance; but now, after allowing our poor and foot-sore animals a short rest, we drove them down, and in less than an hour found ourselves safe in the valley. It was now discovered that two of our men were missing, unable, probably, from their own weakness and the jaded condition of their horses, to keep up with the main body. We could only hope that they might be able to follow our trail, and overtake us at our encampment—it was impossible, so weak and lame were all our horses, to go back in search of them.

On reaching the timber of the river banks we immediately encamped, and turned our animals loose to graze and rest themselves after their fatiguing mountain march. The river was found to abound with catfish, and as we had several hooks and lines with us, a sufficient number were caught to give us all a meal. I should perhaps call it a feast; for even without salt or seasoning of any kind, many of our men ate pound after pound of the coarse fish with a relish which a gouty alderman might covet, but could never enjoy over the best bowl of turtle soup the ingenuity of man ever compounded.

Sunset in this secluded valley presented a scene of almost unrivalled magnificence, as well as of mild and heavenly beauty. The tops of the surrounding mountains, upon which the blue vault of heaven seemed to rest, were gilded by the sun's last and most brilliant rays, while the deep-black shadows, as some beam of sunlight would dance around and kiss for the last time a more towering summit, would course hurriedly down the frowning mountain sides, as if to find their homes in the depths below ere darkness assumed her sway. A soothing, an etherial quiet reigned throughout the valley, broken only by the evening hymn of some turtle-dove, avowing anew her constancy to her mate, or by the last bark of the squirrel, as, with light and buoyant leaps, he wended his way from the river to his nest among the mountain cliffs. By-and-by a brood of wild turkeys, which had been hunting for their supper at the base of the rocky steeps, flew over our heads, and sought their roost in a large cotton-wood which overhung the river. The sharp crack of a rifle soon announced the doom of one of the flock, while the report, taken up by a thousand echoes, reverberated from grot and glen, from steep hillside and quiet dell, until lost to the ear in distance. Night had thrown her sable mantle, alike over the valley and the recently-gilded mountain tops, before I could turn from the contemplation of the lovely scene.

Early the next morning, Mr. Hunt, our guide, set off, in company with Captain Sutton, in search of a passage through the mountains, which would lead us along the river banks. They returned in two or three hours with the joyful intelligence that they had discovered an excellent route in a western direction, one which would extricate us from our present dilemma without much labour. To saddle and mount our horses was a work of but few moments, and then, with hearts much lightened, we resumed the journey.

After crossing the river, and emerging from the timber which lined its banks, we entered a narrow but open valley that had been concealed from view by a projecting point of one of the mountains. Two hours' ride brought us into a road which had evidently been used for carts, as we found yoke-keys, standards, and other trappings belonging to a Mexican vehicle, scattered along its sides. On either hand, the frowning and rocky sides of mountains rose high above us, and we now knew and felt that we were in the *Angosturas,* or Narrows of the river so often spoken of by Carlos, where the stream has forced its passage through the eastern spur of the Rocky Mountains. Well do these mountains deserve their name, for they are nothing but immense heaps of stones, irregularly piled up, while but little vegetation is to be found upon their sides save a few stunted pines and cedars.

For three or four miles, after first entering the Angosturas, our road was along a solid ledge of rocks, the river on our right, and running nearly east and west. The greatest width of the pass through which the stream runs, until the traveller leaves the rocky road, cannot be more than half a mile, while the towering fronts of the mountains on either side are so steep that even a goat would find much difficulty in climbing them. On leaving the ledge of rocks the pass grows gradually wider, and the road becomes sandy. We had no sooner struck the latter than the tracks of mules and asses were plainly visible. A little farther on, the footprints of men were also seen, and from every appearance they had been made but a few hours. Not a sign of a human habitation had we discovered, either in the beautiful valley where we had spent the previous night, or along the road we were now travelling, but that we had at length reached an open highway and were close upon a party of Mexicans was evident enough.

With feelings the most joyful we now spurred our animals briskly forward. The sagacious brutes themselves seemed to know that they were near the end of their long and tiresome journey, for they pricked up their ears and willingly responded to our call upon them for a faster pace. Gradually the Narrows became wider, the road grew smoother, and just as the sun was losing itself behind the western mountains we came up with the Mexicans, encamped at the mouth of the gorge at which the river enter the Angosturas. As Carlos had always told us, the river at this point turns immediately north, watering a narrow and fertile valley.

Those of my readers who have ever made a long sea voyage may remember how eagerly, at the approach of its termination, when the pilot first placed his foot upon deck, they crowded around and pressed him with idle questions innumerable: so with us, in coming up with these strangers. Every one among us, who could speak a word of Spanish, earnestly showered upon the ragged, swarthy, and half-frightened Mexicans volumes of interrogations, without giving them time to answer one of them, even had they been able or willing. The fellows were just returning, with a small drove of broken-down mules and donkeys, from a trading trip of some two months' duration among the Caygüas and Camanches. They frankly told us, as soon as we gave them time to breathe and collect the little scattering sense they had, that they had seen us early in the morning, and that such of their companions as were better mounted had instantly fled, in fear that we might rob them.

In answer to the question as to the state of feeling in New Mexico regarding our approach, they could give us no information—upon this point they knew nothing. They had been absent months from the settlements, and were trading with the Caygüas when the unfortunate Hull and his party were killed, although they had no part or lot in that massacre. They also told us that they were in the main camp of the Indians when the murdering party returned, bringing the dead bodies of eleven of their warriors, among whom was a principal chief. The ceremonies and performances on the occasion—the wild dances of the warriors around the scalps of their victims, with the painful penance of the women in token of their grief for the loss of the warriors of the tribe—were described by our new acquaintances with graphic effect. The women smote and cut their breasts, and ran naked through thorns and prickly pear-bushes, to show the intensity of their affection.

We next asked the Mexicans the distance to the Palo Duro, or rather to the spot where our main body with the waggons were encamped. They said that a good mule could travel the distance easily in four days. Upon our telling them the route we had taken, and that we had been thirteen days on the road, they expressed the greatest astonishment—said it was wonderful that we had been able to cross the immense chasms and mountains at all. They said that if we had taken a course directly west, on starting, we should have avoided the deep canons altogether, and had a good smooth road the whole distance. In addition, they informed us that Carlos and his companion had passed them in the morning, completely worn down by hunger and fatigue. By this it would seem that the runaway guide had taken a course too much to the north, and fallen into the same errors which had caused us so much trouble.

As regards provisions, the Mexicans were almost as badly off as ourselves, their stock being nearly exhausted. They gave the mess to which I was attached, however, a small quantity of barley meal; just enough for a taste, and that was all. They said that San Miguel was still some seventy or eighty miles distant, but before reaching it we should fall in with large herds of sheep, and also the little village of Anton Chico. At the latter place we could procure *tortillas* and *atole*; the former a species of thin cake in universal use throughout Mexico, and the latter a thin mush, made of meal and water or cow's or goat's milk, and also a standing dish of the country. Anything, but more especially any preparation of meal or flour, would have been as welcome to us as manna was to the suffering Israelites in the wilderness.

The next morning, three of the Mexicans were hired to go back to our companions, one of our Mexican servants, Matias, disguised completely, so that he might not be suspected by any Indians they should meet on the route, accompanyng them. They were provided with the best and least jaded mules we had, and took with them a package of letters to General M'Leod.

The purport of those letters was, that we had arrived within two or three days' ride of the settlements, and that the best course the command could pursue would be to march immediately, under direction of the guides, towards San Miguel. The Mexicans, after receiving full instructions from Colonel Cooke and Doctor Brenham, set out on their journey across the immense prairie, and, as we afterward learned, were less than four days in going a distance which had occupied us thirteen!

Shortly after Matias and his three companions had left us we resumed our march towards San Miguel. Not a morsel of food did we have during the day, and at night we encamped, supperless, on the banks of a small creek emptying into the Rio Mora. On this stream the Mexicans, who had thus far accompanied us, had their places of residence. After giving us instructions for our route towards San Miguel, they left us on the ensuing morning for their homes in the mountains.

Before we set out, our commander despatched four of our best mounted men in advance to make arrangements for provisions, while the rest of us followed as fast as our weary animals could travel. As we neared the point where we knew that food could be procured in abundance, not only our hunger, but our impatience increased. During the day, I was fortunate enough, in company with the madcap Fitzgerald, to find half a hatful of wild parsley, and this we swallowed raw with the greatest avidity.

About the middle of the afternoon, one of the four who had been sent forward returned with the joyful intelligence that they had fallen in with a herd of no less than seventeen thousand sheep, and had succeeded in purchasing a sufficiency for the whole command. Again we put spurs to our horses, and a ride of half an hour brought us up with the shepherds and their charge, and to a fine camping-ground on the Rio Gallinas.

Here a scene of feasting ensued which beggars description. We had been thirteen days upon the road, with really not provisions enough for three, and now that there was an abundance our starving men at once abandoned themselves to eating—perhaps I should rather call it gormandizing or stuffing. No less than twenty large, fat sheep had been purchased and dressed, and every ramrod, as well as every stick that could be found, was soon graced with smoking ribs and shoulders, livers and hearts. Many made themselves sick by overeating; but an attempt to restrain the appetites of half-starved men, except by main force, would be the very extreme of folly. Had the food been anything but mutton, and had we not procured an ample supply of salt from the Mexicans to season it, our men might have died of the surfeit.

I have never yet seen a treatise or dissertation upon starving to death—I can speak *feelingly* of nearly every stage except the last. For the first two days through which a strong and healthy man is doomed to exist upon nothing, his sufferings are, perhaps, more acute than in the remaining stages—he feels an inordinate, unappeasable craving at the stomach, night and day. The mind runs upon beef, bread, and other substantials; but still, in a great measure, the body retains its strength. On the third and fourth days, but especially on the fourth, this incessant craving gives place to a sinking and weakness of the stomach, accompanied by nausea. The unfortunate sufferer still desires food, but with loss of strength he loses that eager craving which is felt in the earlier stages. Should he chance to obtain a morsel or two of food, as was occasionally the case with us, he swallows it with a wolfish avidity; but five minutes afterward his sufferings are more intense than ever. He feels as if he had swallowed a living lobster, which is clawing and feeding upon the very foundation of his existence. On the fifth day his cheeks suddenly appear hollow and sunken, his body atenuated, his colour an ashy pale, and his eye wild, glassy, cannibalish. The different parts of the system now war with each other. The stomach calls upon the legs to go with it in quest of food: the legs, from very weakness, refuse. The sixth day brings with it increased suffering, although the pangs of hunger are lost in an overpowering langour and sickness. The head becomes giddy—the ghosts of well-remembered dinners pass in hideous procession through the mind. The seventh day comes, bringing increased lacitude and farther prostration of strength. The arms hang listlessly, the legs drag heavily. The desire for food is still left, to a degree, but it must be brought, not sought. The miserable remnant of life which still hangs to the sufferer is a burden almost too grievous to be borne; yet his inherent love of existence induces a desire still to preserve it, if it can be saved without a tax upon bodily exertion. The mind wanders. At one moment he thinks his weary limbs cannot sustain him a mile—the next he is endowed with unnatural strength, and if there be a certainty of relief before him, dashes bravely and strongly onward, wondering whence proceeds this new and sudden impulse.

Farther than this my experience runneth not. The reader may think I have drawn a fancy sketch—that I have coloured the picture too highly; now, while I sincerely trust he may never be in a situation to test its truth from actual experience, I would in all sober seriousness say to him, that many of the sensations I have just described I have myself experienced, and so did the ninety-and-eight persons who were with me from the time when we first entered the grand prairie until we reached the flock of sheep, to which more pleasing subject I will now return.

There were very few men with the immense herd, but in their stead were a large number of noble dogs, which appeared to be peculiarly gifted with the faculty of keeping them together. There was no running about, no barking or biting in their system of tactics; on the contrary, they were continually walking up and down, like faithful sentinels, on the outer side of the flock, and should any sheep chance to stray from his fellows, the dog on duty at that particular post would walk gently up, take him carefully by the ear, and lead him back to the fold. Not the least fear did the sheep manifest at the approach of these dogs; and there was no occasion for it. They appeared to me to be of mongrel breed, somewhat resembling, perhaps, a cross of the Newfoundland or St. Bernard species, with the larger mastiff. They possessed mild, frank, and open countenances, were indefatigable in protecting their charge from wolves, and from what I could learn were extremely sagacious.

The shepherds had crooks in their hands, instruments I had often read of in poets' lays. The uses to which they were put took away much of the romance I had associated with crooks and gentle shepherds. One of the latter, whenever a sheep has been pointed out in the flock, either to be killed or for sale, thrusts the long-hooked stick immediately under the throat of the victim, and holds it fast until its fellows have been driven past on either side. The sheep is then secured by grappling its wool with the hand—an operation, from first to last partaking more of the practical than of the poetic.

Now that we had found provisions in plenty, we considered the dangers, the fatigues, the delays, and the vexations of the march as over, and bright were the anticipations of the future. Every face was animated with joy, every heart was filled with gladness. How different would have been our feelings had we known the sufferings and privations, the indignities, and the cruel maltreatment we were yet to endure—the terrible fate that was awaiting us!

CHAPTER XIII.

Farther Feasting.—Party sent to the Settlements.—Author accompanies it.—Objects of sending the party a-head.—News respecting Howland and his Companions.—Encounter with Mexican Muleteers.—Their fright at our approach.—Farther information in relation to Howland.—Manuel sent back. — Suspicious horsemen seen. — Arrival at Anton Chico. — Consternation of the inhabitants. — Scanty raiment of the women.—Confidence restored.—Description of Anton Chico.—Scantiness of the Furniture.—A Dinner under Cover.—Start for San Miguel.—Compelled to return.—A night at Anton Chico.—Bad Colds, with worse Coughs to match.—A suspicious Visiter.—Report that we were to be arrested.—Start again from Anton Chico.—Valuables concealed.—Arrival at Cuesta.—Commotion in the village.—Our Party surrounded by Mexican Troops.—Apparent Frankness of their Leader, Dimasio Salazar.—Our Arms taken from us.—Consultation of Salazar and his Officers.—We are formed in Line and searched.—Mexican Duplicity.—A trying Scene.—Prompt Interference of Behil in saving our Lives.—We are marched towards San Miguel.—Kindness of the Women.—Don Jesus, and his attempt to tie us.—Description of our Guard.—Puertecito.—More of the Women.—Arrival at San Miguel.—Meanness of the Alcalde and Kindness of the Priest.—Our first Night in Prison.

THE morning after our feast we made another hearty meal of broiled mutton, with *atole con leche,* a mush compounded of flour and goats' milk. The Mexican shepherds, finding the Texans excellent customers, and disposed to pay the highest prices for anything in the shape of bread, had sent to their *rancho,* or farm, during the night, a distance of some twelve miles, and supplied themselves abundantly with flour.

It was now determined, by our principal officers, to

send two men forward to the frontier town of San Miguel, for the purpose of conferring with the authorities. W. P. Lewis, captain of the artillery company, and George Van Ness, secretary of the commissioners, were detailed for this service. Both could speak Spanish, and the former enjoyed in every way the confidence of Colonel Cooke, who had often befriended him. In addition to verbal instructions, the young men were intrusted with letters to the *alcalde*, or principal officer of San Miguel, and both the instructions and letters set forth that a large trading party of Texans was now approaching, that their intention were in every way pacific, and that the leaders of the advance party were anxious to purchase a large quantity of provisions to be sent back to the main command. Several of General Lamar's proclamations were also given to Mr. Van Ness, to be distributed among the principal citizens, the purport of which was that the expedition was sent for the purpose of trading, and that if the inhabitants of New Mexico were not disposed to join, peacefully, the Texan standard, the expedition was to retire immediately. These proclamations were printed in both Spanish and English, and not a doubt existed that the liberal terms offered would be at once acceded to by a population living within the limits of Texas, and who had long been groaning under a misrule the most tyrannical.

At the request of Colonel Cooke and Dr. Brenham, two of the principal merchants, Major Howard, and Mr. Fitzgerald, accompanied Lewis and Van Ness, and as I was in great haste to prosecute my journey through Mexico, I gathered all my effects, packed them in leather panniers made for the purpose, placed them upon my mule, and set off in company. This was on the 14th of September, and when I parted with my friends I certainly did not expect to see them for the first time in the April following, at the city of Mexico and in chains.

The shepherds from whom we had purchased our provisions had informed us that the country was in arms against us, that Howland and his party were prisoners at Santa Fé, and that an American named Rowland, a merchant at San Miguel, had also been imprisoned and his goods confiscated by order of the governor, Armijo. Yet they told these stories in so many different ways, and contradicted themselves so often in the telling, that but little confidence could be placed in them.

After having obtained directions as to our course towards the *camino real,* or principal road, for our camp on the Rio Gallinas was some distance from it, we proceeded on our way, a Mexican servant we had hired at San Antonio, named Manuel,* accompanying us. After reaching the main road, we journeyed briskly forward until nearly two o'clock. An abrupt turn now brought us suddenly upon two Mexican muleteers, enjoying a quiet siesta, while their mules were feeding close by them. Our appearance frightened them exceedingly, and as they quickly caught their mules and commenced putting on their packs, their extreme nervousness was plainly visible. The colour entirely left

* Manuel was shot, a short time afterward, in mere wantonness, by a drummer in Armijo's redoubtable army. His leading characteristics were great good-nature, extreme idleness, and a proneness to telling the most outrageous falsehoods — the two latter very common failings with his countrymen.

the swarthy face of one of these fellows, who, for once, certainly had the appearance of a white man; and as his trembling hands were flying about from one part of his mule to another, fastening the packs, the movements could not have been more rapid had he been executing the Battle of Prague or one of Strauss' quickest and most difficult waltzes on a piano. At first he could not answer a question coherently; but as he gradually found that our intentions were not to eat him up alive, the colour returned to his cheeks, his tongue became loosened, and he was able to give us satisfactory answers.

The fellow said that our approach was well known to the inhabitants, and that the greatest stir and excitement existed in consequence of Armijo's informing them that our intentions were to burn, slay, and destroy as we went. He corroborated the report that Rowland* had been arrested for his supposed connexion with the expedition, as well as the story that Howland, Baker, and Rosenbury were prisoners at Santa Fé, although he asserted that they had the liberty of the town. After telling us that the village of Anton Chico was some two or three miles to our left, and a little off the main road to San Miguel, the muleteer departed, apparently well satisfied that we had let him off without taking his scalp.

It was now deemed advisable to send word back to our friends on the Gallinas of what we had heard, and

* Thomas Rowland, a brother of John Rowland. The name of the latter had appeared in some of the Texan papers as a commissioner in connexion with Dryden, both of whom were residents of New Mexico. The publication of their names, as commissioners friendly to the interests of the Texans, was made without their knowledge or consent.

Manuel was accordingly despatched with a note detailing everything. Mr. Van Ness also sent back a number of letters of introduction to different individuals, with which he had been furnished, and other papers, fearing that he might be arrested, and that blame might fall upon innocent persons if he should be searched and the letters found upon his person. After this we turned off in the direction of Anton Chico.

A ride of half an hour brought us to a small and miserable hovel upon the banks of the Rio Pecos. This is a beautiful, swift-running stream of fresh water, rising in the mountains in the vicinity of Santa Fé, and after fertilizing a succession of narrow but rich valleys, is supposed finally to empty into the Puercos, a tributary of the Rio Grande. We rode up to the low and narrow door of the hovel, at which stood an old, gray-haired man and two or three women, who were all evidently intimidated at the sight of strangers. As this secluded spot is entirely off the trail of the St. Louis traders, these half-civilized people had probably never before seen other than their own mixed race: as for ourselves, it was the first human habitation having any pretensions to civilization we had seen for months, and was certainly a welcome object to all. We did not dismount; but, while inquiring for the most direct route to Anton Chico, one of the women brought us some warm *tortillas* from the interior of the hovel, a little wooden bowl of *miel*—a species of molasses made from the stalk of the common Indian corn—and three or four large slices of goats' milk cheese. These, to us delicacies, they brought without money and without price—an earnest of the universal kindness and hospitality of the *women* of New Mexico. We threw some silver into their hands, wheeled our horses amid a shower of *muchas gracias* and *adios, caballeros,** and left them.

A ride of another half hour brought us in sight of Anton Chico, a village seated upon a little hill overlooking the Pecos, and probably containing some two or three hundred inhabitants. As we caught a first glimpse of the village, a suspicious, piratical-seeming Mexican, armed with a double-barrelled gun, broad-sword, and lance, and splendidly mounted upon a dashing black horse, passed within ten yards of us. Although he did not even nod at our approach, he still eyed us closely. Had he not been confident that his horse could easily outrun our jaded animals, I doubt whether he would have come within gunshot of us. At a distance, on the rising slope of a hill, another man, similarly armed and mounted, was seen; and he, too, was evidently watching our movements.

As we approached the little village, all was excitement and commotion. Women and children were seen running in every direction, climbing the low houses and hiding behind the mud fences and walls. A large horse-mill, at which the inhabitants were grinding corn-stalks for the manufacture of *miel,* was deserted instantly, and everything plainly denoted that our sudden appearance had created the greatest consternation. We rode steadily up to the first door, as though not noticing that we had caused the least alarm, and asked a man of more hardihood than the rest, who had the courage to show his face, although not enough to conceal his trepidation, whether we could purchase some fodder for our animals and bread for ourselves. This question, being in Spanish, was

* Many thanks; farewell, gentlemen; God be with you.

understoood by several of the frightened inhabitants, who were peering at us through the chinks of the surrounding doors, and who, finding that we did not ask them to surrender their lives and property at discretion, gradually gained colour and confidence, and began slowly to issue from their hiding-places. In three minutes we were surrounded by half a hundred men, women, and children some inviting us this way, others that, and all apparently, anxious to serve us, either from love of money or love of life, for many, no doubt, were impressed with the idea that we had come on purpose to do murder. The women and girls were very slightly clad, and many of the children were naked, while the men were so concealed in their coarse blankets that we really could not tell what their dress might be underneath, or whether they had any. On the faces of many of the women and grown-up girls we noticed large, deep-red spots, apparently marks from their childhood, and disfiguring them greatly. I afterward ascertained that these marks were not natural, as my readers will learn in the progress of the narrative.

The little village of Anton Chico is built on a square, the houses fronting on the inner side, although there are entrances, protected by strong doors, on the outer. The houses are of one story only, built of *adobes*, a species of large, sun-dried bricks, while the tops are flat. They have neither windows nor floors, and in point of comfort and convenience are only one degree removed from the rudest wigwam of the Indian. In case of attack from the savages continually hovering and committing depredations upon the frontiers of New Mexico, these little hamlets serve as forts, the Indians rarely pursuing the inhabitants farther than their outer walls, as they carry on their warfare entirely on horseback. This description of Anton Chico will answer for a majority of the *ranchos* and smaller towns of New-Mexico—their buildings being all constructed of the same materials and in the same manner.

We entered the largest house in the place. It had but two rooms, the earthen floor and scanty furniture of which gave them a prison-like and desolate appearance. Not a chair or table, knife or fork, did the occupants possess, and we were given to understand that we were in the house of the "first family" of Anton Chico. We called for something to eat suggesting a somewhat varied "bill of fare" to be spread before us, for which we manifested our readiness to pay the highest prices: our dinner consisted—substantials and extras all enumerated—of tortillas, boiled eggs, and miel, the latter somewhat resembling molasses and water, the water predominating. In the mean while, our animals outside were faring infinitely better than ourselves, for they had an ample supply of corn and fodder—good, legitimate food for them, to which they did most ample justice.

The sun was about setting by the time we had finished our meal; yet we determined upon travelling some eight or ten miles farther towards San Miguel that evening. After paying the master of the house the most exorbitant prices for every article we had procured, and after his daughters had presented each of us with a bundle of *cigarritos** of their own manufacture, we saddled and mounted our horses, and again proceeded for San Miguel.

Immediately on leaving Anton Chico we were com-

* Small cigars, in New Mexico made of *punche*, a species of tobacco, covered with corn-husks or shucks.

pelled to climb a high, steep, and rocky hill, or mountain, and on reaching its summit, by which time darkness had overtaken us, we found ourselves without a road, and completely lost in a grove of stunted pines and cedars. To advance was impossible, and we accordingly retraced our steps to the village we had left but a short time previous. Once more we secured our animals to a hedge fence, near the house where we had procured our homely dinner, and after carrying our saddles, bridles, and other equipments to a corner of the room which had been appropriated to our use, by the master, we rolled ourselves up in our blankets with the vain hope, as it was the first night we had passed under cover for months, of enjoying a refreshing sleep. But no such good luck was in store for us: there was a closeness in the atmosphere to which we had long been strangers, the room was occupied by some thirty men, women, and children, exclusive of our own party, and when all were provided with sleeping room there was scarcely space enough on the hard earthen floor for a hat. The beds of our neighbours were nothing but sheepskins thrown upon the floor—their clothing a blanket, which they spread over themselves after lying down.

Every member of the family, which consisted of a grandfather and grandmother, with their children and their children's children, seemed to be badly affected by a cold, or worse—for the younger branches were all evidently afflicted with the worst form of the whooping-cough. The grown people appeared to have the most distressing coughs to match their colds, while the children seemed at times to be in perfect convulsions. Occasionally the distressing sounds would all die away;

anon, one of the children would begin coughing frightfully, another would join in the discordant din, and immediately the whole family were in full chorus—and thus they barked away the hours.

Notwithstanding the horrible uproar, however, I finally fell into a half-sleep. About one o'clock in the morning I was awakened by some disturbance among our animals and in going out to ascertain the cause I was asked by a Mexican if I was the captain of the party. As this was about all I could at that time understand, I called Lewis, in the belief that the fellow had something important to communicate, and in this I was not deceived. He said that we were all to be taken prisoners on the next day by a party who were then mustering in the valley, near Cuesta. He farther stated that the inhabitants of Anton Chico would fall upon us were they not fearful of our arms. To wind up, he informed us that we should most certainly be shot, and for this peculiarly pleasant news he asked us one dollar! Had his information extended no farther than that we were to be arrested, and had this statement been gratuitous, we might have paid some heed to his story; as it was, it sounded very much as though he had made up what he considered a dollar's worth of bad tidings, and thought us simple enough to pay him for his trouble. Entertaining this belief, of course we returned to our blankets without giving the fellow even so much as the sixteenth of what he charged; yet I could not but think that there might be some truth in his story.

We were up at an early hour in the morning, and after swallowing a bowl of atole sweetened with a little miel, once more took the road for San Miguel. Although the male part of the inhabitants of the village we had just left had every outward appearance of friendship, there was still a something suspicious in their movements which convinced us that they would have acted otherwise had they not been restrained by fear. To show that they were not all honest, some one of them stole a saddle-blanket from me. It was of little value, however, and I made no mention of the circumstance to the man in whose house we had passed the night.

We must have been blind, indeed, to the evidences around us, not to see that the country was in a state of excitement occasioned by the approach of the Texans—the suspicious men who had crossed our route the evening before, the earnestness with which they eyed our movements, and then the arrest of Howland and his companions, all tended to impress us with the belief that we should at least be questioned closely as to our business, and the objects which had induced us to enter the country, if not detained, in case Armijo should oppose the advance of the Texans. But we never thought of being disarmed or imprisoned. I had no inconsiderable sum of money in gold, confined about my body in a linen belt: this I thought it more prudent to conceal under the buttons which graced the sides of my riding pantaloons. There was not room for all the money under the buttons—what was left I still retained in the belt which I now placed in one of my pockets. A valuable breastpin I concealed under one of my waistband buttons, two or three articles of jewelry less costly I hid under the folds of my shirt bosom, and a gold watch and chain I secreted as safely as was possible. In a country filled, as I knew this to be, with thieves and cut-throats of the worst description, I was anxious to conceal the fact entirely that I had valuable property of any kind with me.

On reaching the summit of the steep hill overlooking Anton Chico, and emerging from the cedars in which we were lost the evening before, we found a level table-land spread out before us, of rare beauty. In the distance, to the north, that spur of the Rocky Mountains at the foot of which lies the mud-built city of Santa Fé, was now plainly visible.

We had travelled but two or three miles after reaching the table-land, before a Mexican, who had seen us approaching from a small house some little distance from the roadside, came out to meet us. He graciously informed us, without our asking the question, that the nearest route to San Miguel would take us directly through the little village of Cuesta, and took no inconsiderable pains to give such directions as would preclude the possibility of our missing the road. At the time, we considered this an act of kindness on his part; but after circumstances made it quite certain that he had been employed to draw us into a snare already set for our apprehension.

After thanking the Mexican for his information, we once more proceeded towards San Miguel. About noon we arrived at the brow of a high, steep, and rocky hill, overlooking a narrow and fertile valley through which the Pecos was flowing. Immediately below us was a small collection of houses; and some distance up the stream, but in plain sight, was the little village of Cuesta. The road leading into the valley ran directly down the rocky sides of the hill, and was so rough and broken that we were compelled to dismount, and lead or drive our animals. As we slowly descended, we could plainly see that our approach had been discovered, for there was commotion in all parts of the beautiful valley. Several horsemen were seen emerging from Cuesta, and dashing, at full speed, towards the spot where we must first strike the level land. A point of the hill now concealed them from our sight, and when we finally reached the bottom not a single human being was visible in any direction.

Van Ness, Lewis, and myself arrived in the valley some ten minutes before Howard and Fitzgerald. While our eyes were turned towards the hillside, waiting their approach, we were suddenly surrounded by more then a hundred roughly dressed but well mounted soldiers, armed with lances, swords, bows and arrows, and miserable *escopetas*, or old fashioned carbines. The leader of this band, whom I will at once introduce as the notorious Dimasio Salazar, instantly rode up, and addressed us as *amigos*, or friends, with the greatest apparent cordiality. He asked us who we were, and whether we were not from Texas. Lewis at once informed him that we were, and that we had been detached from the main body, then some thirty miles distant on the Gallinas, for the purpose of consulting with the authorities, either at San Miguel or Santa Fé, and that he was anxious to see the governor. To this Salazar bowed, as much as to say that all was right, and we fairly congratulated ourselves upon our reception. There was a frankness, a plausibility about the miscreant that completely concealed his real intentions.

On the arrival of Howard and Fitzgerald we remounted our horses, and, in company with our new acquaintances, rode to the first house that presented itself. Here Salazar called a halt, and after his men had completely surrounded us on every side, as if to hear any conversation that might ensue, but with no other intentions, their leader remarked, with the utmost blandness, that we must be aware we could not enter their territory with arms in our hands—that it was contrary to the laws and usages of civilized nations—and that he hoped we would have no objections to placing our rifles and pistols in his keeping, each labelled so that its owner might know it again, until the business we had with the authorities should be arranged. He appeared deeply to regret that his duty compelled him to make this request of persons evidently gentlemen, and whose objects, he doubted not, were of the most friendly nature; he had been ordered by his superiors, he said, to request us to deliver up our arms, and sincerely hoped we would excuse him.

Finding themselves surrounded by a force at least twenty times their number, without the remotest chance to escape by flight even if they felt disposed, and completely imposed upon by the apparent fairness and openness of Salazar's conduct, my companions gave up their arms. It was now necessary for me to inform Salazar as to my position and intentions. Through Van Ness I told him that I was a citizen of the United States, that I was merely a traveller on a journey through the interior of Mexico, and that I had a passport from the Mexican consul at New Orleans, which I took from my pocket and handed him. Not a word could the fellow read, but, placing the document in the hands of his second in command, Don Jesus,* who only wanted natural talents to make him even a greater villain than his master, Salazar, who told him to examine it. After reading the passport from first to last, the worthy lieutenant and secretary returned it to his captain, who remarked that he presumed all was right, but he was reluctantly compelled to demand my arms and retain them until I had seen the governor. With even more reluctance I gave my rifle and pistols into the possession of the miscreant, although my companions openly expressed their confidence that they would be returned in good faith. Now that he had our weapons in his power, I thought I could discover a gleam of satisfaction lighting upon Salazar's countenance, yet his feeling did not openly betray him. It was afterward evident enough that he had used dissimulation, and adopted a courteous tone foreign to his nature—even with his myrmidons around him, the cowardly man did not dare peremptorily to demand our rifles and pistols.

Having distributed all our weapons among his principal men, Salazar next drew his officers into the little house in front of which the scene had taken place. In the mean time we were left outside, under no apparent restraint. I led my horse, the faithful old "Jim the Butcher," as he was called, to an irrigating canal close

* I have given this name the Spanish spelling, although it is pronounced *Hesoos*. Among the women of both Mexico and Spain *Jesusa* is a very common, and considered a very pretty name. By the same rule of pronunciation it is called *Hesoosa*. As is remarked above, I have given these names singular and irreverent as they may appear to an American their Spanish orthography. Were a Mexican to see *Hesoosa* in print he would not know it, even were it his own name.

by, and after allowing him to drink his fill of the cool and excellent water, walked back with him to my pack-mule, opened one of the leathern panniers, and commenced feeding him on bread which I had purchased that morning at Anton Chico. While at that village, so great was my craving for bread after being without it for months, I had purchased all that was offered for sale, really thinking that I should eat it all, although I had at least a month's supply. A moment's reflection now taught me that I was in a country where I could have it fresh every day, and as my appetite by this time was somewhat appeased, I began to feed my horse upon the stores I had provided for my own use. A crowd of men and half-naked women and girls pressed around me, apparently astonished that I should give my horse what was really one of their greatest luxuries, and it was while I was thus engaged that Salazar and his officers stepped from the house and a second time approached us.

His first request was that we should form in a line. He then said he was obliged to take from us any papers or articles we might have about our persons—such were his orders from the governor. There was even an approach to delicacy in this command, for the scoundrel had not as yet shown his real colours; and as we were weaponless, and completely in his power, we submitted to the degrading operation of having our pockets turned inside out and our persons searched by a committee of his officers. During this process, very fortunately for me, neither my gold pieces nor my other valuables were discovered; but all my papers, note-book, penknife, with such other articles as I happened to have in my pockets, were taken from me. At one time, one of the fellows had his hands upon the end of the old linen belt in which I had carried my gold, and which still contained nearly a hundred dollars; its ragged appearance alone saved it, for thinking it but a worthless piece of worn-out cloth, he permitted me to retain it in my possession. Had Salazar got hold of this belt he would at once have seen the places from which I had but recently cut a number of doubloons, as well as found such of the gold as was still left; and so great was the scoundrel's avarice that I believe he would have boiled me could he have found no other means to extract my treasures.

Up to this time, the conduct of Salazar, with the arguments he used to sustain him in arresting us and taking our papers and other articles, was to a certain degree honourable, and it was impossible to suspect the deep treachery and atrocious designs lying under an exterior so apparently fair; we were now to read a new chapter in his character, one that broke upon us with all that suddenness and startling effect which fiction-writers strive to attain in their scenes of most thrilling, blood-freezing, horror.

Our papers and effects had been tied in a handkerchief and removed, and we were waiting the next movement of our captors with some little impatience, when Salazar suddenly ordered twelve of his men, all armed with old muskets or carbines, to march up in front of us. The movement appeared strange, more particularly when we noticed that the men, now paraded directly before us, and within three yards, were pale, and fairly trembling as with fright; but still we could not suspect the horrible design of their leader. Our suspense was of short duration, however; for no sooner had he arranged the twelve men in front of us, than it became but too evident his intentions were to shoot us on the spot! Fitzgerald was the first to speak. The brave but eccentric Irishman had seen much service in Spain, understood not only the language, but the treacherous and suspicious character of the Mexicans, and now fathomed the intentions of Salazar. Prefacing his short speech with a strong oath, the excited man, with fists clenched, and a rich brogue, exclaimed, "They're going to shoot us, boys; let's pitch into 'em and die in hot blood; it's much aisier!" At the same moment I cast my eyes around, and noticed that the crowd in the rear were falling back in two straight lines, as if to the escape the balls in their passage, while the women and girls were wringing their hands and flying from point to point, apparently in deep despair.

That we were to be immediately shot was now terribly manifest. We exchanged glances with each other, and those glances plainly told that each of my companions, in obedience to Fitzgerald's emphatic call, was prepared to rush upon the cowardly and faithless miscreants the moment they were in the act of levelling their guns, to wrest their weapons from them, and then to sell his life at as dear a rate as possible. I will give Lewis the credit of acting, in that moment of extreme peril, as became a man. My station happened to be on the extreme left of my companions, the position bringing me within a yard of a young Mexican whom I afterward ascertained to be a son of the Alcalde of San Miguel. Tied loosely around his waist was a coarse cotton handkerchief, in which he had stuck two of Colt's revolving pistols taken from one of my friends. These I instantly determined to seize upon in the *melee,* while each of my companions had singled out his man to spring upon at the signal.

A man lives almost an age in a single moment of imminent danger—his thoughts crowd upon each other with such lightning rapidity, that his past life, its promises and hopes, are reviewed at a glance. I thought of home, relations, friends, in the fleeting moment which passed after Salazar had manifested his inhuman intentions; but the thoughts that came uppermost with all of us were of deep regret that we had given up our arms to such cowardly assassins, mingled with the bitter consciousness that we were to be shot down like dogs, without a possible chance that our friends could ever know the place or manner of our death. But our thoughts were suddenly checked by a motion from Salazar, as if to give the word of command for our execution. I cast hurried glances at Fitzgerald and my comrades for a signal to make a dash; but at this juncturo an altercation ensued between Dimasio and a Mexican named Vigil. Not a word could I understand, but from my companions I learned that the latter was interfering for our lives. He contended that we had entered the settlements openly and peacefully, and that we had asked to see and hold converse with Governor Armijo. With him rested the power of life and death, and before him we must be taken. Vigil prevailed over the bloodthirsty captain, and thus were our lives spared; but in the few moments which had passed since we were first drawn up, we had lived a common lifetime of excitement.

Foiled in his murdcrous intentions by the prompt aid of Don Gregorio Vigil, whom we afterward saw and thanked for his timely interference, Salazar now ordered Don Jesus to march us immediately to San Miguel, where it was thought Armijo had arrived with a large body of troops. With regret we saw our friend Vigil leave us. He was the owner of an estate near San Miguel, a man of good heart and correct principles, and had no little influence with the Mexicans in that quarter.

Under an escort of some half a dozen men, and followed by a rabble of men, women, and children, we now set off on foot for San Miguel, leaving our well-tried animals in the hands of the miscreants who had captured us. Arrived at the little village of Cuesta, we were marched into the house of the alcalde, where, after placing two sentinels over us, Don Jesus left us to make some arrangement for the march. While in this house we were visited by every woman and child in the place, the former giving us bread, cheese, and stewed pumpkins, and appearing deeply to compassionate us in our unfortunate condition. They undoubtedly thought we should be executed immediately on meeting with the governor, who they took every means to inform us was a brutal and unfeeling tyrant, delighting in every act of cruelty which might impress his subjects with fear, and ever anxious to show off his great influence and power by acts of the most atrocious persecution.

In half an hour Don Jesus returned, and ordered us to prepare for instant departure. We were destitute of every article of clothing except what we had on, and as the nights among the mountains were at this season of the year raw and chilly, we asked him to return at least one of our blankets to each of us. Without apparently heeding this request, he turned to one of his men and ordered him to bring three or four lariats, or ropes, with which to tie us, intending, as he said, to take us before the governor in that degrading condition. Our friend Vigil was now out of the way, Salazar had taken the road towards Anton Chico with the main body of his men, and thinking that the heartless villain who now had charge of us might have adopted this plan to place us completely in his power, and then butcher us under orders from his superior, we peremptorily refused to be tied. He still insisted; but on our informing him that we would walk peaceably to San Miguel, he finally gave up his purpose. Forming us in front of the house, he then placed two of the guard in advance with bows and arrows and heavy clubs, two more in the rear armed in the same manner, and all of them barefoot, while he himself mounted a mule, and took his place at the side of our party. He had an American rifle resting before him on the pommel of his saddle, and drawing an old rusty sword, he started us off, simply informing us that the first one who left his place would be rewarded by the loss of his head.

There was something supremely ridiculous, not only in his threat, but in the appearance of our guard, and gloomy as our situation was, we could not help laughing. We could easily have fallen upon the miserable apologies for men who were guarding us and disarmed them in a twinkling; but we had no means of getting clear, and rejoining our men afterward; and as recapture would have been death, thoughts of an escape were not entertained.

A rapid march of an hour, along the valley of the

Pecos, brought us to the little village of Puertecito, the residence of both Salazar and the fellow who now had charge of us. Here we were halted for a short time, to give the inhabitants an opportunity of gazing at five unfortunate prisoners, and to convince them of the great prowess of the redoubtable Dimasio Salazar, and his equally valiant second in command, who had boldly conceived and successfully carried into execution a daring plan for our capture. That the women all pitied us was evident; for the commiserating exclamation of *pobrecitos !** as they gave us bread, cheese, and such food as they had at hand, fell from their tongues in softest and most feeling tones. They knew their husbands and brothers, and knowing them, felt that little mercy or kindness could we expect at their hands.

A short distance above Puertecito we were obliged to ford the Rio Pecos. The water was not more than two feet in depth; but as my lame and weak ankle had now begun to swell from the active and unwonted exercise, I was deterred from taking off my boots by a fear that I could not get them on again. To soak my feet thoroughly, and to continue the march in this disagreeable plight, was therefore my only alternative.

The distance from Cuesta to San Miguel was fourteen or fifteen miles; and it was nearly sundown before the spire of the little church at the latter appeared in sight. Weary and faint from the unusual exercise, and extremely unwell from the great change which had recently

* Poor fellows! I believe, is a literal translation, although it means much more. Nothing can be more touchingly sweet than the pronunciation of this word by a Spanish or Mexican woman. The tones come fresh and warm from the heart when an object worthy of compassion presents itself.

taken place in our diet, we were escorted through the principal square or *plaza*, and taken to a little hole which was dignified with the name of a room. A crowd followed us to our prison doors, and continued to gaze at us until the last minute.

The *alcalde*, a gruff, bad countenanced man, sent us in a miserable meal of tortillas and weak mutton broth, while the priest of the place, more liberal, sent his servant with a generous bowl of hot coffee for each of us. Our scanty supper over, our thoughts were next turned towards sleep; but the earthen floor of our quarters was without a single blanket to relieve its hardness, and the chilling blast that came down from the adjoining mountains as the shades of the evening drew nigh, told us, more plainly than words, that we need expect neither comfort nor sleep that night. We sent word to the alcalde of our unfortunate plight: he answered our petition by saying that he could do nothing for us. A kind hearted woman living close by, however sent us a buffalo skin and a single blanket, and another blanket I purchased of a man in the crowd, for which I gave him an English sovereign. With these we made up a bed for five persons. I suffered more than any of my companions, the bread I had eaten giving me a severe attack of colic; and I crawled from the ground in the morning weak and unrefreshed.

Thus did we spend our first night in prison.

CHAPTER XIV.

Ordered to march towards Santa Fé.—Departure from San Miguel.—Gloomy Anticipations.—Our Guard increased.—A Present from a Woman.—Meet with a Party of Mexican Troops.—Brutality of their Leader.—Lewis, Van Ness, and Fitzgerald tied with Cords.—Description of Don Jesus.—Large Bodies of Troops passed.—Their miserable Appointments.—Our first Interview with Governor Armijo.—His Reception.—Conduct of Lewis.—We are ordered back to San Miguel.—Armijo's last Command.—Carlòs seen.—First Appearance upon a Donkey.—Antics of the Animal.—A heavy night Shower.—Once more at San Miguel.—Barbarous Execution of one of our Comrades.—We are ordered before the Governor.—An exciting Trial.—Howland condemned to Die.—Cruel mode of Execution.—Noble Conduct of Howland. Kindness of a young Priest.—Reflections upon our Situation.—Departure of Mexican Troops for Anton Chico.—News of Colonel Cooke and his Men.—Plans of Armijo.—Particulars of the Capture of Howland.—Description of Manuel Pino.—News of the Capture of our Friends at Anton Chico.—Great Rejoicings at San Miguel.

We had no sooner risen than Don Jesus told us that the govenor had not yet arrived, and that he should march with us directly towards Santa Fé, distant some sixty miles, in the hope of meeting him upon the road. Before starting, we sent out and purchased an entire sheep, an officious fellow, named Tomas Bustamente, whose countenance appeared to indicate that he had some honesty, acting as our agent in the transaction. A part of this sheep Tomas cooked for our breakfast, the priest again sending us a large pitcher of coffee.

It was nearly nine o'clock before everything was in readiness for our departure. Although we were anxious to see the governor and learn the worst, it may be imagined that our anticipations were not of a very pleasant nature. Had we been prisoners in the hands of any other people under the sun our feelings would have been far different; but we were now in the power of men who possessed all the vices of savage life without one of the virtues that civilization teaches. We felt that although our lives had been spared the previous day, it was but a reprieve; that we were still in the hands of a semi-civilized enemy—cruel, relentless, and treacherous—who looked upon us as heretics, and the common enemies of their religion and race; and we had fearful reason to believe that the appearance of Armijo would be the signal for our immediate execution. Surely, the emotions of that hour, when the future was looming up so close and dark upon us, are not to be appreciated by the reader.

Our guard, which on the previous day had only consisted of four, was now increased to eight men, four members of the country militia, armed with bows and arrows, and mounted upon asses, being stationed, two on either side, while Don Jesus on his mule hovered around, as if to guard the weaker points in the order of march. This addition to our escort had been provided by the old alcalde of San Miguel, with the view, probably, of rendering our escape a matter of positive impossibility; yet, enfeebled as we were from our many privations, and the long weary pilgrimage across the prairies, we still felt certain that we could, at any time, capture Don Jesus and all his men with the greatest ease. A determined rush, accompanied by a true Anglo-Saxon shout of defiance, would have brought every one of the cowardly wretches to his knees begging for mercy; yet we should hot have been able successfully to run the gauntlet of well-mounted men stationed at all the passes between us and our friends.

After parading us in front of our miserable quarters, and arranging his guard around us with much pomp and show, Don Jesus ordered us to march. The plaza was again crowded with the women, children, and old men of San Miguel as we hurriedly marched through it, many of the boys following and gazing at us until we reached the extremities of the town. We had not travelled more than a couple of miles before a tolerably well-dressed woman came running towards us from a small house, bringing a bottle of the country whiskey, and saying that it was for our use. This we drank upon the spot, and as we thanked the good-hearted creature for her kindness she appeared to feel deeply for us in our misfortunes. Even after we had been hurried off by our inhuman guard, the woman still remained to gaze upon us, looking her last at the *pobrecitos,* whom she really thought the sun would not set upon alive. The almost universal brutality and cold-heartedness of the men of New Mexico are in strange contrast with the kind dispositions and tender sympathies exhibited by all classes of the women.

A brisk walk of another mile brought us in contact with a party of some two hundred half-dressed and miserably-armed Mexicans, on their march towards San Miguel. Their commander was a brutal piratical-visaged scoundrel, who, after ordering Don Jesus to halt, cursed us with every opprobrious epithet, said we should have been shot when first taken, and then asked why we were not tied. While Don Jesus was stammering forth some excuse, the fellow ordered his trumpeter to sound an advance, and in three minutes a turn of the road concealed this extremely valiant party and their doughty captain from our sight. Before they departed, however, we learned that they were to act against Colonel Cooke, Captain Sutton, and their men, and we were also informed that Armijo had left Santa Fé in the morning with several hundred men, and that we should meet *him* before nightfall.

The miscreant who had charge of us now stated that his imperative duty made it necessary to tie us. With a mock sensibility he pretended that it was against his wish to do this, but as a superior officer had ordered him he must comply, simply for form's sake. After a little hesitation on the part of Van Ness and Fitzgerald they consented to be tied, and a *lariat* was accordingly fastened around their wrists, while the other end was held by one of the guard. Lewis was also tied and led along like a dog; but as Major Howard was suffering from an old wound received in an Indian fight, and as I was also lame, and, as Don Jesus well knew, had slept none the night before, he allowed us to continue the march without being confined. He ordered us, however, whenever we met with any of the different parties of troops we were now constantly passing, to fold our hands upon our breasts as a token of submission. Never shall I forget this Don Jesus. He had a coarse, dark, hang-dog face, a black but vicious eye, a head which I am phrenologist enough to know was as destitute of the organs of benevolence and the better attributes of our nature as outer darkness is of light, and if he had a heart at all, it legitimately belonged to a hyena or a prairie wolf.

He pushed, or rather drove us rapidly onward until past the middle of the afternoon, during which time we must have passed nearly a thousand troops, the larger portion of them armed with bows and arrows or old and worn-out muskets. The sun had hidden himself behind a range of mountains which divides the valley of the Pecos at this point from that of the Rio Grande, and we were approaching an old and ruined mission, which, in former times, had served the double purpose of a church and fortress, when suddenly the sharp and discordant blast of a trumpet announced the approach of General Manuel Armijo, governor of New Mexico. An abrupt turn in the road had at first concealed his ragged but numerous cavalcade from our sight, but a few steps brought us in full view of all the pomp, circumstance and chivalry, bows and arrows, sycophants and rascals, with which the governor is usually surrounded. When I say that our guard had been entertaining us during the day with stories of Armijo's cruelty and barbarity, and that they freely gave it as their opinion that we should be ordered to execution on sight, I need not add that the present moment was exciting to a painful degree.

The governor himself, a fine, portly man, was mounted on a mule of immense size, and gaily as well as richly caparisoned. Don Jesus had formed us into line by the roadside, there to await the advance of Armijo. The moment the quick eye of the latter caught a glance of us he rode directly up to the spot where we where standing, and, without dismounting, addressed us with no little politeness, shook each of us by the hand with much apparent cordiality, called us *amigos,* or friends, and after saying that he had heard of our capture, asked us who we were. Lewis immediately answered—and here the spirit of the craven caitiff first manifested itself—that we were merchants from the United States. Van Ness interrupted him at once by saying that, with the exception of myself, we were all Texans; but, without heeding him, Armijo grasped Lewis by the collar of his dragoon jacket, dragged him up alongside of his mule, and, pointing to the buttons, upon which were a single star and the word "Texas," he sternly said,

"What does this mean? I can read—*Texas!*" at the same time pointing to the latter word and pronouncing it emphatically. Lewis quailed under his iron grasp, but without heeding him the governor continued, "You need not think to deceive *me:* no merchant from the United States ever travels with a Texan military jacket.

After asking several questions, to which Lewis returned stammering answers, Armijo finally spoke of our main party, and inquired its number and the intentions of the commissioners. He was answered by Van Ness and Howard that it was a mercantile expedition from Texas, and that the intentions of the leaders were pacific. Mr. Van Ness then told him that I did not belong to the party any farther than that I accompanied it for the protection it afforded against Indians, and added that I had a passport from the Mexican consul in New Orleans. This passport, with all my papers, was in the hands of Don Jesus, who immediately gave it to Armijo. After reading it aloud in presence of all of us, he gave it back into the hands of the captain of our guard, at the same time remarking that the passport was a good one, but that, as I was found in company with the enemies of New Mexico, he should detain me until he could learn farther of my intentions. My companions had invariably assured me that I should be released immediately on having an interview with the governor; but by this time I had seen enough of the people of New Mexico, and heard enough of Armijo, to convince me that I need not look for justice at his hands, and was therefore but little disappointed at the disposition he made of my case. After what we had heard of the fellow, and his cruel barbarities, we felt in a measure satisfied on ascertaining that we were not to be shot upon the spot, aud without a hearing.

After disposing of my case and passport thus summarily, Armijo gratuitously informed us that he was an honourable man and not an assassin, and, what was more, that he was a great warrior. Whatever doubts we might have entertained on this point, we did not see fit to express any at the time, and the fellow may have taken our silence for a tacit acknowledgment of our belief in his magnanimity and bravery. He next asked us which of our little party best understood the Spanish language, as he wanted one of us to accompany him as interpreter. At this question Lewis eagerly pressed forward, and after asserting that he could speak the language more fluently than any of his companions, at once proffered his services. He really was more fluent with Spanish than any of us, having resided many years in Chihuahua and other parts of Mexico. Armijo immediately ordered a mule for him to ride, and after his hands were untied he mounted the animal and rode in among his new associates. That up to this time he had acted in perfect good faith towards Colonel Cooke and the expedition, I have not the least doubt; but he now saw that he was completely in the power of men whom he understood thoroughly, and from whom he well knew he could expect neither mercy nor justice; he saw, too, that by betraying his former associates, those who had often befriended him, he might gain life and liberty, and for this he at once sundered all the holy ties of religion, honour, companionship, and patriotism. Not one of us suspected him at the time of other than honourable intentions, but after circumstances rendered his base treachery unquestionable.

Armijo now turned to Don Jesus, and in a pompous and bombastic tone ordered him to guard us safely back to San Miguel that night, as he wished to hold a conversation with us early on the ensuing morning.

"But they have already walked ten leagues to day, your excellency, and are hardly able to walk all the way back to-night,"* was the answer of the fellow, who was thinking of his own personal convenience and comfort all the while.

"They are able to walk ten leagues more," retorted Armijo, with a stately wave of his hand. "The Texans are active and untiring people—I know them," he continued; "if one of them *pretends* to be sick or tired on the road, *shoot him down and bring me his ears!* Go!"

"Yes, your excellency," was the obsequious answer of the cringing Don Jesus, and with a flourish of trumpets

* The Spanish league lacks but a small fraction of being equal to three English miles.

the great General Armijo and his motley army now left us. As they filed by, in helter-skelter order, we noticed our former guide, the runaway Carlos, in the crowd. He was seated upon a mule, his arms and breast bandaged, and we afterward learned that he had been stabbed and severely wounded by a nephew of Armijo, for his supposed connexion with the Texan expedition.

The sun had ceased to tinge the highest tops of the eastern mountains ere the last stragglers and camp-followers of Armijo had trotted past us, and we were extremely tired and faint after our weary march of nearly thirty miles ; yet this fellow, who in one breath told us he was " an honourable man," almost in the next ordered us back over the same rough and broken road without food or sleep! The penalty of failure was death, and to be certain that his orders had been strictly fulfilled, or perhaps to gratify his curiosity, he wished to see the *ears* of such of us as might fall by the roadside, unable to endure the excessive fatigue.

As if fearful of not having an opportunity to fulfil Armijo's last command, Don Jesus now rushed us back over the same ground at a more rapid pace than ever. I was not only weary and unwell by this time, but my lame ankle was so swollen and stiff, from the unusual exercise, that I could hardly drag it along ; yet determined that the honourable governor should see something of me in the morning besides my ears, I hired the privilege, at an exorbitant rate, of a seat on the donkey of one of the Mexicans, the owner to ride behind me. The poor, scraggy animal could not be more than eight hands high, and appeared hardly able to bear up under one full-grown man ; yet the Mexican told me he was strong enough to carry two, and hurriedly helped me to mount a miserable apology for a saddle strapped loosely to the back of the donkey. Possessing all the perverseness and obstinacy, and up to all the tricks of his race, he still allowed a perfect stranger, not only to him but his kind, to mount in quietness. Not so when his owner undertook the task of bestriding him; for no sooner had he placed his hands on the donkey's hip joints, in the act of springing to his perch behind me, than the animal kicked violently up—landing him several yards in the rear, flat upon his back, while the same movement hoisted me skyward in a line as straight as a rocket. Although extremely poor in flesh, I still had specific gravity enough to bring me down; and while in the act of descending directly upon the haunches of the ass, another kick-up gave me another hoist in the air. I fortunately made the ground in my second descent, without sustaining the least personal injury. Gloomy as were our prospects, my companions could not resist the temptation to laugh heartily at my ludicrous exhibition of ground and lofty tumbling, and I even took a part myself in the merry outbreak when I ascertained that I was unhurt.

The road between Santa Fé and San Miguel is rough and uneven, running over hills, and crossing deep gullies.* Bad as it was, however, and faint and tired as we were, we reached a small prairie within six miles of the latter place about midnight. The heavens now became suddenly overcast, and a dark thunder cloud soon rendered it impossible for even our guard to see the way

* This road, I believe, was made at the expense of the St. Louis traders, and is the only part of the long route between Independence and Santa Fé upon which any work has been done or money expended.

any farther. Just as the shower commenced falling a halt was called, and lying upon the ground without blankets, and in the midst of a tremendous rain, we slept sound till morning.

A walk, or rather a hobble of two hours, for we were so stiff and foot-sore that we could not walk, brought us once more to the plaza or public square of San Miguel. The place was now literally filled with armed men—a few regular troops being stationed immediately about the person of Armijo, while more than nine-tenths of the so-called soldiers were miserably deficient in every military appointment. A sergeant's guard of the regular troops was immediately detailed to take charge of our little party, and after bidding adieu to Don Jesus, as we hoped for ever, we were marched to a small room adjoining the soldiers' quartel. This room fronted on the plaza, and had a small window looking out in that direction; but the only entrance was from a door of the side. Sentinels were immediately placed at the little window and door, leading us to suppose that this was to be our regular prison-house; but we had scarcely been there ten minutes before a young priest entered at the door, and said that one of our party was to be immediately shot! While gazing at each other with looks of eager inquiry, wondering that one was to be shot and not all, and while each one of us was earnestly and painfully speculating on the question which of his fellows Armijo had singled out for a victim, the young priest raised himself on tiptoe, and looking over our heads, pointed through the windows of our close and narrow prison. We hurriedly turned our eyes in that direction, and were shocked at seeing one of our men, his hands tied behind his back, while a bandage covered his eyes, led across the plaza by a small guard of soldiers. Who the man was we could not ascertain at the time, but that he was one of the Texans was evident enough from his dress. The priest said that he had first been taken prisoner, that while attempting to escape he had been retaken, and was now to suffer death. A horrible death it was, too! His cowardly executioners led him to a house near the same corner of the square we were in, not twenty yards from us, and after heartlessly pushing him upon his knees, with his head against the wall, six of the guard stepped back about three paces, and at the order of the corporal *shot the poor fellow in the back!* Even at that distance the executioners but half did their barbarous work; for the man was only wounded, and lay writhing upon the ground in great agony. The corporal stepped up, and with a pistol ended his sufferings by shooting him through the heart. So close was the pistol that the man's shirt was set on fire, and continued to burn until it was extinguished by his blood!

Scarcely was this horrible scene over before we were taken by a strong guard from our prison. Without even being able to divine their intentions, we were marched directly by our late companion, conducted through two or three streets, and finally paraded in front of a small and gloomy hovel having a single window. The movement was conducted silently, and there was a mysterious solemnity about it which, added to the late barbarous murder of one of our party, overwhelmed us with sensations of doubt and alarm, even more insupportable than would have been an order for our instant execution.

Immediately in front of the little window, and at a

distance of twelve steps, we were next formed in line by our guard, and ordered not to leave our position or move in the least. All was mystery, uncertainty, anxiety. Soon Armijo, dressed in a blue military jacket, with a sword at his side, was seen to approach the window. One by one he pointed us out to some person behind him, of whom we could not obtain even a glimpse, and as he pointed he asked the concealed individual who and what the person was to whom his finger was now directed, his name, business, and the relation in which he stood with the Texan expedition. These questions were asked in a loud tone of voice, and were distinctly heard by all of us, but the answers did not reach our ears, although we listened with an earnestness and intensity that were almost painful. It seemed to us that we were undergoing an arbitrary trial for our lives—a trial in which we could have no friendly counsel, could bring no witnesses, offer no proofs or arguments to the bloodthirsty and lawless wretch who alone constituted the tribunal. But this torturing suspense was of short duration, for, after having questioned his concealed agent as to each of us separately, Armijo issued from the little house on an opposite side from the window, and with a pompous dignity of manner slowly approached the spot where we were standing, awaiting, with deep anxiety, a sentence from which we knew there was no appeal.

"Gentlemen," commenced the governors, stopping in front of us, "gentlemen, you told me the truth yesterday—Don Samuel has corroborarted your statements—I save your lives. I have ordered Don Samuel to be shot—he will be shot in five minutes. He ran away from

Santa Fé, and, in attempting to reach Colonel Cooke's party, has been retaken. You now see the penalty of trying to escape. His fate will be yours if you attempt it. Sergeant of the guard, conduct these gentleman back to prison." This was delivered in a loud, military voice.

While congratulating ourselves upon this most unexpected termination of a trial of such harrowing interest, and wondering who the Don Samuel was whose testimony had thus evidently saved our lives, our old friend and guide, Howland, was led forth from the little room. The truth now flushed upon us—we knew that his name was Samuel, that he had been acquainted in former years with Armijo, and that the Mexicans seldom use other than the Christian appellative when addressing or speaking of a man. Howland's hands were tied closely behind him, and as he approached us we could plainly see that his left ear and cheek had been cut entirely off, and that his left arm was also much hacked, apparently by a sword. The guard conducted their doomed prisoner directly by us on the left, and when within three yards of us the appearance of his scarred cheek was ghastly: but as he turned his head to speak, a placid smile, as of heroic resignation to his fate, lit up the other side of his face, forming a contrast almost unearthly. We eagerly stepped forward to address him, but the miscreants who had charge of us pushed us back with their muskets, refusing even the small boon of exchanging a few words with an old companion now about to suffer an ignominious death. Howland saw and felt the movement on our part. He turned upon us another look, a look full of brave resolution as well as resignation, and, in a low but distinct tone, uttered, "*Good-by, boys; I've got to suffer. You must—*" But the rest of the sentence died on his lips, for he was now some yards in the rear of us, and out of hearing.

The guard who had charge of us now wheeled us round and marched us in the same route taken by our unfortunate guide, and within ten yards of him. A more gloomy procession cannot be imagined. With Howland in advance, we were now conducted to the plaza, and halted close by the spot where, in plain sight, lay the body of our recently-murdered companion. A bandage was placed over the eyes of the new victim, but not until he had seen the corpse of his dead comrade. Worlds would we have given could we be permitted to exchange one word with our unoffending friend—to receive his last dying request—yet even this poor privilege was denied us. After the cords which confined his arms had been tightened, and the bandage pulled down so as to conceal the greater part of his face, Howland was again ordered to march. With a firm, undaunted step he walked up to the place of execution, and there, by the side of his companion, was compelled to fall upon his knees with his face towards the wall. Six of the guard then stepped back a yard or two, took deliberate aim at his back, and before the report of their muskets died away poor Howland was in eternity! Thus fell as noble, as generous, and as brave a man as ever walked the earth. He was a native of New Bedford, Massachusetts, of a good family, and by his gentlemanly and affable deportment had endeared himself to every member of the expedition. In a daring attempt to escape, and reach Colonel Cooke's party, in order to give him important information, he had been retaken after a desperate struggle, and the life he could not lose in the heat of that struggle was taken from him in this base and cowardly manner.

Our feelings, while looking upon this brutal tragedy, it is impossible to describe. A fearful, a terrible thing it is to see a man shot—one who deserves his fate—even when he is allowed to stand bravely up and die facing his executioners; for much as every human being may dread the king of terrors, there is hardly one so base as not to wish, when death makes his last inexorable call, to meet him face to face. How much more terrible, then, to see a brave and honourable being like Howland, full of manhood and capable of no base or craven deed, led out and shot in a manner so cowardly, and to see this, too, without the power to act in his behalf. Tumultuous feelings did the scene call up—feelings of indignation and deep hatred for his worse than savage murderers; and for him, between whom and us the common ties of friendship had become strengthened and drawn into more than fraternal closeness by our long intercourse in the wilderness, were mixed emotions of regret, pity, love, and admiration at a fate so horrible so heroically met.

The barbarous execution was no sooner over than we were conducted to the *portales* in front of the soldiers' quartel, and again placed under a strong guard of the regular troops. The sergeant appeared to have more kindness of heart than his fellows, as he gave one of my companions a blanket to spread upon the hard earthen floor which was chosen as our sleeping-place for the ensuing night. The young priest, who had called upon us in the morning, shortly made us a second visit, telling us that we need be under no alarm, as the governor had determined upon saving our lives unless we made an attempt to escape. There appeared to be an exceeding degree of delicacy, not only in the visits, but in the conversation of this young man, which denoted that he possessed finer feeling than either his master or the herd by whom he was surrounded. He was evidently a man of education, acquainted with the usages of the world; and his actions showed that he was anxious to impress us with a belief in our own personal security while scenes of the most sanguinary nature were going on around us. Often, on that eventful day, did recollections of the French Revolution pass through my mind. Armijo I could not look upon but as a second Robespierre, only requiring a field of equal extent to make him equally an assassin, a murderer, a bloodthirsty tyrant. His power, I knew, had been purchased by blood—I saw that it was sustained by blood. Human life he regarded not, so that his base ends were attained; and he would not shrink from sacrificing one man on the altar of his sanguinary ambition, if by so doing he could impress another with a due sense of his boundless authority and power to do whatever might seem meet unto him. The young priest was well aware that we knew the man Armijo, and hence his benevolent desire to quiet any apprehensions that might arise of our personal safety. It was this feeling which brought him to our prison before the first of our comrades was killed—the same humane motives actuated him in calling upon us after the murder of Howland. But to return to my narrative.

From the time of our first arrival in San Miguel that

morning, to the death of Howland, the plaza had been nearly filled with armed men. Two pieces of artillery, badly mounted and every way ineffective, were standing immediately in front of our quarters, in the porch. These cannon were drawn by oxen, the animals yoked and hitched, but lying down after a hard march from Santa Fé and quietly ruminating within ten yards of us. Immediately after the execution of Howland, detachment after detachment of mounted men left the plaza for Anton Chico, where we now learned that Captain Sutton and Colonel Cooke, with their men, were encamped. Next the two pieces of cannon were dragged off in the same direction, surrounded and followed by a motley collection of Indians and badly-armed, half naked, wretched Mexicans, whom Armijo dignified with the title of *rural militia.* By the middle of the day the town was completely deserted, except by the women and children and some two hundred of the chosen troops and friends of the governor; for, great warrior as he was, he contrived to keep the prudent distance of some thirty miles between himself and the Texans so long as they had arms in their hands. The plans of the very valiant and most puissant Armijo were laid with consummate skill so far as his own personal safety and that of his property were concerned. He had now surrounded Colonel Cooke with at least a thousand of his men, while there were but ninety-four Texans in all. In case the latter defeated the Mexicans—and Armijo trembled and feared lest they should—his plan was to retreat to his residence at Albuquerque as fast as picked horses would carry him, and then, after gathering all his money and valuables, make his escape into the interior of Mexico.

With these intentions he remained behind at San Miguel, and there anxiously awaited the news from the little frontier town of Anton Chico.

The command of the troops, acting against Colonel Cooke, Armijo had assigned to his few personal friends —toadies and sycophants whom he always has about him, and for whose adherence he pays a good round sum. He well knew that nine-tenths of his people inly hated and despised him, and were also inclined for an immediate annexation to Texas; he knew, too, that they feared *him*, and that nothing but their extreme ignorance and timidity had prevented them, years before, from throwing off his yoke. So long as they were commanded by officers in his pay he felt confident that he could make a show if not a fight with them, and he felt equally confident that if parade, fair promises, and treachery could induce the Texans to lay down their arms, he could still retain his ascendancy. Such was his policy, such were his plans, and fate decreed that they should prove successful.

From some of the soldiers of our guard we gathered. during the day, full particulras of Howland and his unfortunate companions. They had reached the settlements some three weeks before us, when Armijo, suspecting their intentions and the object of their mission, had them arrested at San Miguel and sent to Santa Fé. From this place they effected their escape three or four days before we were arrested. Until their recapture they had been secreted in the mountains between the two places, travelling by night only, and using every exertion to reach Colonel Cooke, of whose approach they had heard from their guard at Santa Fé.

Armijo immediately sent out large parties to retake them, being extremely anxious that they should not reach the Texans and give information of his plans. On the morning of September the 17th they were fallen in with on the side of a mountain, near San Miguel, by a company of Mexicans ten times their number. Although armed only with pistols and swords, which they had taken from their guard when they effected their escape, they still made a brave and vigorous resistance. Rosenbury was killed on the spot, and Howland and Baker were not taken until severely wounded and weak from loss of blood. The latter was the man we saw shot a short time before Howland, the bandage over his face preventing us from recognising him. He could not speak Spanish, and the tyrant Armijo ordered him to death without even saying a word to him. Howland, on the contrary, was well known in New Mexico, having lived in Santa Fé several years before. The governor offered him his life and liberty—the same terms Lewis accepted—if he would betray his companions and assist him in capturing them. The brave and noble-spirited man rejected the offer with scorn, and notwithstanding the disgraceful mode of his execution, his death was an honourable one. Grecian or Roman history, or the heroic deeds of later days, can hardly furnish a parallel to that of Howland—to that of one who fearlessly met the most terrible death conceivable rather than betray his friends.

The bodies of the murdered men were allowed to remain where they had fallen until near night, a large pack of dogs congregating around them, licking their blood and tearing their clothes. They were then taken to a prairie near the town, denied a burial, and were finally devoured by wolves!

Several Mexican officers called at our quarters during this eventful afternoon, among them a pursy, bloated sallow-faced wretch, named Manuel Pino. He rode a beautiful and spirited black horse, of which he was so proud that he was continually galloping and fretting him about the square, and spurring him to the execution of such curvettings as would most induce a rattling of his sword, spurs, holsters, and the other jingling appointments of a Mexican horseman. Ever and anon he would dash up to our quarters, throw himself heavily from his truly gallant animal, and recount some exploit which he vainly hoped might excite our admiration. He said that he had not only begged, but prayed Armijo to allow him to lead a charge against our friends at Anton Chico, but that the governor would not consent that so brave a man should leave his side for a moment. In short, this fellow took such particular pains, on all occasions, to impress us with a belief in his prowess and bravery, that we finally became thoroughly convinced of his being an arrant coward; and after circumstances fully justified our opinions.

Not only Pino, but the other Mexican officers attached to the personal staff of Armijo, informed us that a nephew of the latter, in company with Lewis, had departed for Anton Chico with the hope of bringing the Texans to terms. They also said that our friends were surrounded by more than a thousand of the best troops in New Mexico, and that re-enforcements were hourly reaching the spot; and they even went so far as to assure us that, if they did not surrender quietly, our own lives would be sacrificed by a lawless and unrestrainable mob—anything but a consoling assurance to men who were perfectly confident that our friends would never surrender without a desperate struggle. That they did not come to the country to make war upon the inhabitants we well knew ; we were equally well convinced that such men as Colonel Cooke, Dr. Brenham, Captain Sutton, and the brave spirits under their command, would not tamely submit to be deprived of their arms and made prisoners, intrenched, as we had been informed they were, in a ravine, and so fortified that they could easily defeat ten or even twenty times their number of such cowardly and badly-appointed men as they would have to contend with.

The hours flew swiftly by, couriers constantly departing to, and arriving from Anton Chico. At one time it was represented to us that a dreadful battle was raging —then, that the parties would come to terms. At sundown, a Mexican came riding into the square with the intelligence that the Texans had all surrendered. Instantly the air was filled with *vivas*, and in ten minutes we received a visit from the governor's secretary and the brute Manuel Pino, corroborating the news. They said the terms were an unconditional surrender; but this we could not believe. Even at this time it was suggested by one of our little party that if Colonel Cooke had surrendered without a terrible fight, treachery had done the work, and that Lewis was the instrument; but such was our confidence in the man that a majority of us could not believe he had turned traitor.

It was but too apparent, however, that our comrades had been taken. Nothing was heard, in any quarter, but rejoicings and congratulation. Shouts of "Long live the Mexican Republic!" "Long live the brave General Armijo!" "Long live the laws!" and "*Death to the Texans!*" were heard on every side, and these were followed by discharges of musketry, ringing of bells, blowing of trumpets, and such music as may be produced by cracked mandolins and ricketty fiddles when execrably played upon. A *Te Deum* was in the mean while sung in the church, a short distance from the plaza, and the guardian saint of the place, San Miguel, with all his finery, feathers, and wings, was dragged from his resting-place to take part in the show. Fandangoes were got up in the different houses on the plaza, a drunken poet was straggling about singing his own hastily-made-up verses in praise of Armijo, taking his pay, probably, in liquor—all went perfectly mad, and spent the night in revel, riot, and rejoicing. A grim, swarthy sentinel, with a face hideously ugly, was stationed directly in front of the little porch where we had cast our weary limbs. As if to add to the general din, he howled forth the dismal "*Centinela alerta!*"* every ten minutes during the night, and his cry appeared to be the signal for some six or eight others, stationed in different parts of the plaza, to join in the doleful chorus. This startling watchword I thought the most discordant, grating, and hideous sound that had ever greeted my ears. Drawled out to a distressing length by a voice hoarse, cracked, and scarcely human, and then caught up in different parts of the square by men who appeared emulous of making a still more doleful and wo-be-gone noise, and I, all the while, ignorant of its import—what with all these hellish orgies and cabalistic sounds in our

* Sentinal, be on the look out, or alert.

ears, and with all the startling and horrible incidents of the day in our minds, it may be imagined that we slept but little that night.

The shouting, firing, ringing, dancing, and carousing were kept up until morning; and why? Because some fifteen hundred or two thousand cowardly wretches had succeeded in capturing ninety-four half starved Texans —not by the intervention of battle or military strategy, but by the blackest piece of treachery to be found on record.

CHAPTER XV.

New Quarters.—Our Party taken before Armijo.—Reception by that Functionary.—His bombastic Account of the Soldiers of New Mexico.—Again taken to Prison.—Appearance of Armijo.—Description of our Prison.—Overrun with Chinches.—The Family next Door.—The Zapatero's Wife.—A singular Custom.—The Senora Francisca abandons her Paint.—Dress of the Females of New Mexico.—Its Scantiness.—Freaks of Fashion.—Description of the Reboso and Mantilla.—Beauties of the Women of Mexico.—Kindness of the Girls of San Miguel.—Colonel Cooke's Men marched through San Miguel.—Lieutenant Lubbock's Account of the Surrender.—Agency of Lewis in the Affair.—Change of Quarters.—Prison Occupations.—Manner of passing our Time.—Chances of an Escape canvassed.—Arrival of Caravans from the United States.—We are not permitted Conversation with our Countrymen.—A seasonable Supply of Luxuries.—The Author assured of his personal Release.—A Mexican Loafer.—Tomas Bustamente.—Employ him as our principal Agent.—Thomas Rowland.—His Release from Arrest.—Bustamente sent on a Mission to Lewis.—Its unsuccessful Result.—Thoughts upon Pipes.—Bustamente's Trickery found out.—Confidence lost in the Man.—Come to the Conclusion that the Mexicans will bear watching.

On the morning which followed the night described in the last chapter, we were taken to new quarters in another part of the town, where a small room was provided for our prison. We had barely time to examine our new quarters before the governor sent a guard to escort us to his lodgings at the priest's house. On being brought before him we found the great man surrounded by his principal officers, both military and civil, and from their obsequious manner it was evident enough that Armijo's power was supreme.

The governor did not rise as we entered his room, but still waved his hand with great natural dignity and politeness, and bade us good-morning with a frankness and cordiality which he well knew how to assume. Remarking that he was aware, from our appearance and Howland's declarations, of our being *caballeros,* or gentlemen, in our own country, he ordered his officers to make room for us on the different boxes and trunks scattered about the room. He then asked several questions in relation to General M'Leod and his party, said that he was going immediately with all his force to meet him, and that if the Texans resisted, every one of them would be killed. He next spoke of the strength of New Mexico, its great resources, the prowess and daring bravery of himself and the resistless soldiers under his command, and drew such a ludicrous picture, and relieved it with such a tissue of bombastic fanfaronade, that we could hardly maintain our gravity. If we had not met and seen the brave soldiers of whom he spoke, his words might have gone for something; but the whole of them had passed in review before us, and

> " Such a tattered host of mounted scarecrows,
> So bare, so withered, famished in the march,
> That their executors, the greedy crows,
> Flew hovering o'er their heads, impatient for
> Their lean inheritance!"

In short such a motley, half-naked, ill appointed set of ragamuffins constituted his army, that we could with difficulty believe that the great Armijo was not quizzing us in his grandiloquent description.

After a little commonplace conversation, Armijo next gave special directions to the old alcalde of San Miguel that we should be well treated, that all our wants should be provided for, and that no one could insult or impose upon us without incurring his most fierce and vindictive wrath. He then dismissed us, remarking as we were leaving the room, that if one of us attempted to escape during his absence life should be the forfeit.

We were then marched back to our new quarters, and a very small guard placed over us—a guard we could at any time have seized upon, tied neck and heels, and locked in our own prison. Scarcely had we returned to our *carcel* before a blast from one of Armijo's trumpets announced his immediate departure; and ere the sounds had died away, the great man and his followers dashed passed us, evidently going some hundred yards out of his way for no other purpose than to give us one more opportunity of seeing him. His appearance was certainly imposing, even unto magnificence. On this occasion he was mounted on a richly-caparisoned mule, of immense size and of a beautiful dun colour. In stature Armijo is over six feet, stout and well built, and with an air decidedly military. Over his uniform he now wore a *poncho* of the finest blue broadcloth, inwrought with various devices in gold and silver, and through the hole in the centre peered the head to which the inhabitants of New Mexico are compelled to bow in fear and much trembling. Armijo is certainly one of the best-appearing men I met in the country, and were he not such a cowardly braggart, and so utterly destitute of all moral principle, is not wanting in the other qualities of a good governor.

On his departure, San Miguel, which ordinarily contained some two or three hundred able-bodied men, was left with scarcely a dozen, he having dragged away with him every one old and active enough to carry a lance or bow and arrow, in the direction of the great prairie, to meet the force under General M'Leod.

The room assigned us as a prison was immediately adjoining the little *adobe* church of San Miguel, with its small belfry and clear-sounding bell, and its rude turret surmounted by a large wooden cross. Had this room not been completely overrun with *chinches*, which, when night came, issued from every crack and crevice in the walls in myriads, it would have been very comfortable. Our guard was soon on the most sociable terms with us, allowing us to sit in front of our door, and kindly doing any little errand which might add to our limited stock of comforts. In the room adjoining ours, the two doors not being four yards apart, lived a Mexican family, the head of which was a *zapatero*, or shoemaker. His wife was a young, chatty, well-formed woman, and had not one side of her face been marked by a large, ugly red spot, would have been exceedingly comely. Two thirds, at least, of the women we had seen were more or less disfigured by these deep-red marks; and we could not but think that nature, in this mountain climate, had dealt unkindly with them. Not for one moment did it occur to us that these red blotches, which frequently gave the countenance an expression absolutely hideous, had been placed there by other than the partial fingers of nature. I knew that fancy frequently led the votaries of fashion to strange and most unseemly lengths, but I could not believe that in her wildest caprice she had instituted such revolting adornments for the "human face divine."

On the following morning, it appeared to us that the mark on the face of our female neighbour had changed its position. Not a little did we marvel at this; for all were sure the spot had been on the opposite cheek the day before, and still we could not believe that it was other than a mark she had carried from her birth. Early on the third morning she appeared before us with a face not only fair, but very pretty—not a spot or blemish to be discovered. At first we did not recognize her, but on inquiring, we found that all the spots which had so much disfigured her had been placed there by herself, the juice of some red berry being used for the purpose. We told the Senora Francisca that she looked much better *plain,* and without those extraneous ornaments, and after this she *beautified* herself no more. The custom is universal among the females of New Mexico, and when there is no weed or berry that furnishes a deep-red tint, they use vermillion, or even a reddish clay. How they can imagine that these vile marks improve their appearance it is difficult to conceive, and the fact can only be accounted for upon the principle that there is no accounting for taste. The belles of New Mexico appear to be ignorant of the aphorism that "beauty when unadorned is adorned the most."

The dress worn by the females of Northern Mexico, in fact all over the country, is a cotton or linen chemise and a blue or red short woollen petticoat—frequently, among the more wealthy, the latter is made of a gaudy figured merino, imported expressly for the purpose. These simple articles of raiment are usually made with no little degree of neatness, the chemise, in particular, being in many cases elaborately worked with flowers and different conceits, while the edges are tastefully decorated with ruffles or laces, if it lies within the power of the wearer to procure them. On first entering the country, the Anglo-Saxon traveller, who has been used to see the gentler sex of his native land in more full, and perhaps I should say more becoming costume, feels not a little astonished at the Eve-like and scanty garments of the females he meets; he thinks that they are but half-dressed, and wonders how they can have the indelicacy, or, as he would deem it at home, brazen impudence, to appear before him in dishabille so immodest. But he soon learns that it is the custom and fashion of the country—that, to use a common Yankee expression, the women "don't know any better." He soon looks, with an eye of some leniency, at such little deficiencies of dress as the absence of a gown, and is not long in coming to the honest conclusion, as the eye becomes more weaned from the fastidiousness of early habit and association, that a pretty girl is quite as pretty without as with that garment. By-and-by, he is even led to think that the dress of the women, among whom fate, business, or a desire to see the world may have thrown him, is really graceful, easy—ay, becoming: he next wonders how the females of his native land can press and confine, can twist and contort themselves out of all proportion, causing the most gracefully-curving lines of beauty to become straight and rigid, the exquisite undulations of the natural form to become flat, or angular, or conical, or jutting, and all in homage to a fickle and capricious goddess — a heathen goddess, whose worshippers are Christians! He looks around him, he compares, he deliberates—the result is altogether in favour of his new-found friends.

Among the Mexican women, young and old, corsets are unknown, and, by a majority of them, probably unheard of. I travelled nearly seven hundred miles through the country without seeing a single gown—all the females were dressed in the same style, with the same *abandon*. The consequence any one may readily imagine: the forms of the gentler sex obtain a roundness, a fulness which the divinity of tight lacing never allows her votaries. The Mexican belles certainly have studied, too, their personal comfort in the costume they have adopted, and it is impossible to see the prettier of the dark-eyed *senoras* of the northern departments without acknowledging that their personal appearance and attractions are materially enhanced by the *negligé* style. Moore's beautiful lines to Nora Creina appear to apply especially to the Mexican girls, for their dress certainly leaves

"—— every beauty free
To sink or swell as Heaven pleases."

But by all this the reader must not understand that the traveller sees no full-dressed ladies in Mexico. In the great city of the Montezumas, in fact in all the larger towns where foreigners and French milliners have settled, he sees them habited after the fashion of his own land, although he cannot but notice that a large portion of those so attired feel constrained and ill at ease under the infliction. I have seen, in one of the larger cities, a lady with the body and sleeves of a fashionable frock hanging dangling at her back, without even attempting to conceal what many would call a gross departure from all rules and reasons.*

Bonnets are never worn, either by rich or poor, high or low; but in their stead the *mantilla* and *reboso,* more especially the latter, are in general use among all classes. The latter is a species of long, narrow scarf, made of cotton, and in a majority of cases figured with two colours only, blue and white. These indispensable articles in the toilet of the Mexican female serve not only the uses of parasol and bonnet, but also of shawl, veil, and work-bag. The manner of wearing them is extremely graceful—sometimes upon the head, at others over the shoulders, and again round the waist, with the ends hanging across the arms; in the streets they are worn almost invariably over the head, and so archly and coquettishly does the fair Mexican draw the reboso around her face, that the inquisitive beholder is frequently repaid with no other than the sight of a dark and lustrous eye peering out from amid its folds.

The ends of the reboso are frequently used as an apron,

* Since my return to the United States I have been informed, by traders who have visited Santa Fé, that many of the women of that place have adopted the *tunica,* or gown. The fashion was first introduced, as is almost invariably the case, by a French woman. Her name was Madame Tule, or Toulouse, or something of the kind. How she happened to stray so far from comfort and civilization as Santa Fé, or by what road she reached it, is a matter of which I am ignorant; I only know that she visited the place, opened a monte, or gambling-house, and set the fashion of dress to the belles. The traders, as a matter of policy, favoured the introduction, as it afforded them a more ready market for the sale of silks, satins, and calicoes. By nearly the same means the fashion has spread as far as Chihuahua.

to carry any little articles that cannot be held in the hands, and seldom is a female seen without one of them, from the extreme north of Mexico to its southernmost boundaries. From childhood it is worn, and long habit has so accustomed them to its use that it is not laid aside when engaged in common household labour.

It is really surprising with what facility the Mexican females perform their household duties encumbered by this garment. An American lady would as easily manage her affairs with her hands tied behind her back as with the *reboso* about her, yet it is never in the way of the Mexican. The *mantilla* resembles it in many respects, but is made of finer material, rather wider, and worn more among the fashionables in the larger cities. An extremely beautiful ornament it is, too, when worn with that peculiar grace which no other than the lady of Spanish origin can affect.

The more striking beauties of the women of Northern Mexico are their small feet, finely-turned ankles, well-developed busts, small and classically formed hands, dark and lustrous eyes, teeth of beautiful shape and dazzling whiteness, and hair of that rich and jetty blackness peculiar to the Creole girls of Louisiana, and some of the West India islands. Generally their complexions are far from good, the mixture of Spanish and Indian blood giving a sallow, clayish hue to their skin; neither are their features comely, although frequently a face may be met with which might serve as a perfect model of beauty. But then they are joyous, sociable, kind-hearted creatures almost universally, liberal to a fault, easy and naturally graceful in their manners, and really appear to have more understanding than the men. Had we fallen into the hands of the women instead of the men, our treatment would have been far different while in New Mexico.

During our tedious and annoying confinement at San Miguel, we were visited by every girl in the town, and from the *ranchos* in the vicinity. Each time they brought us some little delicacy to eat; and if ever men came near being killed with kindness, we were the victims. One party would arrive with a dish of *chile guisado*, an olla podrida, or hash of stewed mutton, strongly seasoned with red pepper, and really excellent when well made. Scarcely would this party leave us before another would come in, bringing *atole* and *miel;* others milk, eggs, tortillas, or bread. Of all these different dishes we were obliged to partake, or wound the feelings of our kind-hearted friends; and the consequence was, that we were frequently compelled to swallow a dozen meals a-day for the first week or two of our imprisonment. That we did fair justice to the hospitality of the women, I am frank to confess, for our previous long starvation had given us most excellent and not easily appeased appetites; but if "*enough* is as *good* as a feast"—and an old adage says that it is—I can argue from experience that *too much* is *worse* even than a brief famine, when personal comfort is taken into consideration. No slight can be greater than the rejection of any eatable proffered by a Mexican girl; and so numerously attended were our *levées* at San Miguel, that we were frequently employed half the day in paying due honour to our *presentations.*

It was on the afternoon of the 17th of September that Colonel Cooke and his men surrendered themselves at Anton Chico. On the morning of the 20th these betrayed and unfortunate men passed through the edge of San Miguel on their long and gloomy march towards the city of Mexico. We were not permitted to see them, but were informed by the women who visited us, that they had been stripped of nearly everything, and were badly treated in every way.

At this point of my narrative—for I cannot find a more fitting place—I will give my readers an account of the agency Lewis had in inducing our companions to surrender their arms at Anton Chico. To show him in his true colours, I will make a few extracts from a statement of the particulars of the surrender made by Lieutenant Lubbock, one of Captain Sutton's officers. Lieutenant L. was taken to the city of Mexico with the rest of the party, but while confined in the convent of Santiago, made a daring escape by leaping from a balcony in the second story, and afterward succeeded in reaching Texas in safety.

It seems that the day after the small party which I accompanied, consisting of Howard, Fitzgerald, Van Ness and Lewis, left the large sheepfold on the Gallinas, the main body of the Texans took up the line of march, and travelled as far as Anton Chico. They did not enter the town, but encamped on the edge of a ravine within some two hundred yards, a strong position in case of attack, with an abundance of water running almost at the very feet of the men. Three or four of the Texans, who crossed the river, and entered the small town to purchase provisions, were arrested by Dimasio Salazar, who was then encamped at the place with several hundred men. Salazar immediately sent one of them back to Colonel

Cooke and Dr. Brenham, with a request that they would come over to the village and hold a consultation with him. These officers very properly sent back word to him that if he wished to see them he must come to *their* camp. He came over, and the conference resulted in the liberation of the men. Colonel Cooke then asked Salazar what had become of Van Ness, Lewis, Howard, Fitzgerald, and myself. He answered that he had met us, was satisfied with the objects of the mission as we had explained them, had treated us as friends, and sent us on to the governor. That night, according to Lieutenant L., Salazar was re-enforced by a hundred and fifty men, but the rest of his account of the surrender I will give in his own words.

"About ten o'clock on the morning of the 17th of September, it was determined to take up the line of march, when a message was received from Captain Salazar, stating that Governor Armijo would arrive in a few hours, and that, as an evidence of his friendly disposition, he would cross the river that intervened between our encampments, and encamp near us. As he took up the line of march, our men were formed to receive him *en militaire,* and in a proper manner. He marched, however, entirely around our line, and took his position within two hundred yards of us, having received farther re-enforcements, and now numbering about four hundred men. We were thon dismissed, but with orders to be ready to seize our arms at a moment's notice. In about fifteen minutes we perceived a party of about a hundred and fifty or two hundred men, advancing to our right and rear. This gave a cause for a suspicion of danger, and Colonel Cooke immediately ordered Captain

Sutton to form the men for action. In five minutes battle to the death would have been commenced—but some one exclaimed that Captain Lewis was at the head of the party. The order was therefore given to stand at ease, the advancing party uniting, in the mean while with the party in our front. We then perceived Captain Lewis advancing towards us, with another, whom we afterward ascertained to be the nephew of the governor. Lewis told us that the people were exasperated at our coming, and were in arms; that, in addition to the six hundred troops before us, he himself had seen four thousand of the best equipped men he had ever met with; that they were on the march, and would be on the ground in a few hours. He farther stated that five thousand men were marching from Chihuahua, and were expected daily, but that the governor had commissioned him to offer, if we would give up our arms, permission to come in and trade, and that at the end of eight days they would be returned to us, together with our recruited horses. He farther stated that *he knew* this to be the custom of the St. Louis traders visiting Santa Fé, that no possible harm would result from such a course, and for the truth of these statements Lewis pledged *his honour*. It was observed, during the conference, that Lewis, in his language, disconnected himself from us, using continually the pronoun *you* instead of *we*. This aroused the suspicions of one of the officers, who proposed that we should return to our companions as we came; and if we could not do better, walk, and live upon the horses we had left. The nephew of the governor replied that such a course would never do; that his uncle knew Americans were gentlemen, and that such inhumanity could not be permitted towards them; and again urged us to accept the proposition, and comply with the requisitious made upon all traders visiting Santa Fé. They then started for their camp. While our officers were in consultation, one of them reminded Colonel Cooke of the peculiarity he had observed in Lewis's conversation, and told him that his suspicions were aroused, for the very countenance of the man foreboded evil. Colonel Cooke went after Lewis, and held a private conversation with him. On returning, he said that the officer must be wrong, for Lewis had pledged to him his masonic faith for the correctness of his statements. *That day our arms and equipments were taken from us.*

"We were among strangers—destitute of the very necessaries of life—broken down physically, and well-nigh mentally—two hundred and fifty miles from our companions, and there were no means on the route of supporting nature in an effort to reach them; added to all these, we had the assurance of one of our companions, who had ever been considered a man of honour—we had his plighted faith, that we were among friends, and would be treated accordingly. Could we, would any one have done otherwise than capitulate upon the terms offered? It is painful to denounce one with whom I have associated as a brother-officer and fellow-soldier upon a dangerous expedition, one whom I have looked upon as a man, as a Texan; it is painful, I say, to denounce any one thus situated as a villain and traitor; but the facts are too conclusive—William P. Lewis betrayed his associates to a cruel and inhuman enemy. He has the mark upon his forehead; and will yet be found, recognised, and punished as the Judas of the nineteenth century.

"Just before dark we were ordered to form, and then Mexican faith began to show itself. While we were forming, however, the treachery of Lewis becoming apparent, Colonel Cooke called to him, and in the hearing of his *betrayed,* as well of his *newly-found associates,* denounced him in language which, if he had any soul at all, must have reached it. He reminded him of his pledged honour, which had been forgotten—of his plighted masonic faith, which had been broken—and declared that but for him his former associates would have died in the ditch.

"After we were formed, our knives, watches, and indeed every article of personal property were taken from us, together with all our baggage except one blanket each. We were then formed double file, marched nearer the *rancho,* or town, and then encamped for the night with our guards all around us."

Such is Lieutenant Lubbock's account of the agency of Lewis in inducing the surrender of his former friends and companions. The same officer then goes on to speak of the arrival of Armijo on the day after the surrender, saying that the petty tyrant was much exasperated on seeing that the betrayed prisoners were not tied. By his orders they were then bound—four, six, or eight together, as many as the different lariats would confine. The cries among the more open friends of Armijo, during this operation, were, *"Kill them! kill them! Death to the Americans!"* After nightfall a consultation was held by the officers more immediately in the interest of Armijo, and directly within hearing of the Texans, as to the propriety of either executing them all upon the spot, or sending them forthwith to the city of Mexico as trophies of the valour of the New Mexicans. The party in favour of the latter course prevailed by a majority of only *one vote!*

The day following that on which Colonel Cooke and his comrades were marched through San Miguel, we petitioned the old alcalde for a change of quarters, the room we were then occupying, although comfortable in every other respect, being so completely overrun with *chinchees* and other vermin, that it was impossible to sleep at night. After we had waited with great impatience two days, and passed two more sleepless nights, the old fellow finally procured us a clean and comfortable room directly on the plaza. A hint from Van Ness, to the effect that Armijo should be made acquainted with the kind of room the old alcalde had furnished us, probably induced that functionary to hasten our removal. When once establised in our new quarters, our time passed more agreeably. Our only occupations were eating, drinking, sleeping, chatting with the girls who made us daily visits, and speculating upon our past reverses, our present position, and future prospects. At dark we would build a fire, for the evenings were now cool among the mountains, and then probably spend half the night in song and story. Each one of our little party had a checkered experience to relate, and the recital of some ludicrous adventure would bring forth a peal of uproarious laughter, much to the astonishment of the little knot of Mexicans congregated among us, who could not conceive how prisoners, in the power of such a man as Armijo, could indulge in such boisterous mirth. For myself, I must say that I have never laughed more heartily than while confined in that little prison-house on the plaza of San Miguel; and could our anxious friends have been *spirited* into that wild and romantic land, and permitted to eavesdrop under the walls of our *carcel* on some of those evenings, they could hardly have deemed us other than a party of merry fellows holding a jolly carousal.

But with all this hilarity, thoughts of an escape frequently entered our minds. The members of our guard, who manifested the greatest astonishment at our indifference to imprisonment, we could at any time have captured and tied, and with their bows and arrows, and a German double-barrelled gun in their possession, we could next have taken the town of San Miguel with the greatest ease. On several occasions, so careless was the guard, we made trials of skill with them with the bow and arrow, Major Howard beating the best of them at a game which may be considered their own; but, even with their arms in our possession, where were we to go? Had we known then, what we afterward ascertained, that so many dreary months of toil and captivity were in store for us; had we been aware that by forced marches we could have reached Bent's Fort in three or four days, we might have made the attempt. There was no one, however, to give us advice, no friend without to aid us in an undertaking of the kind, we knew nothing of the country, and thus were we compelled to give up all thoughts of an escape at a time when the chances of its successful results were altogether in our favour. With the knowledge we have since gained, I doubt whether the same party could be safely kept another month in San Miguel, at least with so weak a guard, under like circumstances.

We had been but a week in our new quarters before a caravan arrived direct from St. Louis, owned by one of the Chavez family, a rich and powerful connection in New Mexico. Chavez himself, in a neat buggy waggon, accompanied his men. I could not help reflecting, while gazing at him in the plaza, upon the difference of treatment he had experienced in the United States from that I had met with in his country, knowing, as I did, that my feelings and intentions on entering the latter were precisely the same as his on first setting his foot on that soil where I claimed citizenship. I would cheerfully have endured a month's extra imprisonment for an opportunity of making known my reflections and feelings to Chavez; but this might not be—he did not come within speaking distance.

Three or four days after Chavez passed through San Miguel, another caravan, made up of Americans on their way to California, arrived from St. Louis, and after resting themselves for one day, again took their departure for their new homes west of the Rocky Mountains. Anxious as we were to converse with these men, and gather news of the world without from which we had now been cut off more than four months, we were forbidden the privilege. The alcalde undoubtedly had his orders not to allow any intetcourse, and scrupulously did he obey them.

Following close upon the heels of this party of Americans, or but three or four days later, came still another caravan, belonging to Mr. Samuel Magoffin, a native of the United States, but at this time a merchant of Chihuahua, who was now on his way to that city with more than forty waggons heavily laden with goods. Mr. Magoffin sent us word, through a Mexican, that he had had an interview with Armijo, who had granted him permission to visit us; but as he had not brought a written order to that effect, the old alcalde would not allow him even to approach within a hundred yards of our prison-house. By the same messenger we were informed that we need not be under the least apprehension for our lives; and in addition, he brought the positive assurance that I was shortly to be liberated, the governor not having any charges against me, and not wishing to detain me after the termination of his expedition against the party of Texans now approaching under General M'Leod. This was good news; too good, as I then justly thought, to be true, although at that time, I have little doubt, Armijo intended to give me my liberty, and would have done so had it not been for Lewis.

From Mr. Magoffin we received a generous supply of coffee and tobacco, luxuries more welcome than anything he could have sent us. The old alcalde furnished us regularly with tortillas, atole, and occasionally with an earthen pot of boiled mutton; but as we had saved our money, we had the means to purchase occasionally a fat sheep, eggs, good bread, and any little necessary we might wish for; and now that we had coffee and tobacco, and had no employment save the dressing and cooking of our meals, we fared most sumptuously. We contrived to manufacture excellent pipes of corn-cobs; for stems we were indebted to a monkey-faced Mexican named Juan Sandobal, who brought us some branches from a small bush growing upon the river bank, the pith of which could be easily extracted. This fellow Sandobal was a regular loafer in and about our premises, ready at any time to mend our shoes, run on errands, wash our handkerchiefs, or play us a rude air on a cracked mandolin of which he was the proprietor, and all "for a consideration." He invariably contrived to cheat us in every transaction we had with him, and we as invariably made it a point to tell him that we considered him an arrant knave; yet the fellow had made one trip with the traders to St. Louis, spoke some half dozen words of English, and as he had associated on the road with Americans in the capacity of servant, made bold to call us his *amigos*, or particular friends. There was no such thing as getting rid of his importunities: hints he would not understand, and kicks he appeared to look upon as little innocent familiarities between intimates. Our principal out-door agent, when his time was not otherwise occupied, was Tomas Bustamente, the same personage who purchased the sheep for us on the morning after our first arrival at San Miguel. Don Tomas, as we called him, was always bringing us information of all the movements of Armijo, and was ready at any time to make up a story in case nothing had occurred that might in any way interest us. For us he always manifested the greatest friendship; and as he was a specious, honest-seeming, and open countenanced fellow, accommodating to a fault, and with far more integrity than Sandobal even pretended to, to him we always intrusted our important commissions. All our little purchases were made by him; and with such scrupulous exactness did he give us the price of every little article bought, and so honestly did he return us our change for the money we placed in his hands, that for a long time we gave him credit for being a perfect *rara avis* among the lower classes in New Mexico—an honest man. But an unfortunate accident —unfortunate, at least, for Don Tomas—completely overthrew our good opinions of him.

I have before mentioned that an American merchant of San Miguel, Mr. Thomas Rowland, had been arrested by Armijo about the time when Howland was first taken, and that his goods and effects had been confiscated. We had been confined but a couple of weeks before Rowland was released, his effects were given up to him, and he had once more opened his store. Some half dozen times a day our countryman passed within a few yards of our prison, yet was not allowed to cemmunicate with us by word, or even gesture. We knew the circumstances of his arrest, and the constraints under which he laboured; yet I am confident we were indebted to Rowland for many little favours, and I have little doubt that he sent us many luxuries which never reached us, all through the rascality of Tomas Bustamente. The little circumstance, which brought this fellow out in his true colours, I will here relate.

Hearing that our former companion, Lewis, was at a rancho but a few leagues distant, and not knowing at this time of his traitorous conduct, Van Ness and Howard despatched Bustamente to see him, in the hope that we might gain news, or at least obtain a change of linen, our entire wardrobe now consisting simply of what we had upon our backs. As a token that Van Ness had sent this fellow, he placed a ring upon his finger which Lewis well knew, and which would convince him that there was no deceit in the transaction. This was early in the morning. At night our agent returned unsuccessful from his mission, saying that he had been unable to find Lewis or obtain our much-needed supply. While we were regretting the unsuccessful termination of an attempt which we had fondly hoped would give each of us a clean shirt, if nothing more, Don Tomas casually remarked that the Senora Rowland had accidentally seen the ring sent by Van Ness, and had taken a great fancy to it, at the same time desiring him to ask whether it could be disposed of, and the price. So plausible was this story that not one of us suspected fraud; and as it was impossible to *sell* the ring, valuable as it was, to one who had constantly been sending us many little delicacies, it was at once despatched to her as a present, accompanied by the usual ceremonious compliments. This little incident over, nothing more was thought of the ring, and we filled our pipes and began smoking and talking over the unfortunate result of our mission to Lewis.

Than our pipe—our homely, oblivious pipe—we found no greater solace during the many hours of affliction. Far be it from me to say that any pipe is preferable to a cool, finely-flavoured Havana, or that I esteem it under ordinary circumstances; but in a time of adversity and trial, when the mind has no employment but to brood over unavoidable misfortunes, there is more real comfort, more forgetfulness of the present, to be drawn from even a cob pipe, well filled with Virginia tobacco, than from any cigar that has ever been twisted since the day when Sir Walter Raleigh was supposed by his servant to be on fire, and deluged with a flood of cold water. If any of my readers do not credit this assertion, let them ask old campaigners, those who have had abundant experience, and from whose judgment there is no appeal—in the woods. I know that I have drawn much solid comfort from a pipe, and puffed away many weary hours of captivity.

The evening following the return of Don Tomas from his unsuccessful trip, one of our female visiters remarked that the ring Senora *Bustamenta* had received from Van Ness was a beautiful present, and that she was so extremely proud of it that she was showing it about among all her acquaintances! Here was a discovery, and it is almost unnecessary to say that after this Don Tomas fell most essentially in our esteem. We did not let him know, however, that we had detected him in his little swindling operation. He was useful in doing errands, and probably took as little toll out of our money as any of the natives would have done. His delinquency, too, taught us all a useful lesson—it proved to us that the most specious and honest-seeming among this class of Mexicans had their tricks and failings, and that the best men among them were worthy of close watching.

CHAPTER XVI.

Arrival of a Party of our Companions as Prisoners.—Great Excitement in San Miguel.—Recognition of our Friends, and their Departure.—Don Antonio Baca.—Attachment of one of his Daughters for a Texan Prisoner.—"Old Paint" Caldwell and Nine of his Men brought in Prisoners.—Still greater Excitement in San Miguel.—The Patron Saint brought from his Niche in the Church.—A Mexican Procession.—A funny Figure.—Programme of the Procession.—An old Priest with queer Spectacles.—A Pair of Musicians.—More of San Miguel, the Patron Saint.—End of the Procession.—Startling Information.—Bustamente informs us that all our Comrades have been taken Prisoners.—Great Rejoicing in San Miguel.—General M'Leod and other Texans brought into the Plaza.—Mr. Falconer.—Arrival of all the Prisoners.—Dreadful Appearance of the Texans.—Lewis arrives.—News that the Author is to be liberated.—Division of the Spoils.—Agency of Lewis in the Transaction.—A Visit from Lewis.—More of his Treachery and Rascality.—His Departure for Santa Fé.—A veritable History of Don Manuel Armijo, from his Youth upward, being a short but faithful Narrative of his thieving, gambling, assassinating, and other base Acts and Propensities.

WE had now whiled away some eighteen or twenty days in our prison-house at San Miguel, and were anxiously awaiting news of General M,Leod's party and of Armijo's success with this second band of Texans, when Bustamente came hurriedly into our apartment, just as we had finished a late breakfast, and informed us that three or four of our companions had been taken, and were then coming into the town. A crowd of women, girls, and boys, congregrated upon the neighbouring housetops and around the door of the alcalde on the opposite side of the plaza, soon convinced us that something had occurred to disturb the ordinary quiet which reigned in San Miguel.

We hurried through the door of our room to a little porch, which was our prison limits, anxiously eyeing every figure within view to see if we could discover an acquaintance. Soon a small cavalcade of ragged Mexicans, guarding two mules, upon each of which a couple of men were packed, were seen turning the corner of a street leading into the plaza—the same street by which we had first entered the town. At first we were not near enough to distinguish the faces of the prisoners, but after they had been halted at the door of the alcalde we made them out to be Lieutenants Scot and Burgess, young John Howard, a brother of the major who was a prisoner with us, and the Mexican servant named Matias, whom Colonel Cooke had sent back to the prairies, from the Angosturas, with the guide to conduct General M'Leod to the settlements. We bowed to our friends, and made signs and gestures that we knew and would like to converse with them; they returned our distant salutations in kind, but farther intercourse than this was not allowed by our guards. After remaining a short time at the alcalde's, our friends were sent to a rancho some three miles from San Miguel, and there quartered in the family of a kind-hearted old Mexican, named Don Antonio Baca, a man who had frequently visited us during our imprisonment, and who had never called without bringing us eggs or some little delicacy. Although we had been denied the satisfaction of conversing with our friends, and learning something of their own movements and the position and prospects of the main party, it was still a source of congratulation to know that excellent quarters had been provided for them. Don Antonio had two or three daughters, pretty, and accomplished too for that country; we afterward learned that one of them formed an ardent attachment—fell in love, in more common parlance—with one of our young friends, and was affected even to tears and hysterics when he was ordered to the city of Mexico. It is said that no attachment can be stronger, no love more enduring, than that of the better-informed Mexican doncella, when once her heart is touched by the blue eyes, light hair, and fair complexion of some roving Anglo-Saxon. She may not "live and love for ever," as did a certain maid mentioned by some poet; but she loves as long as she lives, and that is long enough in all reason.

A day or two after the party of Texans I have just referred to were conducted through the town, another party, numbering ten, also arrived. They were prisoners, and had the good fortune to be quartered at the house of our old friend Vigil, the man who had saved our lives when we were first captured by Salazar. We did not see this party, but from descriptions given us of their leader by our guard and the girls who visited us, we felt confident he could be no other than "Old Paint" Caldwell, the well-known leader of our spy company, and in this conjecture we were not wrong. Bustamente informed us that they had been taken prisoners by a large party of Mexicans south of the Angosturas, and that the main body of the Texans was rapidly approaching. We at once came to the conclusion that the two small parties of our friends, now in prison near us, had been sent on in advance, and, as in our case, had been overpowered in numbers, and forced to give up their arms.

A most unwonted excitement was now created in San Miguel. The rumours rife among the people were, that the much-dreaded Texans, whom Armijo had taught them to look upon as so many blood-thirsty cannibals, were advancing in countless numbers, threatening the country with fire, devastation, and the sword. The wax figure of the patron saint of the place, San Miguel, or St. Michael as it is rendered in the English, was dragged from his niche in the little church, mounted upon a large platform, and carried about in procession. A more comical figure than this same San Miguel it would be difficult either to imagine or discover. I cannot say that his saintship had ever been tarred, but he had certainly been feathered from head to foot. From his shoulders hung listlessly a pair of huge, ill-constructed wings, his face was that of a large doll, while his head, to complete the ludicrous *tout énsemble,* was covered with a lace cap of the fashion of our grandmothers. Another figure, intended to represent the Virgin, but nothing more than a doll of the largest size, was carried in state upon the same platform, and over all was a canopy of faded yellow and pink satin, trimmed with fringe, spangles, and tassels. The platform rested upon a litter formed of two long poles, upon which were nailed cross-pieces, and into these cross-pieces were inserted four loose, ricketty legs, hardly firm enough to sustain the wax and feathers, satin and spangles, which reclined above them. Whenever the procession was about to move, the entire fabric would be lifted from the ground, and the ends of the poles placed upon the shoulders of four men.

I will endeavour to give my readers a programme of this singular procession. First came an old, bald-headed priest, a coarse, dirty blanket tied about him with a piece of rope, an open prayer-book in his hand, a rude wooden cross hanging from his neck, and a pair of spectacles on his nose which my companions at first insisted were leather, but which afterward proved to be of glass, about the size of common teacups, and set in wide rims of buffalo horn. Following close at the heels of this odd figure came our particular friend, Juan Sandobal, strumming his crazy mandolin, and digging from it the only tune within his musical scope. By his side walked a brother artist, zealously sawing away upon a rusty violin, the softest tone from which would have set Ole Bull or Wallace raving mad. As each of these performers knew but one tune, and as both were playing at the same time, the reader who may have an ear to detect a crack in a piece of china by the ring, can easily imagine the effect produced by such a mixture of anything but sweet sounds. On either side of the musicians, as flankers, walked half a score of ragged, dirty-faced urchins; then came the four men bearing the car, the patron saint in a sitting posture in front, and his head, either from being hung on a pivot or from having become loose in some way, bowing and bobbing to the multitude like the figures of Chinese mandarins in some of the tea shops. Nothing could be more grotesque and laughable than this comical head of St. Michael, enveloped in an old-fashioned lady's cap, and rising and falling with every motion of the ear upon which it was borne. On the same platform, and immediately behind the figure I have just described, stood the Virgin, dressed in pink satin and spangles, as stiff and inanimate as wood and wax could make her. In the rear of the car followed the women, children, and rabble generally of the town, the faces of a majority of the girls stained, either with vermillion or the juice of some red berry, and many of them presenting an appearance truly hideous.

At different points of the plaza the procession would halt, the bearers of the car would set down their burden, and all would kneel and cross themselves while the old priest read a sentence from the open book before him. One of the principal stopping-places appeared to be directly in front of our little window, and solemn as the affair was intended to be, it was impossible for us to retain our gravity with two such figures as the old priest and the patron saint staring us in the face. Those huge spectacles of the former alone would have drawn a smile from the gloomiest misanthrope that ever lived; and then the comical aspect of the droll figure of San Miguel—waggish in more ways than one, for while it wagged its head it also had a quaint and knowing leer about its eyes—whenever this counterfeit presentment of the saint was brought fairly in sight, we lost our gravity entirely, and were compelled to turn aside to conceal our laughter.

After the procession had knelt in front of our prison, the old priest would call upon every saint in the calendar in general, and San Miguel in particular, to aid the populace against, and protect them from, the vile horde of heretics and barbarians marching against their country. All would then respond by crossing themselves and giving utterance to groans, the *band* would next strike up, and the procession then move slowly to some other point, there to repeat the same ceremony. In this way the time passed, from the day on which the ten prisoners alluded to a few pages back arrived at San Miguel, to the 9th of October.

At an early hour on the morning of the 9th, our guard gave us the startling information that all the Texans had been captured in the vicinity of the Laguna Colorada, or Red Lake, a body of water some thirty or forty miles south of the Angosturas. At first we could not believe this news, but it was soon confirmed by the ringing of bells, general congratulations and rejoicings, and by a grand procession in honour of the victory. Again was the patron saint of the town mounted on the car, accompanied by the ever attendant Virgin, and borne about in triumph through the plaza and all the principal streets. Nothing could exceed the joy and enthusiasm of the inhabitants. The only gun in the place—the double-barrelled German affair I have already mentioned, and which had been used to guard and terrify us—was now brought into requisition to give greater spirit to the rejoicing. The fellow who had charge of this piece followed in the rear of the ragged rabble which formed the procession, and, as fast as he could load and fire, kept up an incessant cracking and banging, much to the delight, in particular, of a troop of graceless urchins who hovered about him on the march. At each of the four corners, and at each of the four sides of the plaza, did the procession stop, kneel down, and publicly thank San Miguel for thus keeping his charge out of the hands of heretics, and all this while the comical image, now arrayed with an extra load of furbelows, feathers, and finery, bowed his acknowledgments to the crowd of ragged worshippers in a style which would have done credit to any merry-andrew.

Scarcely were these nonsensical mummeries over, before General M'Leod and Mr. Navarro, with some ten or fifteen Texan officers and servants, were escorted under a strong guard into the plaza, and placed for safe-keeping in the old quartel we had occupied on the day when Howland and his comrades were shot. Mr. Falconer was seen in this little party by all of us, and although grieved to see him in plight so gloomy, I was still rejoiced to notice that he was in good health. Some of the members of this small party of prisoners were continually passing and repassing our room, within twenty yards of us, on their way to the river for water; they recognised and bowed to us as they passed, but we were not allowed to communicate with them in any way, and were consequently kept in ignorance of the terms of their surrender, and the disposition that was to be made of them.

On the 12th of October, two days after, the rest of the Texan prisoners, more than a hundred and fifty in number, where marched into the plaza. Worn down and emaciated by hunger and fatigue, their pale and haggard countenances showed but too plainly that they had suffered dreadfully after we left them on the Palo Duro. The clothing of many of these poor fellows consisted of but a shirt and pair of pantaloons, and the single blanket which had been left them by the brave and "honourable" Armijo was the poorest they were the possessors of at the time of their capture. They were all taken to a room on the opposite side of the square, and then huddled in like so many sheep in a butcher's pen!

Scarcely were these unfortunate men driven into their close and uncomfortable quarters before Lewis, well mounted and extremely well dressed, rode up to our quarters, and took lodgings in the same house in which we were confined, although in a different room. He bowed to us as he passed our window, said that "all was right," and remarked that he would call and see us in a short time. The day wore away, however, without his fulfilling his promise, although he passed within a few yards of us several times. There appeared to be a sneaking and uneasy expression about the fellow, which we all remarked; yet we could hardly believe that he had been playing a traitorous or unmanly game.

After dark, on the same day, Bustamente came into our room, and declared, positively, that I was to be released by Armijo so soon as all the prisoners had been sent off to the city of Mexico, that being their destination. This information he had from the principal priest of San Miguel, who has the reputation, among the Americans, of being an honest and worthy man. From what Bustamente could learn, by listening to the conversations of the officers attached to the staff of the governor, he was of opinion that Howard, Van Ness, and Fitzgerald, my three companions, would be taken by Armijo to Santa Fé, and shortly liberated. The same story was told by several Mexicans who visited us during the evening—that I was to be liberated was certain.

On the following morning the waggons—the same waggons with which we had set out, more than four months before, from Austin—were drawn up in line in the plaza of San Miguel, and immediate preparations were made for dividing the goods of the Texan merchants. As the merchandise was unloaded, Lewis was seen by all of us standing by the side of Armijo, and frequently pointing out a box or bale of goods, which was placed in a large pile, apparently for him. All the while he appeared to be on excellent and most sociable terms with the governor and the Mexican officers, and was plainly seen and heard laughing and joking with them. How the abandoned man could carry out his villany, and act thus in the very faces, as it were, of his betrayed associates, is a mystery to me.

The distribution of the goods continued nearly the whole of the day, each company of the valorous warriors of Armijo receiving a share of the plunder in proportion to the time they had been in service against the Texans. In the mean time, four of our men, a gunsmith, a blacksmith, a musician, and the hospital steward of the expedition, were liberated by Armijo, and from our window we could see them walking about at liberty. They were not allowed to communicate with us, however, in any way. The governor wanted the services of these men—his only reason for giving them their liberty.

Lewis frequently passed our window on the 14th and 15th of the month, but not once did he offer to speak to us, although he always bowed as he went by. That the man had been acting badly we had now little doubt, but the extent of his treachery was far from being suspected. After dusk of the last-mentioned day a nephew of Armijo called in to see us. He spoke of my release as a measure fully determined on by his uncle, and also gave it as his opinion that my three companions would be set free.

An early hour on the following morning, and for the first and only time, Lewis entered our room. There was a hang-dog expression, if I may so call it, about him, which denoted that he had committed some base action, and it seemed as if he could not look one of us in the face. He, however, tried to convince us that he was glad at having an opportunity, at last, of calling to bid us good-by, assuming an openness and frankness of demeanour which but ill became him. Howard asked him how it happened that the two main parties of Texans had surrendered without firing a single shot, to which Lewis gave an evasive and stammering reply. He was then asked by what means he had been fortunate enough to obtain his liberty: a question he answered by saying that the governor, for some reason unknown to him, had given him his release without his even asking for it. He then added that I was to be set free on the following morning; and, after telling my companions that he had already made every endeavour to procure their release, and that he would have one more interview with Armijo upon the subject, he hurriedly shook hands with each of us and departed. Five minutes afterward, as we learned from several visitors, he was on his way to Santa Fé, without having gone near the governor.

It may appear singular to many of my readers, that we did did not at once suspect Lewis of having played a treacherous game, especially with the evidence that the party under Colonel Cooke had not made even a show of resistance; but they should recollect that we were entirely cut off from all direct communication, and also that Lewis bore an excellent reputation, and was universally esteemed by all. Under these circumstances they will feel that we must have been slow to harbour suspicion against him. It is hard to suspect one with whom we have long associated on terms of intimacy, whose life has been unstained by a single bad act, of the blackest crime in the catalogue.

On the night before Lewis's departure for Santa Fé a young Mexican called at our room and inquired the value of several gold pieces in his possession, among them English sovereigns, French twenty-franc pieces, and different American coins. He spoke broken English, and we afterwards ascertained that Lewis had recommended him to some of our poor prisoners as a trustworthy fellow. They had given him this money, a pittance they had contrived to secrete when they were searched and robbed by Armijo, on his promising that he would procure them small silver change for it. The young scoundrel, with all this money in his pockets, left for Santa Fé the next morning in company with Lewis —*par nobile fratrum.*

Another circumstance has been related to me by the sufferers themselves, which goes to show that to treachery Lewis added the most pitiful swindling. Two members of the expedition, one of them named Farley, and belonging to the company of which Lewis was captain, the other a Mr. Houghtaling, a merchant, had succeeded, during the search made at the time of the surrender, in secreting their watches, both of them valuable. With this fact Lewis became acquainted, and just before starting for Santa Fé he called upon his quandam friends, and said that he would take their watches and sell them for a heavy sum. He said they would need the money on the road, and that it would be impossible for them to dispose of the watches after leaving San Miguel, but that, on the contrary, they would lose them if the Mexicans should by chance discover them about their persons. Farley was an intimate friend of the scoundrel, and gave him his watch with little hesitation. Houghtaling did the same. That was the last they saw of their property.

One other circumstance illustrative of his character, and I have done with Lewis for the present. While at Chihuahua, on our march to the city of Mexico, I saw a copy of *La Luna*, a small paper published there. It contained a letter from Armijo to Garcia Condé, governor of Chihuahua, in which, after stating that he had been successful in capturing all the Texans, he added: "In consideration of the great service rendered by Captain W. P. Lewis, in assisting me to capture these Texans, I have given him his liberty and his goods, and earnestly recommend him to the notice of the Central Government." When it is known that all the goods Lewis had with him he could carry in his hat, it is more than probable that the governor hired him to claim a large portion of the merchandise, which he afterward divided with him, and thus defrauded the government, to which he was obliged to render an account of all the spoils taken.

The history of this petty, yet most absolute and despotic monarch, Armijo, is singular, and as I happen to have the materials at hand, no matter to him how obtained, I will here present my readers with a brief yet truthful sketch of his career, from his boyhood upward.

However much he may be amazed at seeing his own history in veritable print, he cannot but acknowledge that I have done him ample justice—that his portrait is drawn with strict fidelity in every particular.

Manuel Armijo, the subject of the present memoir, as the story-books commence, was born of low and disreputable parents at or near Albuquerque, a town of no inconsiderable importance some sixty miles south of Santa Fé. From his earliest childhood his habits were bad. He commenced his career by petty pilfering, and as he advanced in years extended his operations until they grew into important larcenies. While yet a youth, he carried on an extensive business in sheep-stealing, admitted, I believe, to be the lowest species of robbery; yet so lucrative did the young Armijo find the business, that in his own neighbourhood he gave it a tone of respectability. A wealthy *haciendero,* or large plantation owner, in the vicinity of Albuquerque, named Francisco Chavez, suffered not a little from the exceedingly liberal system of helping himself adopted by the embryo governor. Chavez possessed his thousands and tens of thousands of sheep, large numbers of which he yearly drove to the southern cities of Mexico, and there disposed of for ready cash. At home, his business was to purchase at reduced prices all the sheep offered by his poorer neighbours, and so numerous were his flocks that he could not mark, much less recognise, one-tenth of what he possessed. Yet he always employed shepherds to watch his flocks, and used every precaution in his power to prevent his sheep from straying or being stolen.

But to guard against a person of young Armijo's tact and perseverance was impossible. The scape-grace would enter his flocks while the shepherds were asleep, or suborn them if awake, and by much shrewd artifice contrived to levy a continual and profitable tax upon the substance of the elderly haciendero. The animals thus stolen, in good time would be sold for cash to their rightful but unsuspecting owner, and thus it sometimes happened that Armijo would re-steal and re-sell, time after time, the same identical sheep. Up to this day, when among his intimate friends, General Manuel Armijo boastingly relates the exploit of having sold to "Old Chavez" the same ewe *fourteen different times*, and of having stolen her from him even in the first instance. By this means, and by having what is termed a good run of luck at dealing *monte*, he amassed no inconsiderable fortune, and as his ambition now led him to learn to read and write, the foundation of his future influence and greatness among his timid and ignorant countrymen was substantially laid.

As it would fill a volume to trace all Armijo's steps, I will at once jump from the sheep-folds of Chavez and the monte table, and take him up again after he had been appointed *Administrador de Rentas*, or principal custom-house officer at Santa Fé, in the year 1837. It is proper to mention that, during this hiatus, somewhere between the years 1825 and 1830, he had been, by a federal appointment under the old territorial laws, clothed with the executive authority in New Mexico, and that his short administration was signalized by acts of cruelty and reckless injustice. In consequence of some misdemeanor, he was soon deposed from his place at the head of the customs by the then governor, Don Albino Perez, and another person was appointed in his stead.

The effects of the central form of government were now just beginning to be felt in this isolated department of Mexico, and the people were beginning to manifest no inconsiderable discontent at the new order of things. Armijo, perceiving that there was now a chance, not only to signalize himself, but to reap a rich harvest of revenge against his enemies then in power, took advantage of this feeling by secretly fomenting a conspiracy. An insurrection was soon in agitation, and early in August, 1837, a heterogeneous force, numbering more than one thousand men, among whom where a large number of *pueblos*, or town Indians, assembled at La Canada, a village about twenty-five miles north of the capital. Governor Perez conducted a small force against the insurgents; but a majority of his men went over at the outset, leaving him with only twenty five personal friends to contend with odds the most fearful. A slight skirmish told the story: one of his men was killed, two were wounded, while the rest fled precipitately towards Santa Fé. The insurgents pursued them to the city, from which they were obliged to flee; but they were captured the next day, and fourteen of them, including all the officers of state, were most inhumanly put to death. Among the slain were three brothers named Abreu: Governor Perez was also butchered in the suburbs of Santa Fé, his head cut off, and kicked about the streets by the populace. His body remained where it had fallen, a prey to the vultures and wolves, no friend daring to offer it sepulture!

Shrewdly conjecturing, now that he had raised a whirlwind, that he might easily direct the storm to his own personal advancement, Armijo, after the manner of his great prototype, Santa Anna, suddenly left his hacienda and made his appearance at Santa Fé. There he found every thing in a state of frightful anarchy—the place in the hands of an ignorant mob, and the American and other foreign merchants in hourly expectation that their houses and stores would be sacked, and even their lives taken. The rabble dispersed, however, committing no other outrage than electing one of their own leaders, an ignorant and unlettered fellow named José Gonzalez, governor of New Mexico. They paid no attention to the claim set up by Armijo, the fomenter, as he had exposed himself in no way to the anticipated hard blows and knocks which had given them the ascendancy.

Foiled in his ambition, Armijo once more retired to his hacienda, a fine estate he had purchased at Albuquerque with the proceeds of his cheating, stealing, and gambling transactions. But an active and ambitious mind like his could not long remain inert. Through secret intrigues, he managed, after the lapse of three or four months, to organize a counter-revolution, and collecting a numerous force, he declared in favour of Federalism, and marched towards Santa Fé. He took quiet possession of this place, as Governor Gonzalez, finding himself without an army, had fled to the north. The latter was soon enabled, however, to rally around him no inconsiderable mob; but Armijo, in the mean time, had received heavy re-enforcements from the south, and succeeded in routing Gonzalez without loss, taking him and many of his principal men prisoners. The unfortunate governor was immediately shot, and four of his chief officers met with the same fate by order of Armijo. The latter were put out of the way more, it is said, to prevent disclosures than for any crime they had committed; for they had been Armijo's confidential emissaries in the formation of his original plot.

The ambitious tyrant, now that his enemies were either murdered or dispersed, reigned supreme in New Mexico. One of his first steps was to bribe the army to proclaim him governor and commander-in-chief; his next, to send off a highly-coloured account of his own exploits in favour of Federalism to the city of Mexico, and no officer can more adroitly adopt the high-sounding fanfaronade style in wording a dispatch or an address than Manuel Armijo. Such disinterested patriotism, such love of the confederacy, and such daring bravery as he had manifested could not go unrewarded, and a return of post from Mexico brought documents confirming him in his station of governor, with the additional title of colonel of cavalry. The sheep-thief is now rising in the world!

The year 1838 passed off without any event of great importance—Armijo still governor, and ruling his vassals with a rod of iron. In the early part of 1839, without a shadow of law or authority, he deposed all the custom-house officers and appointed his own brother and his other creatures in their stead, in order that he might have the exclusive control and management of the customs in his own hands. He next, without regard to the federal tariff, established an arbitrary duty upon all merchandise entering from the United States—$500 upon each waggon-load, without reference to the quality of the goods it might contain, or their value. To some of the traders, whose waggons happen to be heavily laden with the finer kinds of merchandise, this singular imposition is exceedingly favourable; while to others, with light or not valuable loading, it is equally oppressive.

From the material which I have at hand, I could give a connected detail of weekly acts of cruel injustice and most glaring partiality. Fénélon's graphic picture of a bad ruler has a living and faithful counterpart in the present governor of New Mexico. Foreigners are the especial objects of his hatred; and acts and decisions affecting the well-being of his whole province are as often founded upon a feeling of hatred towards a small class, or, perhaps, some luckless individual who has excited his jealousy or fallen under the ban of his most unaccountable caprice, as upon a sentiment of justice and necessity. Still oftener do his acts of public administration have their source in some private advantage to which he has a single eye—it may be in the furthering of some libertine and lustful scheme that would disgrace the veriest roué in Christendom. Still, there is not that overt demonstration of malice towards foreigners that he daily makes towards his own cringing and servile countrymen. He is afraid of Anglo-Saxon blood, and he seeks to spill it by protecting the knife of the secret assassin, or by influencing, to most outrageous decisions, his farcical courts of law. Not unfrequently do his own lusty sinews find congenial employment, in the open streets of Santa Fé, in wielding the cane and cudgel about the ears of his native subjects, and never yet has one been found bold enough to strike back. He raps them over the sconce with more impunity, because with vastly less sentiment, than did Hamlet the grinning scull of "poór Yorick."

Out of a multiplicity I will record two anecdotes, in order to illustrate his system of righting wrongs. The first came near resulting in a serious quarrel between the American residents and the governor, and the difficulty was only avoided by the latter abandoning his objectionable ground. An American named Daley was wantonly murdered at tho gold mines near Santa Fé, by two ruffians engaged in robbing a store which he was keeping at that place. The murderers, through the energy of foreigners, were soon apprehended, and fully convicted of the crime; but as they were Mexicans, and had only shed the blood of a heretic, were permitted to go unwhipped of justice. In July, 1839 these murderers were again arrested through the interposition of the Americans, and a second time brought to Santa Fé for trial. The friends of the murdered man now drew up a petition to the governor, in the most decorous language, praying him to mete out full justice to the assassins. Armijo, although he knew full well the justice of their prayer, affected to believe it a threat against his authority and govérnment — a conspiracy! Upon this pretence he immediately collected all the militia he could raise, and made preparations for one of his bravado demonstrations. The Americans, convinced that no justice could be expected from a tyrant so unprincipled, and fully understanding the "bluffing game" he had resorted to, at once, with characteristic spirit, prepared to defend themselves. Their firmness and cool determination frightened the cowardly governor, and induced him to send them an apologetical communication, in which he protested that he had entirely misconstrued the petition, and that their just request should have due attention.

In the year 1840, I think on the first day of January, two most respectable foreigners had the misfortune to kill a Mexican lad by the accidental discharge of one of their guns. They were returning to Santa Fé from the gold mines when the unfortunate accident occurred, and brought the body of the boy into town and at once reported the circumstance to the authorities. The principal alcalde consulted with Armijo as to the steps he should take, and the decision was, without form of trial, that the unfortunate foreigners should be put in prison and held responsible for murder, unless they could *prove themselves innocent!* This is a very common instance of the manner in which the potentate administers justice. But there was something in this case so palpably unjust in the eyes of those who knew the men and the facts, as once more to call out such manifestations of public disapprobation as induced him to retract so outrageous a sentence.

In the early part of February, 1840, a concurrence of two or three acts of most wanton injustice, conceived in cupidity and lust, came near resulting in revolution. Armijo is an extensive merchant, and it becomes a part of his policy to pay off the public dues in his own merchandise at most enormous profits. When it is remembered that he is at once governor, commander-in-chief, legislator, custom-house officer, auditor, treasurer, and judge, the practicability of this policy becomes apparent. Public creditors can get no money from the treasury because it is always bankrupt, or at least so represented, notwithstanding the custom-house receipts on importations are more than enough to pay the army, to to which purpose they are especially set apart. On the occasion alluded to, some twenty regular soldiers, stationed at Santa Fé, were thrown into prison and loaded with irons as malcontents for refusing to receive their wages in corn from Armijo's granary at four dollars a *fanega* — a measure containing about two bushels — when they could purchase in market for cash at one-third of the price. This outrageous act of tyranny created an unwonted excitement against its author, so much so, that he found it necessary to resort to a specious kind of trickery, a display of disinterestedness, to allay the popular clamour. He advertised a contract to the lowest bidder, to furnish the soldiers with corn. But this Mexican display of honesty neither deceived nor satisfied even his stupid countrymen; for they at once declared that no one but Armijo could take the contract at any price, as the insolvent government never paid any creditor but him. Thus the matter remained just as it had begun, and just as this most patriotic governor intended it should, with this exception —the manifestations of discontent became more open and threatening. Two young officers of the army in particular, had fallen under the ban of the governor's displeasure before, and were now suspected of having used their influence in fomenting the disaffection that seemed universal among the soldiers. His hatred of these young and meritorious officers had its origin in an *affaire d'amour*, which, as it exhibits a new phase in the multiplex character of

Armijo—multiplex in all that is corrupt and debasing—I will here relate.

Don Santiago Abreu,* a minister in the administration of Governor Perez, and massacred in the former revolution, left a handsome, and, in such advantages as her country afforded, an accomplished daughter, Dona Soledad Abreu; a maiden whom fifteen summers had ripened into early womanhood. After Armijo's elevation, he insiduously beset the fair doncella with libertine intentions; but she proudly and scornfully resisted all his advances, fortified not more, perhaps, by a sentiment of intrinsic virtue than by the inveterate hatred she entertained for the governor. She knew that he had been the mortal enemy of her father—the undoubted instigator of his assassination—such a miscreant could find little pity with the pretty Soledad. But this great man was not to be so easily foiled, and attempted by intrigue what he had failed to accomplish in a direct way. He influenced a match between Dona Soledad and Esquipulas Caballero, one of his ensigns, and in the plenitude of his good-nature honoured their nuptials by officiating as sponsor at the ceremony.

He now renewed his vile importunities, and, as he supposed, with better prospect of success. He held, in a manner, the destiny of the young officer in his hands; but in every attempt to accomplish his unholy object he was most signally baffled. The maiden and the wife proved alike invulnerable to his solicitations and his threats. At last, convinced of the impregnable virtue

* I believe that this man was governor of New Mexico about the year 1832.

of Soledad, he gave up the pursuit, and began making good the deep oaths of vengeance he had often sworn. Her he could not reach directly, but he found means to degrade her unoffending husband and her favourite uncle, who was also a young ensign in his army, named Ramon Baca. Ordering a grand review of the troops, with no other intention than to humble these young cadets, he publicly promoted to a rank above them several officers of inferior grade—a most galling slight in the eyes of a young military aspirant, and a kind of vengeance worthy only of the great Armijo. He even promoted, from the rank of common soldier to a grade above them, a fellow who had been an agent and panderer in many of his licentious transactions. The young officers, who were the most deserving and meritorious in the whole corps, now finding themselves at the tail of the army, presented a respectful petition to his excellency, praying to be reinstated. This so irritated the tyrant, that he threatened them with instant death if they ever ventured to molest him again with similar importunities, and Caballero, the husband of the pretty Soledad, upon affected suspicion of favouring the disaffected soldiers, was cast into prison with them and heavily ironed!

Baca, upon some frivolous charge, was ordered out of the country. The 9th of February was the day fixed by the governor for his banishment; but when the time came the young man declared to his friends that he would not depart, but would raise an insurrection and sacrifice his and their oppressor, or perish in the attempt. With a sword at his side he promenaded the streets of Santa Fé during the forenoon, with great boldness walked directly under Armijo's windows and held conferences with the soldiers. Without a friend to inform him of the young officer's intentions, Armijo remained in utter ignorance of the plot; yet the inhabitants were all aware of the intended revolution, and anxiously awaited an outbreak they deemed inevitable. But the good fortune of the despot did not desert him in this extremity. Had a single blow been struck, his power and his oppressions would have ended! for, whenever the star of his destiny tends downward, it will gravitate with a velocity vastly accelerated by the universal hatred in which he is held by his subjects; but when called upon by the heroic Baca the soldiers at first hesitated, and then declared that they would render him no assistance. They had promised to aid, to join him; but either from lack of confidence in him as a leader, or from craven fear of Armijo, they were deterred from an open demonstration. Thus was this embryo revolution, which gave such excellent promise, crushed through the timidity of a handful of soldiers.

In the afternoon, young Baca mounted his horse, and riding to the barracks, made a short speech to his brethren in arms. It was a farewell address, couched in decorous terms, and at its conclusion the really gallant officer departed on his exile. But by this time Armijo had obtained information of the contemplated revolt, and immediately sent off a detachment of dragoons with orders to bring back the young officer, dead or alive. He was overtaken, and thinking himself betrayed by the soldiery, quietly gave up his arms, was guarded back to Santa Fé, and thrust into the same dungeon with his friend Caballero. At first it was thought that

Armijo would order them to immediate execution; but fearing the populace, among whom they had so many friends, he finally sent them off to the city of Mexico to be tried for treason, himself to furnish all the proof. The father of young Caballero, a brave and meritorious officer, but broken down by age and dissipation, was carried to the door of Armijo to intercede for his son; but the tyrant denied him an audience. The shock was too much for the old man; he was borne to his home only to be carried thence to his gaave, and his loss was much lamented by both foreigners and natives.

The young officers were released on reaching Chihuahua, and afterward visited the city of Mexico with the hope of obtaining redress. They were unable to effect anything, however, for by the time they were allowed a hearing, the Texan expedition to New Mexico began to be agitated, and the aspect of affairs at Santa Fé was now too critical for the General Government to think of tampering with her tyrannical governor.

In his rude *palocio* at Santa Fé he is more the despot than anywhere else, maintaining himself proudly, and enforcing all the regal homage and courtly ceremonial exacted by the veriest tyrant. A guard, musket on shoulder, marches before the entrance to his door, denying entrance to all unless they have first obtained the royal permission. Should his excellency feel in the humour of walking out, the cry from the *centinela* is, "The governor and commander-in-chief appears!" and this is echoed and re-echoed from every guard in and about the barracks. When his majesty is in the street, each dutiful subject takes off whatever apology for a hat he may have on his head. Should the governor's wife, a gross, brazen-faced woman issue from the building, the form is even more ridiculous, for then the cry of "*La gob nadora!*" or "*La commandante generala!*" resounds on every side. This woman is contaminated with every depraved habit known to human nature; and as her husband is a debauchéo by "special prerogative," she does not scruple to act as his *alcaheuta* in all his amours. In the mean time she is not without her own lovers—a worthy couple, truly!

It is strange how this man has been able to maintain his despotic and arbitrary sway among a people acknowledging no law but that of force. The inhabitants are far more dissatisfied with his administration than they were with that of Perez and his cabinet of Abreus; yet so far they have dared to do no more than plot revolutions against their oppressor. He continues to hold sway in a country where he has not a real friend upon whom he can depend; even his sycophantic favourites would prove his bitterest enemies were he once in adversity. Could the Texans have entered New Mexico in a body, with plenty of provisions, Armijo would have fled with his ill-gotten wealth, and the new-comers would have been hailed by all parties as deliverers.

I might diversify this hasty biography of Don Manuel Armijo, from the abundant material which I have yet by me unused, with stories of his atrocious acts that would bring a blush upon the brow of tyranny. I might detail many horrible murders which he has committed. I could relate many a thrilling story of his abuse of the rights of women, that would make Saxon hearts burn with indignant fire; for Saxon hearts enshrine the mothers of men as objects sacred and apart. I might speak of his conniving with the Apache Indians, in their robberies of his neighbours of the State of Chihuahua, by furnishing this hardy mountain tribe with powder, and balls, and guns, knowing that with them they would fall, like the eagle, from their fastnesses, upon his own countrymen. I could give a catalogue of men's names whom he has banished from their own families and homes, for no reason but because they were in his way. Assassinations, robberies, violent debauchery, extortions, and innumerable acts of broken faith are themes upon which I am armed with abundant and most veritable detail; but my readers would sicken, and my narrative leads me another way. A few remarks and I have done with him.

The mien and deportment of Armijo are not ill calculated to strike a timorous people with awe; for, as I have before remarked, he is a large, portly man, of stern countenance and blustering manner. Not one jot or tittle of personal bravery does he possess, but is known to be a most arrant coward. In all the revolutions that have taken place since he first courted power, his own person has never been exposed, if we except one instance. In a skirmish with some Indians he received a wound in the leg, from which he still limps; but the action was not of his own seeking, and his conduct on this occasion was that of a man engaged in a business anything but to his liking. He has made great capital, however, of his crippled leg, and, like his great exemplar, Santa Anna, is determined that his subjects shall never forget that he received it while encountering their enemy. But the master-stroke of this great man was the capturing the Texan Santa Fé Expedition. These small squads of tattered soldiers, taken piecemeal, in his grandiloquent bulletin he multiplied into a legion of Buckramites—for which act of most heroic daring he was, all in good time, knighted by Santa Anna. He knows his people thoroughly, having studied their character with a most acute discernment. A common remark of his is, "*Vale mas estar tomado por valiente que serlo*"—it is better to be thought brave than really to be so—and thus, by blustering and swaggering, he keeps the timid natives in subjection.

It may be thought singular that no attention is paid to Armijo's tyranny by the general goverment; but his policy is only part of that which has obtained in many of the departments. In our own confederacy, we regard intelligence as the great bond of union; the reverse is the case in Mexico—a sufficient test to prove that the so-called Republic is no Republic at all. To General Manuel Armijo I will now bid adieu; but I cannot do it without again saying, that, however much he may be astonished at seeing his portrait thus taken, he cannot urge a single syllable against its fidelity.

CHAPTER XVII.

Unrealized Hopes.—A Brood of unhatched Chickens.—We are quartered with our Companions.—Arrival of " Old Paint."—Joy at seeing the Veteran.—Another Meeting with Friends.—Stories of Suffering.—Liberated Prisoners again confined.—Armijo and Lewis.—Departure for the City of Mexico—A long and gloomy March before us.—The Brute Salazar in Command.—Bustamente and the Women of San Miguel.—Causes of the Failure of the Santa Fé Expedition.—Arrival at a deserted Mission.—Sufferings of the Prisoners from Cold.—More of Salazar's Brutalities.—The dreary March continued.—Arrival at Pino's Rancho.—Farther Sufferings.—A cold Camping-ground.—Hard Fare.—Frostbitten Feet.—Horrible Threat of Salazar.—San Domingo.—Kindness of the Women.—San Felipe.—First Sight of the Rio Grande.—Algodones.—A Second " Black Hole of Calcutta."—Arrival at the Indian Village of Sandia.—A singular Rite.—Description of the Inhabitants.—Alameda.—Scene in an Oven.—Misery makes us acquainted with strange Bedfellows.—Sufferings on the Increase.—Bottoms of the Rio Grande; their Fertility.—Albuquerque in Sight—Herons and Wild Geese.—A dashing Mexican Horseman.—Lieutenant Hornsby abducted.—Arrival at Albuquerque.—The Family of Armijo.—Farther Kindness of the Women.—General Pike's Journal.—The Pretty Girl of Albuquerque.

I AWOKE on the morning of the 17th of October with full confidence that I had passed my last night in prison. Neither myself nor my companions thought it could be otherwise. I had received assurance after assurance, from every quarter, that as soon as the Texans were on the march an order for my release would be made out and issued by Armijo; and so sanguine were my illusory hopes that such would be the case, that the evening previous I had spent in speculations as to my future movements. On leaving New Orleans, in the preceding May, I had fondly anticipated reaching Santa Fé by the 1st of August, at farthest, and the city of Mexico by the 1st October, after having seen all the "sights" between the two points. It was now the middle of the latter month, a period só late in the season as to render my returning to the United States, by way of Bent's Fort and Independence, impracticable, so that I should be forced, as I then thought, to go as far as Chihuahua, at least, into the interior of Mexico. From that point I determined, if it would facilitate my journey home, to leave the main route to Mexico and travel directly to Matamoros. I even made my calculations, in case Armijo would not give up my horse, to purchase him of his present owner if possible; or if I was disappointed in once more obtaining possession of this tried and faithful steed, I at least determined upon purchasing a large and untiring mule which had belonged to Van Ness.

A larger brood of unhatched chickens has probably never been counted. When the sun had appeared above the eastern summits of the mountains which environ San Miguel, I was ordered to march, with my three companions, to the quarters occupied by the main body of Texan prisoners. Our meeting was an occasion of strong and diverse emotions—joy once more to shake the hands of those with whom we had shared the perils and hardships óf the prairies, gloom to see those friends in plight so miserable.

But a few minutes elapsed ere "Old Paint" Caldwell, with his nine comrades, was escorted from the house of our friend Vigil and placed in line with the other prisoners. A low but cordial shout of welcome arose on the still morning air as the men saw the veteran approach, and warm were the greetings as he shook hands with the eager crowd that pressed around him. Question followed question in such quick succession that no time was given to answer; stories of suffering and of wrong were broken off half finished, in such haste was each man to unbosom his rapid-crowding thoughts. The burden of the stories on every side was of starvation, murdered friends and broken Mexican faith, mixed with deep curses upon the head of Lewis, whose perfidy was by this time generally known.

Before these first greetings were over, Lieutenants Scott and Burgess, with young Howard, were escorted in from the rancho of old Antonio Baca. Here was another meeting of deep joy alloyed with melancholy; the latter had a brother among us, and all had warm friends. My friend Falconer, too, reduced in flesh, but still preserving the full measure of his buoyant spirits, we found in the crowd.

Even up to this period I had not lost all hope of being liberated: Armijo had released four of the Texans, then why not me? He had all my papers in his possession—documents proving incontestibly that I had no part or lot with the expedition he had been fortunate enough to capture—and with such proofs in his hands, upon what grounds could he detain me longer? He had none other than his arbitrary will—the supreme law of New Mexico. But whatever hopes I might have entertained, up to this time, of being released, they were now banished on seeing the four Texans, who had for several days enjoyed unconditional liberty, marched in among us. They knew not the cause, could divine no motive which might have induced Armijo to this singular step, unless Lewis was at the bottom of it. At one moment the governor had liberated these men, and assigned them all lucrative situations: they had scarcely tasted the sweets of freedom before they were again arrested, brought in, and penned with their imprisoned comrades. Not a doubt exists that to Lewis these four men, as well as myself, were indebted for months of suffering, peril, and imprisonment: the traitor probably thought that we had found out and would make his treachery known to the Americans at Santa Fé, and thus render the place too hot for his comfort or safety. He had a certain influence with Armijo, which he might have used for the melioration of our lot; but the same cowardly impulse which urged him, by base means, to save himself from the Mexicans, now caused him, in a more traitorous way, to save himself from his own countrymen.

After we had been paraded in the plaza of San Miguel, and the ceremony of counting us had been gone through, it was ascertained that the notorious Salazar—the greatest brute among Armijo's officers—was to have charge of us. This was considered unfortunate by all, and even our old and tricky friend Bustamente, who came up to bid us farewell, privately took occasion to manifest his regret that such a cold-blooded wretch was to have charge of us. The women, too, who had been so kind to myself and companions while in San Miguel, now came up and shook our hands for the last time, many of the girls affected even to tears at the gloomy prospect before us, and openly warning us to beware crossing Salazar in any of his demands or wishes.

The beginning of a cold and disagreeable winter was at hand, as we set off on foot upon a journey of over *two thousand miles*—we were in the hands of a brute whose only delight was in cruelty and blood—should we be fortunate enough to withstand the fatigues attendant upon the journey, an uncertain fate awaited us at its termination; thus, with hope lending hardly a gleam of sunshine to the dark clouds before us, the reader can easily imagine that our condition was gloomy in the extreme.

And what mistake had brought this sorrowful issue to our enterprise? In as few words as possible I will answer the question. In the first place, the expedition began its march too late in the season by at least six weeks. Had it left Austin on the 1st of May, the grass would have been much better, and we should have had little difficulty in finding good water both for ourselves and cattle. In the second place, we were disappointed in obtaining a party of the Lipan Indians as guides, and were consequently obliged to take a route some three hundred miles out of the way, and in many places extremely difficult of travel. Thirdly, the government of Texas did not furnish waggons and oxen enough to transport the goods of the merchants, and this, as a matter of course, caused tedious delays. Fourthly, cattle enough on the hoof were not provided, even with the second supply sent for by the commissioners from Little River. Again, the distance was vastly greater than we had anticipated in our widest and wildest calculations, owing to which circumstance, and an improvident waste of provisions while in the buffalo range, we found ourselves upon half allowance in the very middle of our long jouruey—a privation which weakened, dispirited, and rendered the men unfit for duty. The Indians also annoyed us much, by their harrassing and continual attempts to cut off our small parties and steal our horses. Finally, the character of the governor of New Mexico was far from being understood, and his power was underrated by all. General Lamar's estimate of the views and feelings of the people of Santa Fé and the vicinity was perfectly correct: not a doubt can exist that they all were and are anxious to throw off the oppressive yoke of Armijo, and come under the liberal institutions of Texas; but the governor found us divided into small parties, broken down by long marches and want of food, discovered a traitor among us, too, and taking advantage of these circumstances, his course was plain and his conquest easy.

Far different would have been the result had the expedition reached the confines of New Mexico a month earlier, and in a body. Then, with fresh horses, and a sufficiency of provisions for the men, the feelings of the inhabitants could have been ascertained; the proclamations of General Lamar would have been distributed among them; the people would have had an opportunity to come over to Texas without fear, and the feeble opposition Armijo could have made, and I doubt whether he would have made any against the Texans in a body, could have been put down with ease. Had it been evident that a majority of the inhabitants were satisfied under their present government, and unfriendly to a union with Texas, then the goods would have been sold, and the force withdrawn—at least, such was the tenour of the proclamations. No attack would have been made upon the inhabitants—that was expressly understood; but had Armijo seen fit to commence hostilities, his power in New Mexico would have been at an end. Fate decreed otherwise, and by a series of unforeseen and unfortunate circumstances the expedition was thrown into his hands.

To return to our present gloomy situation. A guard numbering nearly two hundred men, mounted upon horses, mules, and asses, and miserably armed with bows and arrows, lances, or worthless muskets, rode upon either side of us, single file, as we trudged along on foot. We had questions innumerable to ask each other, and during the day I learned from Mr. Falconer and others the particulars of their journey across the Grand Prairie,* and of their capture. The story was one of great hardship and suffering. The implacable Caygüas had harrassed them continually, killed several of their men, and at one time rode directly through the camp, and succeeded in *stampeding* no less than eighty-seven horses, which were never recovered. When we left them, on the 31st of August, it was thought that they would hear from us at farthest by the 10th of September, but the 15th of that month came, and still no tidings. On that day a council of officers was held, at which it was determined to wait five days longer, and then, if no news should be received of Colonel Cooke's party, it was resolved to burn the waggons and goods, and make the best of their way back to Texas by forced marches, living upon their horses and mules, after the beef should have been exhausted, until they could reach the buffalo

* By this name I designate the immense prairie we crossed after ascending the *steppe*, or chain of high hills, west of the Palo Duro. It is the *Llano Estacado* of the New Mexicans.

and hunting range. Unfortunately the guides sent back by us, after we had passed the Angosturas, reached General M'Leod's encampment on the 17th of September, when immediate orders were given to resume the march towards Santa Fé.

To show how unfortunate had been our choice of route, after leaving the main party on the Palo Duro, it is sufficient to say that the guides we sent back traversed the distance in three days and a half—whereas it had taken us fourteen. The distance must have been, by their route, nearly two hundred miles; yet by travelling night and day they were enabled to make their journey in the short time mentioned. The guides, too, were enabled to find, what we had supposed impracticable, a road for the waggons up the high and precipitous steppe, and when once on the summit, instead of taking the northwest course which had brought us directly upon the deep chasms and other obstructions, they guided the command in a due west direction, finding a smooth road, and heading the chasms entirely. Had Colonel Cooke known this route on leaving the main body, the fate of the expedition might have been different.

But even on gaining the Grand Prairie, and with the bright hopes of soon reaching the settlements, and a sufficiency of food before them, the sufferings of the men composing the main party were still intolerable. The Caygüas pursued them some distance, hovering upon their flanks and rear, and cutting off several small parties who had been driven by hunger to seek for grapes, plums, or game. The men were out of salt, heir daily allowance was only one pound and a half of starved and sickly beef, which was probably two thirds bone, and their wants had caused great debility and disease among them. It is only necessary to mention, in order to show the great sufferings they endured, that every dog in camp—and several of the Indian curs had followed us—was killed and greedily devoured. Snakes, lizards, tortoises, polecats—in short, almost every living and creeping thing upon the face of the prairie, were eaten with avidity, so ravenous was their hunger. Not a vestige, save the horns, hoofs, and larger bones of the beeves, was left—the wolves and buzzards were even cheated of their just allowance, the hide and entrails, for all was devoured.

On arriving at the Laguna Colorada, a small sheet of reddish water south of the Angosturas, the advance of General M'Leod was opposed by the Mexicans under Colonel Archulete. Out of more than two hundred men, it was now found that the Taxans could muster but about ninety who were really fit for active service, and these would have been obliged to act on foot entirely, as their horses had been either run off in the *stampede* on the Palo Duro, or kept so closely within the lines that they could not obtain grass enough to sustain their strength. Many of the men who had lost their horses, weak and dispirited from long marches and want of food, had secretly thrown away their arms to lighten themselves upon the road, and, in the mean time, that subordination, without which all efforts are useless, was in a measure lost. In this desperate condition, unable to hear a word concerning the fate of either Colonel Cooke or of two small parties they had sent out, and with the promise of good treatment and that their personal effects would be retured to them, a surrender was made. Many of the men, as well as officers, were ready and willing to bide the issue of an action in case their advance was opposed; but they were overruled by the majority, and thus was the fate of the expedition sealed. The men had no sooner laid down their arms than they were searched, robbed, tied, and most grossly insulted, and then, with hardly provisions enough to sustain nature, marched hurriedly to San Miguel. Of their arrival in that place I have already made mention. I will now continue the journey towards the city of Mexico.

The 17th of October, the day on which we started from San Miguel, was warm and showery. Our route lay towards Santa Fé, and over the same ground myself and companions had travelled the day on which we first met Armijo. About sundown, foot-sore and completely exhausted after a hurried march of thirty miles over a rough and hilly road, we reached the old ruin of Pecos—in former times a mission and a fortress, but now uninhabitable, and fast crumbling to decay. Salazar drove us into an enclosure amid the ruins, and there herded us for the night in quarters not fit even for brutes, and without giving us a morsel of food.

Immediately to the north of Pecos, and within a few miles, rose a lofty mountain whose summit was now covered with snow. On the other side of this mountain, and immediately at its base, lies the little mud-built city of Santa Fé, a place towards which we had been journeying for months, but which we were not destined to see.*

* General Zebulon M. Pike, in the narrative of his imprisonment in New Mexico, says that Santa Fé, from the mountain's sides, has the appearance an immense fleet of flat-boats on the Mississippi, while Albert Pike, in

As I have before remarked, the day had been hot and sultry, with a shower in the afternoon sufficient to moisten the ground. The only baggage in possession of the prisoners, besides the slight and ragged clothing upon their backs, was a single blanket for each man. In this each immediately rolled himself, and then stretched his weary limbs upon the cold, damp earth, vainly hoping that he might obtain rest and forgetfulness in sleep—but no such good fortune awaited us.

As if to increase our sufferings, a chill, biting wind sprang up, at dusk, fresh from the snow-clad mountain north of us, and in less than an hour it was so bitterly cold that to sleep was impossible. In vain did we crowd close to each other, in vain did we nestle in the little hollows formed in the uneven ground; the piercing wind penetrated our scanty covering and benumbed our every energy. I tried to rise, as did many of the unfortunate prisoners; but the cold wind had so stiffened our limbs, rendered in the first place heated and sore by the long mountain march, that we could scarcely move or turn over without enduring tortures the most excruciating. In this way, and without an hour's sleep, we passed our first night on the long road to Mexico.

Early in the morning we were ordered to continue the march, and without food. Salazar did, previous to starting, distribute some fifty small cakes among one hundred and eighty-seven half-starved men; and the manner of this distribution showed the brutal nature of

his interesting sketches, likens its general features to those of an extensive brick kiln, or rather a succession of brick-kilns. Either comparison is doubtless correct, for such certainly is the appearance of all the towns in Northern Mexico through which I travelled.

the wretch. Calling the prisoners around him, each with the hope that he was to receive something to allay the sharp cravings of hunger, he would toss one of these cakes high in the air, and then, with a glee absolutely demoniacal, watch the scramble that ensued as it fell among the suffering throng. It was a game of the strong against the weak, this struggle for the few mouthfuls of food which Salazar threw among them. The better attributes of our nature, the kind sympathies and generous forbearance which lift man above the brutes, were for a time overwhelmed, in a majority of the prisoners, by long starvation and great bodily suffering; and now, as the savage who had charge of them tossed the miserable pittance in the air, it was a study to watch their eager faces as it descended, to see with what wolf-like ferocity they would rush to secure the prize, and the terrible struggle which was sure to ensue ere some one, stronger than his fellows, could secure it. Salazar was accompanied by our old acquaintance, Don Jesus, in this distribution; and the satisfaction with which they watched the fierce conflicts marked a new leaf in the dreadful chapter of human depravity.

This revolting scene was scarcely over before we were ordered to commence the day's march. Sore and stiff in every bone and joint, we started, many of the men being hardly able to hobble and halt along over the rough and rocky hills which now intervened between Pecos and the valley of the Rio Grande; but as the sun gradually dispersed the morning mists, and exercise warmed our limbs and reduced the stiffness in our joints, we were enabled to move with less pain. Our course was now nearly south. The road forks near Pecos, the right-hand branch leading directly towards Santa Fé, while the left, which we were now to take, is the regular thoroughfare towards Albuquerque and the other towns on the Rio Grande.

After a march of some thirty miles, during which the men suffered incredibly from hunger, thirst, and extreme lameness, night overtook us at the small rancho of a man named Pino, a brother of the brute of that name mentioned in a former chapter. Before reaching it my feet were so badly swollen and blistered that I was obliged to draw off my boots, and finish the march with no other protection against the short and prickly grass than my stockings; yet many of my fellow-prisoners were unfortunately worse off than myself, their feet bleeding at every step.

We were driven, one by one, into a cow-pen or yard, and there encamped for the night, Salazar distributing a pint cup of meal to each man after having satisfied himself that none of us were missing. Even in his mode of counting us he exhibited his characteristic brutality; for just as they drive sheep or cattle into pens in New Mexico, with the intention of enumerating them, so had he driven us!

A fence, which enclosed our pen, here partially protected us from the biting north wind, and in the early part of the night we were enabled to catch a little sleep. Towards morning, however, the weather changed to such a degree of coldness that farther repose was impossible—it was so cold that the frost was plainly visible on our thin blankets. So stiff and benumbed were the men by this time, from cold, want of sleep, and the excessive fatigue they had undergone, that even an order to rise at daybreak and continue the march was received with joy by all—it would at least enable us to obtain warmth, and lessen the acute pains we felt in every bone.

From Pino we learned that General M'Leod, Mr. Navarro, Dr. Whittaker, Captains Houghton and Hudson, with two or three other officers, had passed the previous night at his rancho, and were provided with comfortable quarters. They had been sent forward one day in advance of the main body, on horseback, and as they were fortunate enough to fall into the hands of an officer of humane feeling, were well treated. The name of this officer, if I remember aright, was Quintana, and our friends who were under his charge always spoke of him as a kind-hearted, gentlemanly man.

A walk of two or three hours, after leaving the rancho, relieved our limbs of the torturing pains felt during the latter part of the night, but our frostbitten feet now began swelling and paining us severely. The road of the two previous days had led over mountains and rugged hills; we now struck upon the valley of a small stream running into the Rio Grande a short distance to our right. After a long and toilsome march, our men suffering at every step, we encamped upon the borders of the little stream for the night. Here we experienced great relief from bathing our inflamed and swollen feet in its cold waters.

After issuing to each man a miserable pittance of barley-bread, so hard that it was impossible to eat it without much boiling, Salazar told us that his orders from Armijo were to tie us every night; but, as we were very tired, his *humanity* prevented him from carrying out the orders! He placed a strong guard around us, however, and coolly remarked that if a single man was missing in the morning the *whole party* would be instantly shot! The heartless wretch took especial good care that none should make an attempt of this kind, by working the men so hard during the day that they willingly sank upon the ground at night with hardly the power of moving.

A biting, chilly evening was followed by a heavy frost towards morning. Sleep was out of the question—we could only curl up, and by nestling close to each other upon the cold ground, keep from freezing. At daylight we were ordered to be ready to march, and before sunrise were again upon the road, with nothing to eat. To let my readers know the horrible condition of our feet, I will here state, that, for the next ten days after this, I was unable to pull off my stockings without bringing the skin with them. The large blisters would break during the day, and the exudation, as it dried, adhere firmly to my stockings, so that I was obliged to keep them on although full of gravel, and torturing me at every step. Many of my companions suffered much more from frostbitten feet than myself, their toe-nails coming off, in consequence, before we got through our journey.

At a brisk pace we were hurried forward, reaching the little village of Santo Domingo before it was yet noon, a distance of eighteen miles from our camping-ground of the previous night. At this village our men first had cause to thank the women for their kindness. The latter came running out of the mud houses in every direction, bringing tortillas, baked pumpkins, and dry ears of corn, and fairly shedding tears at our forlorn and miserable appearance. The corn was our principal food, and was swallowed after simply roasting the ears a short time before the fire, although many of the more hungry among our men ate it raw.

A little farther on, we entered the village of San Felipe, the banks of the Rio Grande now seen to the right. Our course was nearly south, occasionally approaching the banks of the river, and then leaving it as the turns threw us off. The women of San Felipe were in every way as charitable as those of Santo Domingo. Many of them openly reproached Armijo as a brute unfit to live, and even the men took every opportunity to manifest their sorrow that we had fallen into his hands.

Towards night we reached Algodnes, a small village near the Rio Grande, and here we encamped. That the night would be unusually cold we were well aware, and Mr. Van Ness was requested by the men to ask Salazar if he could possibly procure shelter. Two small rooms, with a door leading from one to the other, and together hardly large enough for twenty men, were provided, and into these over one hundred and eighty of us were driven like so many sheep, and the heavy wooden door locked upon us. To lie down, or even sit down, was out of the question, and a scene of misery and desperation soon ensued which beggars description.

In the rear room there was no window, or other opening for a circulation of the air, except the door which opened into the front room, and this was blocked up by the mass who had crowded towards it. In the front room was a single open window, two feet in height, perhaps, by eighteen inches in width, and through this small aperture came all the fresh air that was to be inhaled by nearly two hundred persons! In this room, and within three yards of the window, I stood firmly wedged and jammed by human flesh, unable to move either forward or backward, to the right or to the left; yet even at this short distance from the window I soon felt sensations of suffocation — what, then, must have been the feelings of those in the farther room?

Soon outcries arose from those in the rear. Half-stifled, they shouted aloud to those in front to break open or tear down the door, and madly pressed forward as if to assist in accomplishing the object of their wishes. In the mean time, those nearest the window, who could speak Spanish, begged the guard to open the door and allow at least a part to leave the house; but the latter either could not hear their entreaties above the din, or heeded them not. Half-suffocated, and with sensations of sickness and giddiness, thoughts of the Black Hole of Calcutta, with its attendant train of horrors, now came over us; and I am confident that an order for instant execution would have been preferred, by many, to passing the night in that dismal, dark and horrible place. An attempt to open the door inwardly was now made, but so great was the press in that direction that it was found impossible to effect this desirable object; a battering-ram of human flesh was next brought to bear upon it, and with all the energy which desperation lends did our men endeavour to burst lock or hinges —but it gave not away. In the midst of cries, imprecations, and half-smothered anathemas, we now heard a key turning in the clumsy and ponderous lock

—Salazar had consented to pass fifty of us out, but no more.

Being near the door, as the guard without opened it, I was carried out in the current among the first. How grateful, how instantaneous was the relief! Cold as was the northern blast, it was pure—we could now breathe. The guard escorted us to a cow-yard, and there herded us for the night. I crawled under the lee of a low mud wall, still reeking with the perspiration which had issued from every pore while undergoing the tortures of heat and suffocation—the cold wind penetrated my blanket and chilled me through, yet I was content. So piercing was the blast, that even our guard left their posts, and sought the friendly shelter of the neighbouring houses, yet we had neither the power nor inclination to attempt an escape. Huddled together under the walls, shivering with the cold and without a minute's sleep, we passed the hours until morning came; yet even for this poor boon we felt thankful—felt rejoiced that we had escaped the horrid tortures of suffocation.

On the 21st of October, Salazar giving us no other rations before starting than an ear of dry, hard corn to each man, we reached the large Indian village of San Dias. The *pueblos*, or town Indians of New Mexico, are by far the better part of the population—are frugal industrious, and honest—cultivate the land, and are very kind-hearted and hospitable to all strangers. Their religion is Roman Catholic, mixed up with many of their own superstitious rites and ceremonies, and the same may be said of nearly all the inhabitants of New Mexico. The Indians certainly retain, to the present day, many of their original rituals, feasts, and ceremonies, having ingrafted such of the Romish rites only as were calculated to strike the eye by their imposing pageantry. Stories of their strange ceremonies I myself heard, while at Sandia and other towns upon our march, but one that was told General Pike is more singular than all. If this tale be true, it would seem that once a-year there is a great feast, prepared for three successive days, which time is spent in eating, drinking, and dancing. Near this scene of amusement is a dismal, gloomy cave, into which not a glimpse of light can penetrate, and where places of repose are provided for the revellers. To this cave, after dark, repair grown persons of every age and sex, who pass the night in indulgences of the most gross and sensual description. Such is the account given of one of their ceremonies, which bears strong resemblance to some of the mystic revels of the ancients.

At Sandia the population came out in a body to see us, and during a short halt the women gave to each of our men a watermelon, besides apples, cakes, and, in fact, everything they could spare. A gray-headed old man who had been in St. Louis several times and who spoke a little English, told us that the people were in our favour, and that Armijo was universally hated and despised. He would have said more, but our guard hurried us from the place. The dress of these people varies but little from that of the Mexicans; that of the men being a coarse cotton shirt and loose and flowing drawers of the same material, over which they draw a pair of leather or cloth pantaloons, open from the knee downward, and flapping about whenever they are in motion. The women —and, for Indian women, many of them had strong pretensions to beauty—were attired simply in a chemise and blue woollen petticoat.

The inhabitants cultivate the soil, live principally upon corn and pumkins, and appear to be a simple, mild, and inoffensive people—not having the spirit to rise upon their cowardly oppressors. Their complexion is a light, clear brown, or copper; their limbs are symmetrical, and denoting great activity and strength, while their eyes are dark and piercing, yet possessing a singular mildness and an expression of resignation.

We should have remained a night at Sandia; but the policy of Salazar being to tire and worry us down to such a degree that there would be no possibility of our attempting an escape, we were barely allowed to pass some five minutes in the place. After a long and tedious march in the afternoon, many of our men nearly ready to drop from pain and exhaustion, we finally reached a little village called Alameda. Here we were penned in a large yard, without any protection from the cold. In the early part of the night I made out to catch a little sleep, but before midnight it was so cold that I rose, to find, if possible, a warmer location. I tried to crawl into a large oven standing in the yard, but found it already occupied by two or three of my companions. Surely, misery not only makes us acquainted with strange bedfellows, but also with strange beds.

In the morning, and after we had each received our day's ration—a hard ear of corn—the tiresome march was continued. Passing through the fertile bottoms of the Rio Grande, the land on either side of the road covered with cornstalks from which the ears had but recently been plucked, about ten o'clock the still distant church of

Albuquerque appeared in view. The land in the vicinity of this city appears to be under a higher degree of cultivation than in any other part of New Nexico. The inhabitants do not depend upon rain in making their crops, but, on the contrary, the entire valley appears intersected by irrigating canals, from which the waters drawn from the broad but shallow Rio Grande can at any time be let upon the earth. Among the stubble, on either side of the road, we noticed immense flocks of blue and white herons and wild geese, so exceedingly tame that we could approach within a few yards of them. The Mexicans seldom kill them, and hence their tameness.

We were yet some two or three miles distant from Albuquerque, journeying along at a rapid pace, when a single horseman was seen speeding across the fields and making directly towards us at a sweeping gallop. Soon he was up with the rear of the party, when checking his horse into a prancing canter, he politely raised his hat and with great cordiality addressed the prisoners as gentlemen, while riding up the line towards the head. His horse was a beautiful black, of glossy skin, clean and well-made limbs, spirited eye, expanded nostrils, and proud and gallant action—the rider, a gay, dashing, and handsome Mexican, dressed in a pair of green velvet trousers, slashed at the sides, and with a profusion of bell buttons, while his close, neatly-fitting jacket, although now somewhat faded and worn, showed him a fashionable blade among his countrymen, and altogether a different personage from the ragged rabble by whom we were surrounded. There was a flashing, dare-devil expression in his eye, too, and a jounty set to his hat—and then he sat so fearlessly in his saddle while his proud steed curvetted and caracoled along as if impatient of the slow pace at which he was compelled to amble, that we could not but look with admiration at both horse and rider, so gallant was their bearing.

The horseman rode twice up and down the line of prisoners, nodding gracefully as he passed, and eyeing the crowd as if in search of a friend. By-and-by his eye fell upon one of our officers, Lieutenant Hornsby, who happened to be the best-dressed man in the party. His well-wadded and full-buttoned Texan dragoon-jacket was new, or nearly new, his cap and military trousers had seen but little service, while his blanket was of that fiery and showy red which could not fail to attract in a country where gaudy and glaring colours are so much sought after and admired.

The Mexican cavalier at once checked his steed on seeing Hornsby, and immediately asked him if he was tired. This was a question he could not but answer in the affirmative. The horseman than asked H. to jump up behind him—his horse, he said, could easily carry double, and a short ride would rest the weary limbs of *el prisionero.* Instantly Hornsby was comfortably seated behind his new friend. The Mexican told him to place one arm around his waist, and then to hold fast: Hornsby did so. The next moment the horseman suddenly wheeled his steed in an opposite direction from that we were pursuing, plunged his heavy Mexican spurs in the animal's sides, and dashed off at a speed which was truly astonishing considering the heavy weight his steed was obliged to carry. He did not pursue the road over which we had just travelled, but leaving it a little to the right, struck off diagonally across fields and pastures. Here was an abduction, and we could not help congratulating our friend upon his good fortune. Whenever the party came to an irrigating ditch the horse would stop, brace himself, settle firmly upon his haunches, and then at a bound carry both his riders safely across. In the mean time we continued our journey towards Albuquerque, yet we could not but turn our eyes, ever and anon, to gaze at our rapidly-receding comrade. We watched him until naught could be seen but his red blanket rising and falling gently in the distance from the motion of the horse, and when we finally turned from gazing it was with the firm belief that we were not soon to look upon him again.

About noon we entered Albuquerque, somewhat famed for the beauty of its women, besides being the largest place in the province of New Mexico, and the residence of Armijo a part of the year.* His family

* General Pike, in his *Narrative*, speaks of having met with numbers of beautiful women at this place during a couple of days he spent there, in the winter of 1807, while on his journey from Santa Fé to Chihuahua, a prisoner. The following I quote from his journal: "We were received, at Albuquerque, by Father Ambrosio Guerra in a very flattering manner, and led into his hall. From thence, after taking some refreshment, into an inner apartment, where he ordered his adopted children, of the female sex, to appear, when they came in by turns, Indians of various nations, Spanish, French, and finally, two young girls, whom, from their complexion, I conceived to be English: on perceiving I noticed them, he ordered the rest to retire, many of whom were beautiful, and directed those to sit down on the sofa beside me; thus situated he told me they had been taken to the east by the Tetaus, passed from one nation to another until he purchased them, at that time infants, but they could recollect neither their names nor language; but concluding they were my countrywomen, he ordered them to embrace me as a mark of friendship, to which they appeared nothing loath. We then sat down to dinner, which consisted of various dishes, excellent

were living here when we passed through, and treated Van Ness, who was allowed many liberties by Salazar, with much respect and consideration—loading him with excellent bread and other luxuries on his departure. As we were marched directly through the principal streets the inhabitants were gathered on either side to gaze at the *estrangeros*, as we were called. The women, with all kindness of heart, gave our men corn, pumpkins, bread, and everything they could spare from their scanty store as we passed, and had Salazar allowed us to remain but an hour, all our immediate wants would have been supplied; but the hard-hearted wretch appeared to delight in acts of cruelty, and drove us through with scarcely a halt of ten minutes.

It was at Albuquerque that I saw a perfect specimen of female loveliness. The girl was poor, being dressed only in a chemise and coarse woollen petticoat; yet there was an air of grace, a charm about her, that neither birth nor fortune can bestow. She was standing upon a mud-wall, the taper fingers of her right hand supporting a large pumpkin upon her head, while her left was gracefully resting upon her hip. Her dark, full, and lustrous eyes overarched with brows of pencilled regularity, and fringed with lashes of long and silken texture, beamed upon us full of tenderness and pity, while an unbidden

wines, and to crown all, we were waited on by half a dozen of those beautiful girls, who, like Hebe at the feast of the gods, converted our wine into nectar, and with their ambrosial breath shed incense on our cups." Now, I neither saw as much nor enjoyed myself as well while a prisoner at Albuquerque, as did General Pike when he passed through there under circumstances somewhat similar; still I saw enough to convince me that the race of pretty girls has not altogether degenerated, a fact of which my reader will be acquainted by reading the two following pages.

tear of sorrow at our misfortunes was coursing down a cheek of the purest and richest olive. Her beautifully-curved lips, half opened as if in pity and astonishment at a scene so uncommon, disclosed teeth of pearly, dazzling whiteness. Innocence and the best feelings of our nature were playing in every lineament of that lovely face, and ever and anon, as some one of us more unfortunate than the rest would limp halting by, again her tears would gush from their fountains and illumine a countenance of purity. If

> "Crystal tears from pity's eye
> Are the stars in heaven high,"

some of them fell that day from the poor village girl, drawn from their firmament to lighten the sorrows of those upon whom misfortune had laid her heavy hand. She could not be more than fifteen; yet her loose and flowing dress, but half concealing a bust of surpassing beauty and loveliness, plainly disclosed that she was just entering womanhood. Her figure was faultless, and even the chisel of Praxiteles himself never modelled ankles of such pure and classic elegance.

As the long and straggling line of prisoners passed the spot upon which this lovely form was standing, sore and worn down by long marches, and wont of food and sleep, her rare beauty drew the eyes of all towards her, and exclamations of wonder were upon every lip. She understood not our language, and in the artless simplicity of her nature knew not that her singular loveliness, combined with the display of charms her unstudied yet graceful attitude and scanty dress had given, was the theme of almost universal admiration.

She beckoned to a youth among the prisoners, a German lad but little older than herself, and presented him the pumpkin with infinite delicacy and grace; and as she did it, the exclamation *pobrecito* was heard gently falling from her lips in tones of softest pity. The fairest flowers are oftenest found in obscurity, and I trust my readers will not doubt my sincerity when I assert that the prettiest girl I ever saw was selling woollen stockings at twenty-five cents a pair at Holme's Hole, Massachusetts —her twin-sister in beauty was standing on her bare feet upon a mud-wall at Albuquerque, New Mexico, with a pumpkin on her head!

I lingered to take a last look at the beautiful girl, and when I turned from the spot I could not but regret that the lot of one so kind-hearted and so fair had been cast in such a place. There are faces we see in our journey through life surpassingly beautiful, faces that leave a deep and lasting impression on the beholders, and hers was one of them. Among the crowds of beauty her image will stand out in bold relief, and not one of those who saw her on the day we passed through Albuquerque will ever forget her.

CHAPTER XVIII.

Los Placeres.—Another dark Leaf in Salazar's Character.—Women and Water-melons.—Re-appearance of Lieutenant Hornsby.—His singular Story of Adventure.—The dashing Horseman and his gentle and generous Wife.—Arrival at Valencia.—Farther Sufferings of the Prisoners.—Kindness of an old Woman.—Death of Ernest.—An American Traveller.—Cruel Murder of M'Allister.—Its Effect upon the Prisoners.—Casa Colorada.—A comfortable Camp.—Appearance of the Valley of the Rio Grande.—Uses of the Cotton-wood.—Salazar and the Alcaldes.—The Mexican Button Market.—Straits to which the Prisoners were driven.—A Story of Stump.—Magoffin's Waggons passed.—American Drivers.—Not allowed to hold converse with them.—Arrival at Joya.—A Fandango.—Salazar Drunk.—Conduct of the American Drivers on the occasion.—Parrida.—Crossing the Rio Grande.—Arrival at Socorro.—A short Rest allowed.—Character of the Inhabitants.—A Party of Apaches.—Anecdote of the Priest of Socorro.—Head Chief of the Apaches.—His dignified Bearing.—Obsequiousness of Salazar.—Bosque de los Apaches.—Re-crossing the Rio Grande.—The Camp of Fray Cristobal.—A Snow-storm at Night.—Appearance of the Prisoners by Daylight.—Colds and Coughs.

After leaving Albuquerque, we continued our march through a succession of cultivated fields and pastures until we reached a small rancho called Los Placeres, and here we were encamped for the night. Nothing was given us to eat, and on complaining to Salazar that we were very hungry, he pointed to the spot where his mules and horses were feeding, and said that the *grazing was excellent!* Because many of the prisoners swallowed the corn given them by the women raw, the fellow called them wolves and hogs.

At this place we were visited by a family of Mexican women of no inconsiderable wealth, who lived at a rancho some little distance from our road. It consisted of a mother and her two daughters, and I will venture the assertion that either of the latter weighed more than two hundred pounds, and will also declare positively that neither of them was very prepossessing in appearance. They had brought two large water-melons as a present, and while one of the girls bestowed a melon upon one of my companions, her sister made choice of me as the recipient of the other. I gave the girl the customary *mil gracias*, or thousand thanks, as I received the melon; had the pretty one of Albuquerque given me that pumpkin I should have been far better satisfied.

Not a little astonished were we, when, towards evening, our absent comrade, Hornsby, with a chopfallen countenance and a half-worn jacket a world too small for him, was seen approaching, his Mexican friend, the dashing horseman, setting him down near our quarters and then galloping off in the direction of his home. A singular story did the lieutenant tell of his adventure, the substance of which was as follows:—

On first mounting behind the Mexican, he supposed that the fellow simply intended carrying him a mile or two on the route—perhaps to Albuquerque, which was then in sight; but to his astonishment the man wheeled his horse suddenly round, and struck off across the fields at a tremendous pace. Hornsby had employment enough in hanging on to his new friend, to avoid being thrown off as the gallant horse leaped the irrigating canals, so that, to use his own words, he had no time to speculate upon the singularity of his adventure, or upon the intentions of the wild horseman who was giving him such a race. A hard ride of three or four miles brought them to a house of neater construction and finish than were possessed by the generality of Mexican dwellings. It was a solitary house, and appeared to be about half a mile from the road he had walked over but a short time previous. Once at the door, the Mexican threw himself lightly from his animal, and, after assisting Hornsby to dismount, politely asked him to enter his dwelling. There was an air of neatness and comfort within, and the furniture betokened a style of living which formed a singular contrast with the destitution apparent in even the better class of houses upon the road.

His strange host led the way into a room in which the furniture and appointments were absolutely luxurious. Over the fireplace was a large mirror; two or three scriptural paintings, one of them a well-executed portrait of the Virgin, adorned the walls; while upon a sideboard was neatly arranged a set of decanters and tumblers, all of cut glass, and of admirable workmanship. Here the Mexican left him for a moment, but soon returned with a massive silver pitcher filled with cool water.

Unfortunately, Hornsby could speak but little Spanish, and was, consequently, unable to carry on a regular conversation with his host; but when the latter pointed to a tumbler, and then to a decanter of brandy, our lieutenant understood him perfectly, and manifested his knowledge of signs by helping himself to a bountiful allowance. At this juncture the wife of the gay cavalier, a mild-eyed, pretty woman, entered the apartment, and, exchanging a few words with her husband, led the way to a table in another room, which was fairly groaning under the weight of a hot and sumptuous breakfast. Hornsby, now more astonished than ever, and wondering how this adventure was to terminate, took a seat at the table in silence, and ate a heartier meal than he had done for months. Both the husband and wife were assiduous in their attentions, and pressed dish after dish upon him with a most zealous courtesy.

Breakfast over, the wife brought in a package of cigarritos, or shuck cigars, and after the husband had lit one of them by means of the flint and steel which every Mexican carries in his pocket, and had politely asked his guest to join him in a smoke, he opened the business which had induced him to *invite* Hornsby to his dwelling. By words, and more particularly by signs, he informed his guest that he had taken a great fancy to his military jacket, and that he must exchange with him. Hornsby responded, with an equal amount of his own vernacular and a corresponding quantity of signs, to the effect that the jacket of his host was much too small for him, and that he was not disposed to trade. The gentle and pretty wife, who had been all the while watching either party, now interfered, her actions plainly denoting that she was anxiously entreating her husband not to entertain their guest thus rudely and uncharitably. Paying no heed to her entreaties, the husband again intimated to Hornsby that he must doff his jacket—he had no money to offer him in exchange, but then he had given him a ride, a drink, and a breakfast, and, as a return for these civilities, only wished to exchange jackets. He stripped off his own, notwithstanding his wife's opposition, and now commenced assisting his guest in taking off the much-desired garment. It was a forced transfer, contrary to the laws of Mexico; but our comrade was driven into the transaction.

The Mexican next brought a coarse, thick, and heavy blanket, which he wished to exchange for the scarlet affair belonging to Hornsby. As there was no such thing as avoiding a trade when his host had determined that it must be, our comrade, with a sorry grace, submitted to his demands: yet this time he really got the best of the bargain, for the blanket he received was much warmer and of infinitely more service than the one forced from him. The Mexican now pointed to his horse, which was still tied in front of the dwelling, and uttered the well-known *bamanos.** It was now Hornsby's turn to take a liberty. Heretofore his host had made himself exceedingly free on very limited acquaintance, as Hornsby dryly expressed it: the latter now bethought him that he would pay off a small portion of the debt in kind. He therefore walked deliberately to the sideboard, poured himself out a stiff glass of brandy, and bowing very respectfully to his host, tossed it off. He then expressed his readiness to depart, and walking out of the house, was soon seated behind his singular host. The wife now made her appearance with the new blanket, in which she had tied a large quantity of dried beef. Watching an opportunity while the eyes of her husband were turned away, she stealthily slipped a quarter of a dollar into the hands of Hornsby—

* Come, let us be moving—a word we heard forty times a-day, and the import of which we soon understood.

probably her little all. A tear stood in her eye as she murmured "*Adios Senor,*" for the kind-hearted creature felt deeply mortified at the inhospitable manner in which her husband had treated a guest. Another moment, and Hornsby was on his way to rejoin his comrades, the Mexican apparently anxious to escape the reproachful looks of his gentle wife; and ere it was yet dark he had discharged his burden within a few yards of our camping-ground. Such was the story told of the gay cavalier, who, by his dashing and fearless riding, had excited our warmest admiration in the morning. Was ever such an ingenious trick to effect an exchange of clothing? Salazar was probably privy to the whole transaction, else he would have never permitted his brother Mexican to carry off one of the prisoners in such a manner. The self-esteem of the highwayman would not allow him openly to rob our comrade he thought that the cloak of hospitality which he threw over his act more than covered its rascality. But I must return to my narrative of more important events.

Late on the evening of the 24th of October, and after a march of uncommon length, we reached the little town of Valencia. Here a pint of flour was distributed to each of the prisoners; but many of the men were so tired, faint, and sore, from the long and continued marches, and from cold and want of sleep at night, that they had neither the will nor strength to cook even this scanty ration. On the contrary, they sunk immediately upon the cold ground, and vainly endeavoured to smother their pains and sorrows in sleep. Fitzgerald and myself had better quarters, or rather a better bed, that night, than our fellows. We were about lying down, immediately in front of a small house, when an old woman threw us out a couple of sheepskins with the wool still on. With these between us and the cold ground we really passed a comfortable night.

Not so one of our unfortunate companions. On rising in the morning, it was found that a man named Ernest had died during the night—died from hunger, cold, and fatigue, and without even the knowledge of the man sleeping by his side! The long march of the previous day had so weakened the poor Texan that on reaching camp he had sunk to the ground exhausted. He soon fell asleep, and with him it proved to be the sleep which knows no waking! Not a murmur, not a groan did he utter; but when his companion shook him in the morning, with the intention of arousing him to the fatigues and sufferings of another day, the lamp of his existence had burned out, or rather had been rudely smothered—he was stiff and cold! Salazar immediately ordered one of his men to cut off and preserve the dead man's ears, as a token that he had not escaped, and by the orders of the same brute the body was thrown into a neighbouring ditch. An American with two or three waggons, who was on his way from the United States to either Monterey or Saltillo with machinery, was within two hundred yards of us all the while, and saw the whole transaction. Salazar would not allow us to hold any conversation or communicate with this man; but we afterward learned that he had been an overseer on some plantation near New Orleans, and that the machinery he had with him was a sugar-mill on a large scale, which he had been employed to set in operation in Mexico. I heard the man's name, but have forgotten it.

Scarcely had the events occurred, of which I have given a brief recital, ere we were ordered to form in line and be counted before resuming the march: even before we could finish the cooking of our scanty supply of meal into thin mush we were compelled to move. Just as we were starting, a man named John M'Allister, a native of Tennessee and of excellent family, complained that one of his ankles was badly sprained, and that it was utterly impossible for him to walk. The unfortunate man was naturally lame in the other ankle, and could never walk but with difficulty and with a limp. On starting, he was now allowed to enter a rude Mexican cart, which had been procured by the Alcalde of Valencia for the purpose of transporting some of the sick and lame prisoners; but before it had proceeded a mile upon the road it either broke down or was found to be too heavily loaded. At all events M'Allister was ordered by Salazar to hobble along as best he might, and to overtake the main body of prisoners, now some quarter of a mile in advance. The wretch had frequently told those who, from inability or weakness, had fallen behind, that he would shoot them rather than have the march delayed; not that there was any necessity for the hot haste with which we were driven, but to gratify his brutal disposition did he make these threats. Although he had struck, and in several cases severely beaten, many of the sick and lame prisoners, we could not believe that he was so utterly destitute of feeling, so brutal as to murder a man in cold blood whose only fault was that he was crippled and unable to walk. He could easily have procured transportation for all if he had wished, and that he would do so rather than shoot down any of the more unfortunate we felt confident: how much we mistook the man.

On being driven from the cart, M'Allister declared his inability to proceed on foot. Salazar drew his sword and peremptorily ordered him to hurry on, and this when he had half a dozen led mules, upon either of which he could have placed the unfortunate man. Again M'Allister, pointing to his swollen and inflamed ankle, declared himself unable to walk. Some half a dozen of his comrades were standing around him, with feelings painfully wrought up, waiting the *denouement* of an affair which, from the angry appearance of Salazar, they now feared would be tragical. Once more the bloodthirsty savage, pointing to the main body of prisoners, ordered the cripple to hurry forward and overtake them —*he could not!* "Forward!" said Salazar, now wrought up to a pitch of phrensy. "Forward, or I'll shoot you on the spot!" "Then shoot!" replied M'Allister, throwing off his blanket and exposing his manly breast, "and the quicker the better!" Salazar took him at his word, and a single ball sent as brave a man as ever trod the earth to eternity! His ears were then cut off, his shirt and pantaloons stripped from him, and his body thrown by the roadside as food for wolves!

A thrill of horror ran through the crowd of prisoners as the news spread that one of our men had been deliberately shot down in cold blood, and deep but whispered threats of vengeance for this most unnatural murder where heard upon every lip. In our present condition we could do nothing. It would have been an easy matter for us to rise and overpower the guard; but their arms were worthless, and it would have been impossible, unacquainted as we were with the country, to cut our way through to Texas without provisions. And then, as I once before remarked, it was part of Salazar's policy to drive us along and tire us down by marches of almost incredible length, and so to weaken us by scanty food that escape would be next to impossible. Weak as we were, however, had our guard been well armed with rifles or muskets, and with plenty of ammunition, we never should have been marched to the Paso del Norte; but those who had charge of us were strong in their very weakness. Thus wretchedly we were compelled to journey forward in dreary hope of falling into more humane hands on reaching the State of Chihuahua.

Late in the afternoon of the day on which M'Allister was murdered we reached the Casa Colorada, or Red House, a large hacienda and trading establishment belonging, I believe, to one of the Chavez family. Passing the little collection of houses, we entered a grove of cotton-woods near the Rio Grande, and there encamped for the night. From the time when we first struck the valley of this stream, after leaving the mountains in the neighbourhood of Santa Fé, to that when we reached the Paso del Norte, but little timber was seen, and that was composed exclusively of cotton-woods. The inhabitants are very saving of this timber, although it is exceedingly soft and brittle; yet, as they can obtain no other for the construction of their rude carts, ploughs, and other implements, its uses to them are invaluable. Sometimes we would journey for days, hardly seeing a tree to each mile we travelled. The few fences, like the houses, are constructed of *adobes*, or sun-dried bricks, square instead of oblong, and perhaps four times the size of ordinary bricks. Of this material nearly all the dwellings of the lower classes in Mexico are constructed. The valley of the Rio Grande, above El Paso, is of unequal width, varying from a mile and a half to four or five miles, and in some places perhaps more. On either side of the valley rises a chain of hills—some of them may deserve the name of mountains—which for the most part appeared sterile and destitute of vegetation. The valley itself is generally fertile, well adapted to the growth of corn, wheat, beans, and pumpkins; not a potato, either sweet or Irish, did we see, although the latter, in particular, would undoubtedly attain great perfection. Under Anglo-Saxon cultivation, this region might support five times the population it now contains; still, the want of timber and the immense distance to a market, will always present obstacles to emigration in that direction.

The custom had been, on nearing the camp each afternoon, for the prisoners to pick up every little chip and twig by the roadside, wherewith to cook their scanty rations of dry corn or meal; for the first time since we had entered the valley, we now found a sufficiency of wood, but a majority of us had nothing to cook. On leaving San Miguel, Armijo had given Salazar eighteen head of cattle, some of the oxen taken from the Texans, and had ordered him to kill them for our use. I will even give the governor credit by believing that he placed a quantity of the goods taken from the Texans in the hands of Salazar, for the purpose of trading them for breadstuff on the road, to be appropriated to our use; yet, up to this time, the scoundrel had neither killed one of the oxen nor disposed of a single article of merchandise for anything but money, all of which he placed in his own pockets. Our sufferings were plainly a gratification to him, and to sustain life he compelled us to depend alone upon the charities of the women, or upon the small supply of corn and meal he wrung, by threats and violence, from the different alcaldes of the villages through which we passed. In the mean time, to still the inordinate cravings of hunger and to procure an occasional ride upon the animals of our guard, the prisoners had disposed of every little article of clothing they could possibly spare, frequently exchanging a pair of their own woollen pantaloons for the ragged breeches of the Mexicans, to purchase a ride of a few miles. The buttons, too from their clothing, they had bartered either for meal or rides; and as by this time they were nearly all expended, the sufferings of the majority may be said to have fairly commenced.*

I cannot leave our encampment among the cotton woods near the Casa Colorada without relating an amusing story told that evening by "Old Paint" Caldwell. The time appeared ill-assorted with merriment and laughter, yet laugh we did, and heartily too, at the recital of the old captain's anecdote.

Among the passengers in the cart with poor M'Allister

* Buttons commanded a high price, for even an ordinary iron or horn article, such as might be easily purchased for six cents per dozen at any shop in the United States, in New Mexico would procure for one of our prisoners a ride of several miles, or bread enough to last him a day. Needles, too, were in great demand; one of our men, a tailor, who had been fortunate enough to save two or three papers, was enabled to procure an ample supply of food, and also to have a mule when his necessities required. This information may be useful to some itinerant pedlar of small "notions," although I cannot conscientiously advise him to visit New Mexico for a market.

were the narrator and a man who went by the soubriquet of "Stump;" there may have been others, but if there were I have now forgotten their names. In the morning, before starting, Stump had declared that he could not walk a mile—to save his life, even—and so positive was he upon this point, that a place was provided for him in the cart. When this vehicle met with the accident, of course Stump was thrown upon his feet with the rest. While the few words were passing between M'Allister and Salazar, and previous to the inhuman murder of the former, Stump was hobbling about, apparently unable to walk at all: his feet were sore, his knees were stiff, and not a bone was there in his body that did not pain him at every movement—he was curled up, the picture of despair; but no sooner did he see his comrade fall, and feel the certainty that he, too, would meet with a similar fate unless he put his powers of locomotion in immediate action, than, to use the old captain's own words, Stump straightened up and started at a pace that would have staggered Captain Barclay, Ellworth, or the greatest pedestrian mentioned in the anuals of "tall walking." Stump went by, first one, then another of his companions, and never abated his stride until he was in the lead of the whole party of prisoners: a position he pertinaciously kept through the remainder of the day, and, in fact, during the march. In the morning he *could not* walk a mile; he afterward *did* walk something like eighteen hundred and without flagging. This story of the old captain's through, we cast our weary limbs upon the earth, and as the grove of trees in which we were encamped materially deadened the force of the wind, we were enabled to pass a more comfortable night than any since we left San Miguel.

On the following day we passed the long train of waggons belonging to Mr. Magoffin, of Chihuahua—the same that had arrived at San Miguel from St. Louis while we were there. The drivers were all Americans—brown, healthy-looking men; and although strict orders were given by Salazar that no communication should be held, we still exhanged a few words with them as we passed. It brought back old times and old recollections to see these men, fresh from my own country, and anxiously did I wish that I might obtain an hour's conversation with them, an opportunity to learn the news from the United States, if nothing more; I could only wish, as Salazar took especial care that my desires should not be gratified.

A little before sundown we reached the village of Joya, and here our men were allowed a shelter for the night in two or three old and abandoned rooms. A fandango was got up during the evening in the town, at which Howard, Van Ness, and two or three of our officers were allowed to be present. Here they met several of the Americans we had passed during the day, their encampment being in the skirts of the village close by. Salazar became much intoxicated during the evening, and with the fumes of Whiskey in his head grew insolent and overbearing towards the drivers. Fortunately they came well provided with bowie-knives, thinking they might possibly be insulted; and no sooner had Salazar commenced his insolence than he was driven —I believe *kicked*—from the room, the cowardly wretch not daring even to open his mouth after their weapons were drawn.

By making an early start on the following morning,

we were enabled to reach Parrida, a small town immediately on the banks of the Rio Grande, by the middle of the afternoon. Here, in the plaza, we stopped for the night; and here, after an allowance of a pint of meal had been measured out to each man by the alcalde and Salazar, we were permitted to make and eat our poor mush in peace and qüietness. At Parrida I was also fortunate in purchasing a pair of heavy and substantial shoes, after walking several days in a pair of soleless moccasins, which let in the gravel at every step upon the numerous blisters that covered my feet. I had not a little difficulty in making change with the *zapatero* of whom I purchased, for the piece of gold I tendered him in payment I was anxious to keep from the eyes of Salazar. The brute knew that I had a small sum of money about me—some few dollars. Had he suspected the large amount in gold and jewelry I had concealed in those ragged and dirty vestments of mine, he would soon have found a pretext for sending me to keep company with the murdered M'Allister.

After a hasty breakfast of mush, on the following morning, we were once more upon our journey. A short walk brought us to the banks of the Rio Grande, here some three or four hundred yards in width. The water was cold and waist deep to our men, yet we were obliged to ford it, and when once safely upon the opposite side, we had entered Mexican territory for the first time. I say for the first time, because Texas claims to the Rio Grande, and, sooner or later, this will be her boundary line.

An hour's brisk march along the river banks brought us to Socorro, the last settlement before reaching El

Paso. What the exact distance between the two places is I have now forgotten, but it cannot be far from two hundred miles. As Salazar had to make a demand on the alcalde for corn and meal enough to sustain us across the long and dreary waste yet to travel, we were permitted to remain at Socorro until the following day. That the inhabitants of this frontier town were a pack of thieving, cheating, swindling scoundrels, we ascertained beyond doubt before we had been in the place two hours. I remember, perfectly well, that a small party of us paid for a supper twice at this place, and that, because we would not pay for it a third time, the master of the house became very much incensed.

When we were at Socorro, a party of Indians, belonging to the large and powerful tribe of Apaches, were encamped in the vicinity. They lived, for the most part, in a rough and mountainous country, yet, like the Camanches and Pawnees, are ever on horseback, and are daring and skilful riders. With the inhabitants of the States of Chihuahua and Durango they are at continual and open war, murdering and robbing the inhabitants whenever opportunity offers; yet with the people of New Mexico they are at peace, and the plunder they obtain in their incursions into the former states is sold to the citizens of the latter, who are ever found ready purchasers! A pretty state of things, truly, but so it is. I was told that many of the horses of New Mexico really belonged to persons in the former states, and that the purchasers bought them with powder and lead, knowing that it was to be used against their neighbours and brethren! Armijo and some of his principal officers probably know more about this singular and most unrighteous compact, and of the profits arising from the trade with these Indian banditti, than any other persons in Mexico.

While at Socorro, one of the prisoners, who was a Catholic, obtained permission to visit the priest of the place. The real object of the man was, to obtain something in the way of solid assistance—something to eat upon the road—temporal rather than spiritual aid and consolation. The priest gave him absolution and a small bundle of shuck cigars! I do not mention this circumstance to stigmatize the holy fathers generally of Mexico, for we found a majority of them liberal and enlightened men, and disposed to assist us as far as was in their power.

On the morning of the 29th of October we left Socorro without regret; for although its name signifies succour or assistance, we found none within its inhospitable gates. We had travelled but a short distance before the head or principal chief of the Apaches, with a small retinue of his warriors, was seen rapidly dashing over a hill, having ridden out especially to see *los Americanos*, as they called us, who had surrendered their arms to the New Mexicans. At one time the inhabitants of Chihuahua had employed a number of American adventurers in different expeditions against the Apaches, and in every engagement the former were able to bring about, the Indians were defeated with no little loss. The rifles of the Americans told with singular advantage against the bows and arrows, lances, and ineffective Spanish carbines of their adversaries, fought they ever so bravely; and now that one of the principal chiefs of the latter had an opportunity of seeing some of the countrymen of their much-dreaded enemies, he did not miss the opportunity.

A more dignified savage in appearance than this chief I have never seen. He was about the middle height, strong and well built, some sixty-five or seventy years of age, and with hair as white as snow. He was dressed in an old-fashioned blue military coat and blue pantaloons; a huge pair of gold epaulettes graced his shoulders, while his head was covered with a Continental tri-cocked hat, such as was worn by our grandfathers in the days of the Revolution. His countenance was stern, strongly marked, and very expressive, and he was mounted upon a large and powerful gray charger of fine action, and apparently of good blood.

He rode up to the head of the line, in company with Salazar. As we passed in review before him, a ragged, beggared, and emaciated throng, the old man examined us with the eye of an eagle—his thoughts could not be divined. Salazar appeared polite even to obsequiousness in presence of this man, and it was intimated at the time that he stood in much fear lest the old chief might take it into his head to rescue us from his hands, a matter he might easily have accomplished. What would have been our fate had he done so—whether he would have sacrificed us on the spot in revenge for the losses he had sustained at the hands of our countrymen, or taken us to the mountains, is a question I am unable to answer. One thing I do know—had he called for volunteers to act against any part of Mexico, and promised to arm all that came, he might have got them to the full extent of our number. After the last stragglers had passed him, the old chief turned his horse and rode over the hills in the direction whence he came. His followers were dressed much in the general Indian costume—buckskin shirts, leggings, and the usual quantity of feathers and finery. I also noticed while in Socorro, that the Apaches have the besetting sin of all the aborigines of America; several of them were seen reeling about upon their horses, so drunk that they could with difficulty keep their seats.

After a walk of unusual length across a bend of the Rio Grande—I say unusual, for it was nearly forty miles—we reached, just at dark, a large grove of cotton-woods close upon the river bank. This grove was called the Bosque de los Apaches, or Wood of the Apaches, and afforded us one of the best camping-grounds on the journey. We re-crossed the river at an early hour on the following morning, and another long and tiresome march brought us to Fray Cristobal, the last camping-ground before entering the noted *Dead Man's Journey!* This is a well-known stretch of ninety miles, across a large bend of the river.* To avoid many weary miles, a road has been worn directly through the centre of this bend by the travel of years. It is a level, sterile, and desolate plain—a desert with no vegetation save here and there a few stunted thorns, different species of the cactus of dwarf-like proportions, and clumps of one of the smaller kinds of palm, growing to the height of some six or seven feet, with long, coarse leaves branching up from the roots, and forming a very mat

* The Mexicans call this noted stretch *La Jornada del Muerto*, or The Journey of the Dead Man—our men gave it the name of the Dead Man's Journey, and by that title I designate it.

from the closeness with which they grow together. These clumps were called *bear grass* by our men, and at a little distance they resembled long and slender bundles of coarse straw. Near the centre of the desert is the *Dead Man's Lake,** which, during the spring and early summer, is filled with water; but when we crossed its bed was perfectly dry.

Immediately on our arrival at the camping-ground of Fray Cristobal, a bleak, sandy point of land formed by a slight curve in the Rio Grande, Salazar ordered that the poorest and most travel-worn of the eighteen oxen given him at San Miguel by Armijo should be killed for the prisoners, taking most especial care, however, that all the better portions—everything really fit to eat—should be reserved for himself and his friends. Poor and tough as was this meat, our men swallowed it with an avidity absolutely wolfish. The scanty meal over, they rolled themselves in their blankets and once more sought such rest as the cold ground might afford them.

During the earlier part of the evening the wind was biting and chilly, but at midnight the weather moderated, and then commenced a violent fall of snow. I drew my blanket entirely over my head, thought of home and its comforts, and while thinking of them fell asleep; for the snow, as it lodged upon my scanty covering, imparted a warmth to which I had long been a stranger.

When morning light came I raised my head and surveyed the scene. Far as the eye could reach the face of nature was clothed in white, the snow having fallen

* Called by the Mexicans, *Laguna del Muerto,* or *Lake of the Dead Man.*

to the depth of five or six inches. My companions were lying thick around me, their heads and all concealed, and more resembled logs imbedded in snow than anything else to which I can compare them. No one would have supposed that animated beings were under those little mounds were it not that from many of them a hollow, hacking, and half-suppressed cough proceeded. The two or three nights we had passed within doors, huddled some thirty or forty in rooms scarcely capacious enough for three or four, had given nearly all extremely bad colds—colds they were unable either to guard against or cure.

END OF VOL. I.

THOMAS HARRILD, Printer, Silver Street, Falcon Square, London.